D0760507

Women and Culture Series

The Women and Culture Series is dedicated to books that illuminate the lives, roles, achievements, and status of women, past or present.

Sacred Queens and Women of Consequence

Boki, Governor of Wáhu, of the Sandwich Islands, and his wife, Liliha.

Sacred Queens and Women of Consequence

*Rank, Gender, and Colonialism
in the Hawaiian Islands*

Jocelyn Linnekin

Ann Arbor
The University of Michigan Press

Copyright © by the University of Michigan 1990
All rights reserved
Published in the United States of America by
The University of Michigan Press
Manufactured in the United States of America
♾ Printed on acid-free paper

2000   1999   1998   1997   8   7   6   5

No part of this publication may be reproduced,
stored in a retrieval system, or transmitted in any form
or by any means, electronic, mechanical, or otherwise,
without the written permission of the publisher.

Library of Congress Cataloging-in-Publication Data

Linnekin, Jocelyn, 1950–
    Sacred queens and women of consequence : rank, gender, and
colonialism in the Hawaiian Islands / Jocelyn Linnekin.
        p.   cm.   —(Women and culture series)
    Includes bibliographical references.
    ISBN 0-472-09423-8. — ISBN 0-472-06423-1 (pbk.)
    1. Women, Hawaiian—Social conditions.   2. Women, Hawaiian—
Economic conditions.   3. Taboo.   4. Hawaiians—History.
5. Hawaiians—Social life and customs.   I. Title.
DU624.65.L57   1990
305.4'09969'09034—dc20   89-20618
                                                                    CIP

Frontispiece: Boki and Liliha. Drawn on stone from the original painting by
Mr. John Hayter. 1824. (Reproduced with permission from Kamehameha
Schools/Bishop Estate.)

Cover illustration: A Young Woman of the Sandwich Islands (Hawaii) with
Feather Leis. After a drawing by Robert Dampier, who sailed with Lord Byron on
the HMS Blonde 1824. (Courtesy of the Bernice Pauahi Bishop Museum.)

For Benjamin and Abigail

Preface

The majority of women . . . had no deity and just worshipped nothing.
—David Malo ([1838] 1951:82)

In their domestic life, they appear to live almost entirely by themselves, and though we did not observe any instances of personal ill-treatment, yet it was evident they had little regard or attention paid them.
—Lt. James King (Cook and King 1784, 3:130)

Women are excluded from the production and cooking of these [important] foods. . . . At most, they are given the task of appropriating some secondary foods—which in a way are "residual," like the women themselves: shellfish, mollusks, seaweed, small crustaceans, and so on. Sometimes they are able to grow sweet potatoes (*'uala*), a little-prized tuber reserved for marginal land, which has the dubious honor of being associated with the excrement of the pig Kamapua'a. . . .
—Valerio Valeri (1985:123)

[I]t is at least possible that women (and, for that matter, commoner men) construed the system quite differently from male chiefs.
—Jocelyn Linnekin (quoted herein, 34)

Believing that all knowledge has a context, I endeavor here to clarify the context of this book and its author. The first quotation above is by a Hawaiian man, a convert to a severe Calvinist form of Protestantism, a scholar and minister who grew to adulthood in the early nineteenth century. The second is taken from the 1779 journal of Lt. (later Captain) James King, an Englishman, officer on the *Resolution* under James Cook, commander of the third voyage after the deaths of captains Cook and Clerke, and second author of the official account of the voyage (Cook and King 1784). The third is by a modern scholar of Mediterranean extraction who traces his family lineage back to the Romans, and draws on the scholarly genealogy of Durkheim and Lévi-Strauss. The last comment is by the author of the present work: an American woman with a personal commitment to feminism and civil liberties, a college student during the late 1960s, and now an anthropologist.

I provide these biographical details because they explain in part the contrasts between these statements about the women of Hawaii two hundred years ago. The authors' biographies have no bearing on the relative validity of their interpretations. Nevertheless, their gender and the times they lived in have influenced the way these writers portray Hawaiian women. Valeri's characterization of Hawaiian women as "marginal" and "passive" in the context of the sacrificial religion strikes me as a characteristically Western male view of women and moreover, if I may be forgiven for indulging in a stereotype myself, a very Mediterranean male attitude. That I have a different interpretation is certainly due in part to my status as an American woman and a member of a generation dedicated—at least during one period of our lives—to challenging conventional views. This biography, and the influence of a decade of feminist scholarship, form the background to this book, and they explain in part why I see Hawaiian women as powerful actors and decision makers with great temporal and symbolic importance—albeit in contexts other than the male-dominated sacrificial religion. This difference of interpretation is not solely a matter of analyzing "data" or summarizing "the facts" but also of acknowledging the different points of view from which we write.

I juxtapose the above citations also to make a point about doing ethnohistory, by way of clarifying the claims I make for the present analysis. The nature of ethnohistorical data, fragmentary at best and filtered through the perceptions of a myriad not-so-disinterested observers, is frustrating to empirically oriented anthropologists. The material defies attempts at "objective" verification. Yet as contemporary scholars working with older ethnographic materials, we tend to consider the statements of Malo and King as "data," and those of later writers and other scholars as interpretations or reconstructions. Clearly the distinction is not so simple. We can treat Malo's and King's words as objectively recorded data only if we assume that they have no biases or, to put it more neutrally, no context; if we use them without evaluating their cultural and temporal context, we implicitly adopt those biases as our own, as Valeri (1985:113) seems to do when he cites Malo's statement as confirmation for his view that women play a marginal role in the Hawaiian religion.

This lengthy caveat is intended to underscore the provisionality of any ethnohistorical analysis. This book presents an interpretation of the cultural position of Hawaiian women in conjunction with certain nineteenth-century events. The subject of this study is a quantitative phenomenon: an apparent shift in the inheritance pattern such that women increasingly came to hold land during the mid-nineteenth century. The meaning of the numerical results is by no means unambiguous, however. And by way of context, it should be noted that I formulated the initial problematic, designed the computer database, constructed the analytic categories, supervised the coding of the land data, and wrote the programs to elicit inheritance patterns over time. I also designed the tabular presentation of the statistical results for this book. Quantification, in other words, is no more context-free than qualitative analysis. Statistical treatment must also be seen as an interpretation, not a presentation of objective "facts" (Linnekin 1987b).

While I stress the provisionality of the analysis presented here, I do maintain that some interpretations are better than others. The injunction to acknowledge and evaluate the context of our sources and our own work should not be taken as nihilism or an invitation to turn non-Western societies into funhouse mirrors for our own psyches or our own political programs; ethnography is still not the same as fiction. In my view good models have greater explanatory power: they take into account, illuminate, and render comprehensible more of the received evidence, whether the latter is experientially or textually derived. I am suspicious of David Malo's assessment of the worship practices of Hawaiian women because it conflicts with certain of his own statements and those of other early sources. In its original textual setting (see King's journal in Beaglehole 1967, 3:624), Lt. King's statement describes his reaction to the *kapu* system with its separation of men and women in certain contexts. It is a valuable observation by a conscientious man, and it must be evaluated in light of other, more specific observations by King and his comrades. I object to Valeri's treatment of Hawaiian women because his model leaves too much unexplained and because to a twentieth-century American woman his statements about eighteenth-century Hawaiian women sound disturbingly familiar.

This study is the summary of work long in progress. I began working on Hawaiian land records and ethnohistorical materials in the early 1970s as research assistant for Marshall Sahlins on his project, "Historical Anthropology of the Hawaiian Kingdom," sponsored by the Bernice

P. Bishop Museum and funded by the National Science Foundation. My later doctoral fieldwork in a Hawaiian community was sponsored by the National Institute of Mental Health and the National Science Foundation (Grant GS-39667). Some of the material collected during that period has informed and augmented the present study. The major source of the quantitative data used here, however, is the corpus of Hawaiian land records compiled by Marshall Sahlins. Dr. Sahlins graciously gave me access to his files and found an initial home and funding (in the form of a Faculty Research Grant) for the computerization project at the University of Chicago. Coding, data entry, and computer time were also supported by a Grant-in-Aid (#4207) to me from the Wenner-Gren Foundation for Anthropological Research. The University of Hawaii also provided funds for computer time at the University of Hawaii Computing Center.

As in any work that has been in the making for several years, I owe thanks to numerous individuals. My greatest debt is to Marshall Sahlins, who first suggested this study to me and provided material assistance and support to make it happen. Dorothy B. Barrère has long been a gracious and expert consultant on things Hawaiian. Aletta Biersack and Raymond C. Kelly offered invaluable suggestions and criticisms on an earlier version of this work. Discussions with Richard Handler and Daniel Segal and a recent work by George Marcus and Michael M.J. Fischer (1986) helped me to clarify some of the epistemological concerns. My husband, William Fay, has been my in-house advisor on the computerization of the land records; I thank him for his goodwill and patience throughout the project. My understanding of the Hawaiian land records and their historical context has been furthered by discussions with Lilikalā Kameʻeleihiwa and Marion Kelly. While I have benefited from the insights of all these individuals, I alone am responsible for the oversights and omissions in this study.

Uncertainty is an inevitable companion of ethnohistorical research, but the provisional nature of one's conclusions also has a perverse appeal: one can be sure that "the vast darkness of the subject" (Alfred North Whitehead, quoted in Bateson 1967:280) has been left for the most part unobscured, and is perhaps destined to remain so.

Contents

Tables

Figures

Note on Sources

An excellent review and evaluation of the Hawaiian ethnohistorical sources has been provided by Valeri (1985:xvii–viii). With this meticulous summary Valeri has performed an inestimable service for those of us who would investigate the Hawaiian past, and I will not recapitulate his overview here. I must, however, briefly clarify the premises that have guided my use of these sources. As I suggested above, ethnohistorical analysis entails continual evaluation and interpretation, and the interpreter's own point of view is a variable in the process. I therefore cite the evidence for my own interpretations in some detail in the text. In general, when making inferences about precontact Hawaiian society I have relied on the older sources, and on the works of the nineteenth-century Hawaiians Malo, 'Ī'ī, and Kamakau. For normative, symbolic, and ideological material—that is, for insights into Hawaiian culture in the Geertzian sense—the writings of the Hawaiians are more trustworthy than the secondary interpretations of Europeans, even though these Hawaiians were themselves living in a much changed era.

I use later ethnographic works such as the writings of twentieth-century scholars for clues and corroboration and never as the only evidence for a point. This book is largely concerned with land relations and the status of women through the 1850s. The Great Māhele, the land division of 1846–55, set the stage for massive land alienation among Hawaiians; dramatic changes took place in Hawaiian communities in the latter half of the nineteenth century, a period of progressive dispossession and proletarianization. The works of Handy and Pukui, for example, are tremendously valuable for insights into modern and early twentieth-century Hawaiian culture, but they cannot be taken as descriptions of the "ancient" society and they often combine ethnographic reporting with reconstructions of the past.

The reader of this book must be equally circumspect about the interpretations presented here. But citing ethnohistorical sources in the text by publication date presents a problem for those who would evaluate the evidence for themselves. The date of a work's publication is often far removed from the time when the observations were made, and in any case tells nothing about how much time the author spent in Hawaii. To specify these details in the text for every citation would become tedious to all but the most dedicated reader. I have therefore used normal anthropological citation style in the text but have added an item to the bibliographic entries for ethnohistorical observers' accounts. The time period reflected in the account appears at the end of the entry in brackets, e.g., [1813–15] for Whitman 1979. Other details about the observer's context are related in the text where appropriate.

Block quotes and bibliographic information are provided as they appear in the original, without adding the diacritics now commonly used for Hawaiian words and phrases. Hawaiian words in the text are spelled as they appear in the Pukui and Elbert (1971) dictionary. For place names, I have used the versions given in Pukui, Elbert, and Mookini (1974). Following a convention utilized by Sahlins (1985) and Valeri (1985), I use Hawaii without the glottal stop to refer to the entire archipelago, and Hawai'i to refer to the island of that name. I am not fully comfortable with this compromise but I recognize that continually counterposing the two spellings in text and quotations—for the diacritics are used in some publications but not in others—is equally confusing. For the proper spelling of personal names, such as of chiefs and gods, I have consulted the genealogies compiled by Marion Kelly in Freycinet (1978) and recent works such as Valeri (1985). Dorothy B. Barrère and Lilikalā Kame'eleihiwa have also assisted with the names of *ali'i.* Where uncertain, I have made a guess based on my analysis of the elements making up the name. In citations the personal names of Hawaiian authors appear as they do in their published writings. When referring to the authors individually, however, I spell their names according to the modern orthography, that is, with diacritics—hence the appearance of both Ii 1959 and 'Ī'ī (cf. Valeri 1985:xiii).

The Land Records

Aside from published and unpublished ethnohistorical accounts, the major data source utilized in this study is the corpus of land records from the Great Māhele. My database contains information on 4,445 claims, or approximately a third of the total filed. Most of these were originally transcribed by Marshall Sahlins during his ethnohistorical researches on the Hawaiian kingdom. I will address the historical context of the Māhele in chapter 1, but discussion of the statistics will be expedited by a preliminary description of the format of the land records and some explication of how I transformed them into a computer database (see also Linnekin 1987b).

Established by statute in 1846, the Board of Commissioners to Quiet Land Titles in the Hawaiian Kingdom was charged with determining who had rights in the lands of Hawaii (see Hawaii 1846:107–10). For a landholder, there were three steps in the process of acquiring title to land: the initial filing of a claim, giving supporting testimony (which occurred from one to seven years later), and finally the award. All citizens who considered that they had ownership rights in land were to present their claims to the Land Commission by February 14, 1848 (Hawaii 1929:12), and were to be prepared to substantiate them with oral testimony. Although chiefs were also required to file claims, the deadline applied most rigorously to commoner Hawaiians. Many chiefs neglected to file claims, but legislative extensions were later granted to 1862 and then 1895 (see Hawaii 1929:53–54). Approximately 13,500 claims were filed between 1848 and 1855, and 11,309 resulted in awards (Alexander 1890:110).

The organization of the Māhele records corresponds to the three stages of the process described above (originals in AH; copies in AH and in the Hawaiian Collection, Hamilton Library, University of Hawaii). The initial claims are preserved in the Native and Foreign Registers. "Native" means that the claims are in Hawaiian, "foreign" in English. The Native Register is the larger document and is the more significant for my purposes, since the Foreign Register comprises largely claims made by foreigners. The Native Register, however, presents serious obstacles to quantitative treatment. Hawaiians were apparently given minimal instructions as to the format of their initial claims, for the information and level of detail provided in the Register vary widely. Some claims are only for a "land right," with the location usually but not always specified. In contrast, a Hawaiian on the north shore of Oʻahu claimed thirty named planted areas located in the bends of a stream. Source information—when and from whom the right was acquired—and the boundaries of land parcels are given only irregularly. Clearly, the Native Register offers invaluable insights into the Hawaiian subsistence economy and the indigenous notion of rights in productive resources. Claims in the Register are not only for land parcels—real estate in the Western sense—but include irrigation ditches, trees, the right to gather firewood, "clumps" of semiwild cultigens, and the right to fish in the sea and streams for certain species at certain times of year.

While the Register is qualitatively rich, the variability of the information provided makes it less amenable to quantification than the Foreign and Native Testimony. The statistics presented in this book derive primarily from the Testimony, which records the corroborating (and sometimes disputing) statements presented in regard to individual claims. Representatives of the Land Commission traveled the islands between 1848 and 1855, collecting the testimony in each *ahupua'a* land section. The Land Commission conducted its deliberations and made the actual decisions in Honolulu. Unfortunately, these proceedings have not been preserved, but in most cases the testimony appears to have been the primary basis for the Land Commissioners' decision. The instructions given to the commoners at this stage have also not been preserved—they would have been conveyed by missionaries or the chief's local land supervisors—but the content of claims in Testimony is far more standardized than in the Native Register. Hawaiians in most areas were apparently warned that claims for streams, trees, and gathering rights could not be sustained. While less rich qualitatively than the Register, the Testimony is more suitable for generating statistics: the claims are primarily for land parcels, and the composition of each claim tends to adhere to a predictable format. In wetland taro-growing areas the typical claim includes taro land, a houselot, and unirrigated open land for dryland plantings or pasturage.

Claimants usually recited when and from whom they received their right, and gave the location and boundaries of land parcels. Longtime residents of the area were sworn in as corroborating witnesses. The chief's local land supervisor was also present when the testimony was taken. If the *konohiki* disputed the claim, it was usually not awarded. Figure 1 shows a sample claim from the Foreign Testimony, by a commoner named Hikiau; it should be noted that this is a simple claim. The Testimony is often much more complex. Some claimants recited a chain of transmission ("I had it from my father . . . who had it from . . . who had it from . . ."). Sometimes disputes are recorded. In giving the bounds claimants cited the names of neighbors, land sections, or physi-

[Oct. 25, 1849]
No. 1745 Hikiau

Kawela sw. [sworn]   This land is in Kanewai, Waititi–
small kula & 4 kalo patches–1 small house–
        Mauka, Kalama; Waialae stream & Kaluahinenui;
Makai Kalaualii; Honolulu Kalama's hog pen–
        Claimant had this from Kalaiheana in time of Kamehameha I
and has held it undisturbed ever since.
        Lehuanui   Confirmed all the testimony given.

Fig. 1. Sample Māhele claim. (From FT 3:173.)

cal features such as a road, wall, or cliff. In figure 1 *mauka,* Waialae, *makai,* and Honolulu are the four directional points, corresponding more or less to north, east, south, and west in this case.

The computer database was created and statistics were generated using the software package SAS (Statistical Analysis System) on an IBM mainframe. Information from the Native Register and the Testimony reside on separate files within the database. A comparison of the data from these two sources is a study in itself. Clearly, we see a gradual process of editing the indigenous system along Western lines in the progression from claim to testimony, and thence to award. The Foreign and Native Testimonies were not segregated because, ideally, they represent English and Hawaiian versions of the same evidence. This is sometimes true, but where there is a difference the Native Testimony tends to be more specific and more reliable. Information from the third major set of Māhele records, the Awards Book, was utilized only for a subset of the sample, in order to compare the claim with the award on a parcel by parcel basis. The latter findings pertain particularly to Hawaiian land alienation, a tangential issue in this book. For the study at hand I have used the database primarily to generate land transmission statistics.

The data items recorded include characteristics of the claimant (gender, social rank, date of death—if known) and of the overall claim (number of parcels claimed and awarded, acreage awarded), as well as attributes of each parcel or item claimed (location by land name, type of land or right, donor and donor's relationship, time acquired). One of the realities of working with older documentary materials is that there are many missing values, even in the Testimony, and these are excluded from tabulations. In Māhele records the names of women are usually annotated with "(w)" for *wahine,* "woman." Gender was inferred in some cases from the use of gender-specific Hawaiian kin terms by witnesses or was established through other archival and documentary sources. The claimant's social rank—chief, *konohiki,* or commoner—is sometimes stated in the testimony. In other cases the identity of the local *konohiki* becomes clear when commoners cite one individual as a frequent donor. I have also relied on my own familiarity with the prominent chiefs and land givers of the early nineteenth century. I am confident that the vast majority of the chiefs and *konohiki* in my sample have been marked as such, but the category "commoner" undoubtedly includes a small number whom I have not yet identified. As an indicator, of the 4,153 claimants in the "commoner" category only 133 (3 percent) were awarded more than ten acres.

Although this book begins with statistics, most of the subsequent narrative is concerned with ethnohistorical reconstruction and cultural analysis. In Sahlins's original research project a subset of *ahupua'a* land sections was selected for intensive follow-up in pre- and post-Māhele archival materials, including missionary reports and journals, probate and other court cases, petitions, letters, tax records, and land conveyance documents. These materials have made it possible to reconstruct many nineteenth-century household groups and family histories; such analysis has particularly informed the discussion in chapter 5. But these sources are valuable for more than reconstructing genealogies and residential groups. In the archival materials we hear nineteenth-century Hawaiians speaking about their marital and kin relationships, their feelings toward the chiefs, their sense of loss during a period of devastating epidemics and progressive land alienation. Only the words of the Hawaiians can convey a sense of their culture in the Geertzian sense, as a "system of symbols and meanings." Without such recorded statements ethnohistorical analysis would be sterile indeed.

Abbreviations and Symbols

AH	Archives of the State of Hawaii, Honolulu
E-0000	Hawaiian Court of Equity case number; originals in AH
F.O. & Ex.	Foreign Office and Executive File; originals in AH
FT (vol.:page)	Foreign Testimony given before the Commission to Quiet Land Titles, Kingdom of Hawaii, 1848–55; copies in AH and on microfilm in the Hamilton Library, University of Hawaii, Honolulu
HMCS	Hawaiian Mission Children's Society Library, Honolulu
L-0000	Hawaiian Court of Law case number; originals in AH
LCA	Land Commission Award
NR (vol.:page)	Native Register of claims presented to the Commission to Quiet Land Titles, 1846–48; copies and translation in AH and on microfilm in the Hamilton Library, University of Hawaii
NT (vol.:page)	Native Testimony given before the Commission to Quiet Land Titles, 1848–55; copies and translation in AH and on microfilm in the Hamilton Library, University of Hawaii
OL	Older
P-0000	Probate Court case number: First Circuit Court unless otherwise noted
YO	Younger
2d C.C.	Second Circuit Court (Maui)
□	Male or female
○	Female
△	Male

⚯	Deceased
=	Marriage
⊔	Marriage
≈	Cohabitation or common-law Marriage
|	Parent/child relationship
⊓	Sibling relationship
● ▲	Land Commission awardees (female and male)

Chapter 1

Introduction

From the indigenous perspective Hawaii represents a worst-case example of colonial conquest. In the century following Captain Cook's arrival in 1778 a Western-modeled monarchy was established, the Hawaiian economy became enmeshed in production for mercantile capital, and commoner Hawaiians were effectively dispossessed of their lands when the government institutionalized private property. By the time the United States annexed Hawaii in 1898, Hawaiians had been outnumbered, dispossessed, and disenfranchised. Today they are a neocolonial minority fighting for the restoration of lands and some form of sovereignty. This study traces the economic and political transformation of Hawaii through the first century of Western contact, focusing on changes in Hawaiian women's status and cultural valuation in the wake of Western contact and asking how women fared in the transition from sacred chieftainship to a secular, Western-dominated kingdom.

In writing this book I have drawn inspiration from the growing anthropological literature that advances a dialectical relationship between structure and history (e.g., Biersack n.d.; Comaroff 1982; Comaroff 1985; Dening 1980; Sahlins 1981, 1985; Valeri 1982). In nineteenth-century Hawaii we see the response of an indigenous social order to some extraordinary, even tragic, historical events. But this work's point of view (I use the phrase advisedly) has also been influenced by the more explicitly critical anthropology of colonialism and political economy, notably by such writers as Talal Asad (1973), Sidney Mintz (1975, 1977, 1985), and Eric Wolf (1982). Especially useful have been recent works that temper the uninflected world-system perspective of Andre Gunder Frank and Immanuel Wallerstein with more culturally nuanced understandings of indigenous cultural response. Examining local forms of articulation with global capitalism is increasingly becoming the dominant problematic in political economy (Roseberry 1988). Works in this genre that I have found particularly successful include Ong (1987), Sider (1986), Taussig (1980), and Verdery (1983).

I will address the question of whether the status of Hawaiian women necessarily declined with Western colonization, a question that Gailey (1987) and Silverblatt (1987) have recently posed in other cultural contexts (cf. Etienne and Leacock 1980), by examining the place of women in Hawaiian culture and offering some hypotheses about the way Hawaiian society worked, both before and after European contact. Using a concept of gender that includes sociological aspects of women's status as well as the ideologies that shape or mask male/female relations, I attempt to pursue a historical anthropology that balances the overwhelming force of Western expansion with the capability of indigenous cultures to resist and bend foreign intrusion. By the end of this study I will reach a conclusion that concurs with Stoler's (1977:76) observation about Javanese culture, namely, that "the introduction of private property, the emergence of class stratification, and the imposition of colonial rule have frequently produced sexual dichotomization, but they do not *necessarily* do so." Asserting Hawaiian women's essential autonomy in spite of the gradual subordination of Hawaiian society as a whole may sound paradoxical, if not revisionist, and there is certainly the danger of "romanticizing the cultural freedom of anthropological subjects" (Roseberry 1988:174), but I will nevertheless argue that the structural importance and the personal authority of women, both chiefly and common, were enhanced *in some contexts* in the early postcontact period, even as women in general were progressively devalued in state-level civil institutions. The important point, as I elaborate below, is that women's status is not a simple matter: not only were there considerable ambiguities, even paradoxes, in indigenous Hawaiian gender relations, but the cultural conjuncture with the West also intensified the contradictions that were already in place.

Questions of women's status often turn on the issue of jural authority or women's activity in the "public domain," that is to say, control over people, resources, and property. Ethnohistorical studies most typically rely on the observations and representations of foreign and mostly male observers to reconstruct women's standing and authority. The present study is unusual in this regard, for it relies on a set of ethnohistorical statistics that provide a reliable measure of jural authority: women's control over land. The initial impetus for this book was a statistical phenomenon that came to light in my analysis of nineteenth-century

Hawaiian land records. The text is broadly structured as an explanation of an apparent change in Hawaiian women's control over property in the mid-nineteenth century: a statistical shift in the inheritance pattern such that land increasingly came into the hands of women. The data that evince this change were compiled and tabulated from testimony given, for the most part, by commoner Hawaiians during the Great Māhele. I begin with this empirical puzzle and will keep returning to it, for the explanation for the inheritance shift must take into account economic history, demographics, and political change as well as cultural precedents: local-level social organization, the nature of the Hawaiian chieftainship, and, perhaps most importantly, a social and symbolic complex that is often summed up as "the status of women."

The Problem of Women

Certain tangents are unavoidable when tackling a complex ethnohistorical problem, but by centripetal force the argument of this book will keep returning to the issue of gender relations. Much of the debate in the gender literature since the mid-1970s has revolved around a seemingly irreconcilable dichotomy: are women universally subordinate to men or not? Most writers have opted to defend some variant of the "yes" or "no" position under the guise of oppositions such as subordination/ dominance, nature/culture, domestic/public domains, influence/power.[1] For all the eloquence of the arguments on either side, the either/or quality of the exchanges has begun to seem unproductive. Much more interesting are studies that view sexual asymmetry as an ethnographic issue (cf. Tiffany 1979) and examine popular generalizations about women's status in a particular context of social action, such as exchange; notable investigations of the latter include Feil (1978), Sexton (1986), Strathern (1972), and Weiner (1976, 1982), among others.

Accordingly, I wish to make it clear that my intent is not to develop what Quinn (1977:182) calls "key" theories—universalistic explanations for a unitary concept of "the status of women." As Quinn points out, part of the problem with the gender literature is that different authors do not agree on what they mean by women's status. Moreover, writers have varying conceptions of such crucial notions as "politics" and "authority," so that their statements about women's participation in jural affairs may not be comparable (Tiffany 1978:47; for an excellent discussion of this issue see Oboler 1985:284–94). In this book I use the phrase "status of women" in the most holistic sense to refer to all aspects of women's social and cultural position: jural and domestic authority, economic and social productivity, the division of labor, participation in both informal and formal exchanges, kinship role expectations, structural position in and between kin groups, sentimental attachments, and symbolic and mythic associations. When we unbundle the status of women into these components and examine them individually in a particular society, it becomes ever more difficult to characterize the status of women simply as high or low, valued or devalued (cf. Sanday 1981; Whyte 1978).

To my mind the most salient and intriguing issue is the relationship between women's categorical status within a normative ideology that is often male dominated—at least as retrieved by anthropologists—and their social efficacy in action and affairs, particularly in material exchanges. The congruence or incongruence of these two aspects of the status of women remains an ethnographic issue. It is not a given that the relationship between ideology and social practice must be homogeneous; studies by Kelly (1977) and Wagner (1967), for example, have shown that every social system embodies internal contradictions.

In the gender literature Feil (1978) has shown that the explicit institutionalization of sexual asymmetry has little bearing on Enga women's control over material exchanges involving men (Friedl 1967 made a similar point about Greek gender relations). The gender literature would benefit from more ethnographic studies (such as Weiner 1976) detailing women's views and diverse spheres of activity. Admittedly, the empiricist approach carries a danger: anthropologists are notorious for countering any sort of generalization with the objection that "my people don't do it that way." This familiar argument—which can be traced to Boasian historical particularism, the conceptual wellsprings of modern American anthropology—leads logically to the conclusion that each case is unique and incomparable. Nonetheless, an examination of the cultural ethos and social position of Hawaiian women does undermine several of the distinctions central to ongoing debates in the gender literature. In subsequent chapters I will argue that Hawaiian women were not relegated to the domestic domain in the indigenous society and that it is not accurate to say that Hawaiian women exerted "influence" in contrast to men's "power."

Again, we may err if we expect to find correspondence between the views and interests of men and women. In the matrix of relationships between male and female ideology and action, there are tensions and countervailing forces, and these shape the outcome of social change. It is particularly difficult to postulate a set of consistent "rules" for Hawaiian social organization. Kinship was reckoned bilaterally and there were no corporate descent groups (see chap. 5). The evidence points to a patrilineal bias in political and property succession, but in the exercise of personal authority women appear to have been the equals of men. Moreover, women figured prominently in adoption and in the transmission of spiritual property. Should we then treat female inheritance in Hawaii as a "deviation" from a norm, or as an alternate normative pattern that became dominant at a particular historical moment? Anthropologists working in societies with patrilineal norms have often seen matrilaterality as a deviation or an exception to the rule. If inheritance is 70 percent patrilineal, that still leaves a sizable incidence of deviations to explain. For the Nuer, Evans-Pritchard asserted that the residential group was bilaterally constituted "on the ground" precisely because Nuer ideology was strongly patrilineal—the famous "Nuer paradox." The point is that alternate practices are never random; they too have a pattern. That pattern may run counter to certain ideological norms but may accord well with other cultural premises.

For early Hawaii the salient question is not simply how we should understand exceptions to the rule. In Hawaiian social organization and gender relations, a major issue remains that of determining what in fact are the rules. Outside the context of the sacrificial religion and the tabu system, it is difficult to find support for the premise that Hawaiian women were considered inferior to men. Although in some societies women are explicitly conceptualized as subordinate, polluting, dangerous, or passive, and they may have correspondingly little influence on affairs, the ideology of male dominance seems weakly developed in early Hawaii and it is well documented that chiefly women at least were autonomous political actors with considerable personal and spiritual power (for missionary attempts to teach Hawaiian women "submissiveness" see Grimshaw 1985).

To use Karen Sacks's (1979) terms, Hawaiian women were "sisters" rather than "wives." Despite an indigenous religion that imposed eating tabus on women and mandated a degree of sexual separation (see chap. 2), the ethnographic evidence suggests that the Hawaiian woman was indeed a "member of a community of owners of the means of production: an equal, an adult among adults, a decision maker" (Sacks 1979:6). Hawaiian women were celebrated as mothers and as sisters and were portrayed as potent beings in myth and symbolism. In politics and social organization women played a crucial role in chiefly rank determination and in the composition of the local group. The role of Hawaiian women as landholders in the mid-nineteenth century was far from unprecedented. The statistical shift in inheritance realized the long-established cultural centrality of Hawaiian women in certain roles and contexts—an alternate normative complex to the statistical dominance of males as landlords and military rulers. I will argue further that the participation of Hawaiian women in land relations cannot be explained economically or demographically but derives from their structural and symbolic position in kinship and the local group.

The Hawaiian case highlights the inadequacy of a purely categorical approach to the status of women. If we analyze women only in light of a dominant ideology that emphasizes their inferiority vis-à-vis men, far too much is left unexplained, even incomprehensible. Edwin Ardener (1972) and Shirley Ardener (1975) have elaborated the idea that women may have their own, alternate ideological models of cosmology and social relations. Given the intrinsic limitations of the ethnohistorical data, this is not a line of argument that I feel qualified to pursue at length here. But there is evidence that Hawaiian women viewed the indigenous religion quite differently from men and that they participated in parallel but separate forms of worship. I will also suggest that the abolition of the aboriginal religion with its system of ritual prohibitions or *kapu* was not induced solely by the intrusion of foreign goods and ideas but was in part provoked by a contradiction between the ritual status of Hawaiian women and their efficacy in temporal (including jural) affairs.

One further note: in early Hawaii chiefs and commoners were linked in a single structure of material relationships and categorical oppositions (see chap. 4). Hierarchy pervaded land relations and stimulated economic productivity, and postcontact Hawaiian history was decisively shaped by the actions and decisions of the chiefs. One cannot address the issue of gender hierarchy without discussing the social and political structures of Hawaiian society as a whole, for the destiny of chiefly women and their vulnerability to the tabu system differed considerably from the life experiences of commoner women. And so this book is also about ordinary Hawaiians living on the land. Their statements are the basis for the statistics that I wish to explain. In this study I attempt to reconstruct what happened to the people on the land after 1778. Changes in the status of Hawaiian women are part of that story.

The Māhele

The Great Māhele[2] is widely considered a watershed in the transformation of Hawaiian society. Except for the overthrow of the monarchy in 1893, no other nineteenth-century event had such far-reaching effects on Hawaiians. Even pro-Western historians now concede that the Māhele's long-term effects were disastrous for the Hawaiian people. Intended to replace tenancy relations with the guarantees of secure title, the Māhele instead set the stage for the alienation of most Hawaiians from the land. I will have more to say about Hawaiian land tenure and dispossession in later chapters (see also Linnekin 1983, 1987a); for now it will suffice to say that land was inalienable in the native conception. Rights to use productive resources—including not only land but forests, streams, and the sea—were allocated through a hierarchy of land giver/tenant relationships, from higher to lesser chiefs to local land supervisors, and thence to commoners.

By the 1840s the Hawaiian government, beset by threats from the major powers, was under considerable internal pressure from resident foreigners to reform the land tenure system (see Kuykendall 1938:271–79). Merchants and entrepreneurs saw the land as potentially productive capital that was going to waste as the native Hawaiian population dwindled due to introduced diseases. The foreigners wanted the right to own, buy, and sell land and were convinced that they could put it to better use than the Hawaiians. Missionaries argued that land ownership would protect the commoners from chiefly tyranny and would encourage industry, to the ultimate economic benefit of the kingdom. Their rationale closely resembled the modern argument for converting rental apartments into condominiums: the belief that owners will take better care of their property and be more industrious in making improvements than renters. The political argument was also made that by instituting land reform the fledgling kingdom would earn the respect of the Western powers and thereby safeguard its autonomy. As for the king and the chiefs, the disastrous sandalwood trade and decades of conspicuous consumption had left many *ali'i* saddled with massive debts to foreign merchants. Some chiefs were persuaded that private title would benefit them economically, either through their own capitalist ventures or through the option of outright sale (see Dorton 1986).

The Land Commission was charged with defining and separating the rights of the various parties having interests in the lands of Hawaii, principally the king, the chiefs, and the commoners. Before the Māhele no one could be said to own land in Hawaii in the Western sense, but as the highest ranking landlord in the social hierarchy the king had the ultimate right to distribute land. From late January to March, 1848, King Kamehameha III divided the lands of the kingdom between himself and 250 prominent chiefs and *konohiki*. This event constituted the Great Māhele proper. As recorded in the Māhele Book, the king and the chiefs signed complementary quitclaims to specific lands, the king giving up all rights in one named land section as the chief surrendered all rights to a different land. The king later separated the Government Lands—those reserved for the Hawaiian government as a formal entity—from the Crown Lands—those reserved for the monarch and his descendants.[3]

The Hawaiian commoners, who lived as tenants under the chiefs, were notably absent from this initial formal division, largely because the king and the chiefs could not agree on a formula for defining their rights. The architects of the Māhele, many of them foreigners, had initially envisioned that the common people would constitute one of the three major parties in the division. But in 1848 the commoners' rights were safeguarded only by a qualifying phrase: the Crown, Government, and *konohiki* lands were apportioned "reserving the rights of native tenants." The specific rights of the common people were to be determined later. The king and the chiefs debated the rights of the *makaʻāinana* in Privy Council in July and August 1850 (Privy Council Minutes, AH). A sticking point was whether commoners should retain their long-established gathering rights in the uplands and forests. The chiefs wanted their lands "in fee simple," unencumbered by residual privileges, but the king was adamant about preserving the commoners' access rights. At his insistence the Kuleana Act of 1850 (Hawaii 1850: 202–4), which authorized the granting of Land Commission awards (*kuleana*) to commoners, included a section safeguarding the people's right to take firewood, timber, and thatch from the chiefs' lands, as well as their water rights.

The king's misgivings about the land division were prophetic; the government's failure to protect *kuleana* holders from large landowners after the Māhele was a contributing factor driving the people from the land. When the division was completed, nearly a million acres were allocated as Crown Lands, a million and a half each went to the government and the chiefs, and fewer than thirty thousand were awarded to the mass of the Hawaiian people (Thrum 1896:40).

The Statistics

The figures presented in tables 1 and 2 are the starting point for this excursion into Hawaiian history and culture. These two tabulations document the rise in female inheritance; further statistical material will be presented and analyzed in chapter 7, where I will elaborate on the historical context of the inheritance data. The number of cases represented in table 1 is far smaller than the total number of claims in the sample: first, this tabulation includes only cases where the donor's relationship, time of acquisition, and gender of recipient were known, either through the testimony or other sources; and second, as is clear from a comparison of the total number of cases in tables 1 and 2, most claimants in Māhele testimony traced their *kuleana* to political superiors rather than relatives. The largest single category of land givers is that of *konohiki*. But land giving from a political superior and transmission through the family were not mutually exclusive. Land was always subject to severance by the chief and *konohiki*, but in practice eviction of the commoners was infrequent (see chap. 4) and particular plots were passed down from parents to children. Both kinds of transmission—

TABLE 1. **Time of Inheritance by Gender of Recipient**

Time of Inheritance	Female N	Female %	Male N	Male %	Total N
Before 1820	11	5.7	182	94.3	193
1820–29	2	5.6	34	94.4	36
1830–39	9	14.8	52	85.2	61
1840–47	17	24.3	53	75.7	70
Total before 1848	39	10.8	322	89.2	361
1848–55	140	58.3	100	41.7	240
Total	179		422		601

Note: The total before 1848 includes 1 case (a male claimant) where it was not possible to pinpoint the time of receipt by decade.

TABLE 2. **Time of Inheritance by Gender of Recipient, Honolulu Area, *Ahupua'a* of Kalihi, Mānoa, and Moanalua**

Time of Inheritance	Female N	Female %	Male N	Male %	Total N
Before 1848	7	24.1	22	75.9	29
1848–55	25	65.8	13	34.2	38
Total	32		35		67

political and familial—took place concurrently. The hierarchical basis of land giving pertained within the extended family also. A senior member of the household group was considered the *haku ʻāina* 'landlord' within the family and had the right to allocate use and residence rights to junior relatives and dependents who then lived "under" the donor.

The land transmission statistics reveal a dramatic shift in female inheritance during the period of the Māhele: the incidence of women inheriting land increases from 10.8 percent before 1848 to 58.3 percent in the 1848–55 period. Bequests to male heirs average 89.2 percent before the Māhele, but 41.7 percent between 1848 and 1855. Moreover, increasing inheritance by women was a trend through the 1830s and 1840s. As stated earlier, the primary source for this tabulation is the Foreign and Native Testimony. However, the figures for the Native Register do support the trend evident in table 1. If there is a pattern of difference between the two sources, it is that the proportion of female inheritance for the pre-1848 decades is higher in the Native Register, averaging around 25 percent. The increase in women inheriting land is even more pronounced in the Honolulu area than in the sample as a whole, as indicated by table 2, which presents figures from three populous land sections around Honolulu. Female inheritance is also more frequent in the Honolulu area in the pre-1848 period. This suggests that it is valid to draw diachronic conclusions from a comparison of *ahupuaʻa* near Honolulu with those in rural and outer-island districts more remote from the market center.

Nearly all of the donations represented in tables 1 and 2 are oral bequests reported by landholders to representatives of the Land Commission. Although the 1850 Session Laws established guidelines for the division of property left by intestates (Hawaii 1850:181–85), these pertained only when the case reached probate court and a judge had to determine the division of the estate. Commoners rarely brought cases to probate during this period; when they did it was often years, even decades, after the awardee's death, when consensual coresidence and use broke down among the surviving heirs. The tabulations do not include cases where a judge divided the property according to the formula set by law, because such divisions do not reflect the express wishes and cultural attitudes of Hawaiians.

Although Hawaiian women's legal rights were successively abridged during the 1840s, such laws had minimal impact on customary land giving within the family through the early 1850s. In other words, the inheritance statistics are not an artifact of Western-influenced laws but instead represent a Hawaiian cultural response to historical contingencies affecting the local community. During this period and in the years following the Māhele, Hawaiian women's formal legal status was markedly at odds with their importance both in government politics and at the local level. This incongruity corresponds in part to the difference between Western and Hawaiian views of women. But an analogous disjunction existed in the indigenous society under the *kapu* system. I will argue that Hawaiian gender relations were characterized by a degree of politicking—men and women competing and vying for authority in certain contexts. Nearly two decades after the overthrow of the tabus—an event instigated by high-ranking chiefly women—male Hawaiian *ali'i* adopted a set of laws authored by Western males who believed in the incompetence and passivity of women. I am not suggesting that the male chiefs necessarily subscribed to the Western view; they may well have considered the legal code a sop to the foreigners and largely irrelevant to their own lives. But after 1819 both male and female chiefs were experimenting with a new set of tabus, and there is an intriguing parallel between the public ritual status of women in the old religion and the "official" position of women under the new laws.

One other possible disqualification must be considered when evaluating the veracity of the land transmission statistics. Could the increase in female inheritance over time be attributed solely to retrospective revision or "structural amnesia"? It is a commonplace in anthropology that retrospective genealogical revision takes place in oral accounts of political and property succession. If one sex is normatively favored, bilateral links tend to be forgotten in time: males in the ascendant generations may be transformed into females, or vice versa. Sahlins (1985:21) has pointed out that male links predominate in the more ancient Hawaiian chiefly genealogies, which then become "a reticulate network of relationships through men and women in the most recent generations." In land succession, temporary custodianship by someone other than the eventual heir would probably not be recited in a retrospective account of the chain of transmission. Admittedly, temporary placeholding by women was probably long established in Hawaiian land tenure. The inheritance statistics may therefore reflect a degree of retrospective revision, although it is impossible to gauge the effect precisely. But I do not believe that the increase in women inheriting is solely an artifact of structural amnesia. Most of the bequests are relatively recent—within approximately two generations prior to 1850—and the numerical pattern is too pronounced to be explained away that easily. In my view, tables 1 and 2 summarize individual events occurring over time: instances where particular individuals were given control over family resources.

Two interpretations of the land transmission statistics are possible. One is that the increase in female inheritance represents radical culture change, a thorough transformation of Hawaiian values and social patterns. The other is that female inheritance was always a structural possibility, and the increase therefore represents not much of a change after all. Perhaps neither conclusion is accurate as stated; in rationalist style I will take an intermediate position, maintaining that the increase in women inheriting land was part of an ongoing transformation of Hawaiian gender relations during the nineteenth century. I will argue that Hawaiian women saw themselves as placeholders on the land rather than as permanent heirs, a role that not only resonated with the indigenous notion of land tenure as guardianship rather than owning, but was also precedented in women's position in the local group and accorded well with the Hawaiian symbolic association of land with woman and femaleness. As mothers and as sisters, women took control of the land on behalf of those whom they saw as the rightful heirs in the next generation—their own or their siblings' children. In this sense, female inheritance had a conservative intent—that of reproducing the prior social pattern. But as Sahlins (1981) has eloquently argued, such attempts at reproduction are likely to have unintended consequences (see Giddens 1979) and often entail transformation.

During the nineteenth century Hawaiians as a people and Hawaiian women in particular were progressively devalued from the point of view of Western white society, which became politically and socially dominant in the islands. Yet, paradoxically, Hawaiian women at the same time assumed an increasingly active and structurally central role at the local level. Granted, there were precedents for them to do so. Nonetheless, the social and personal dominance of women in Hawaiian communities—a theme that pervades twentieth-century Hawaiian ethnography—represents a change of emphasis and ethos and a transformation of gender relations from the era of the sacred chieftainship, when male chiefs could put women to death for eating forbidden foods.

Chapter 2

Women and Tabu

Most writers in the anthropology of gender address either ideological or behavioral aspects of women's roles but not both. In Polynesia particularly, a focus on issues of purity and pollution has tended to divert attention from women's temporal and political activities. There are a number of excellent discussions of the cultural ethos and symbolic status of Polynesian women (Hanson 1982; Hecht 1977; Huntsman and Hooper 1975; G. Rogers 1977; Shore 1981), but with the exception of Weiner (1982, 1985), few have thus far attempted to reconcile women's symbolic valuation with their productive and exchange activities. In this and the following chapter I will discuss the status of women in later precontact and early postcontact Hawaii, focusing on the interaction between categorical and symbolic aspects of women's cultural position and their roles in production and exchange.

Inescapable problems arise when one analyzes the status of Polynesian women in exclusively categorical terms. Such a perspective tends either to underemphasize women's power or to overdraw the incongruity between women's ritual valuation and their social importance. Particularly problematic is the premise that *noa* 'free, common' is an unchanging female state and an irreducible ritual disability. The apparent contradictions are particularly striking in the Hawaiian case: women were categorically *noa*—common, profane, or perhaps more accurately "free of kapu" (Hanson 1982:344)—but chiefly women were vessels of the highest *kapu* rank and were critical to the dynastic aspirations of their frequently lower-ranking husbands; women were barred from full participation in the sacrificial ceremonies that sedimented chiefly conquest, but the products of impure women (fine mats and tapa cloth) performed the function of consecration when they were used to wrap offerings and idols; and women were forbidden the choicest foods, but they manufactured some of the highest valuables of the society—mats, tapas, loincloths, and possibly feather cloaks—goods that figured prominently in tributary prestations, chiefly gift giving, and religious offerings. Even if we accept the thesis of female pollution and assume that Hawaiian women were ritually devalued or considered contaminating in some contexts, what does that ideology have to do with women's social efficacy, their temporal or secular power? The answer in the Hawaiian case is, as the evidence suggests, very little.

The abolition of the indigenous religion in 1819 marked a watershed in Hawaiian history, for the Hawaiian religion had embodied an elaborate system of *kapu* 'tabus, prohibitions' that impinged on day-to-day relations between men and women. Like any reconstruction, what follows is an interpretation of ethnohistorical materials. Since all of the available sources are postcontact, and many of them are post-1819, my statements should not be applied uncritically to the pre-European period. However, I believe that much of the following discussion holds true for the late precontact, conquest period. In this chapter I address categorical issues, primarily the standing of Hawaiian women within the native ideology and religion, while in the following chapter I deal with women at work and in action, as producers and exchangers.

The *Kapu* System

Early Western visitors interpreted the ritually mandated segregation of Hawaiian men and women in certain contexts as an indicator of a general low valuation of women in Hawaiian society (e.g., Ellis 1969:126, 390–91; Whitman 1979:22; see also Malo 1951:51). This book advances the argument that women are multivalent in Hawaiian thought, that their symbolic valuation cannot be characterized simply as high or low, positive or negative. Nonetheless, there is good evidence that Hawaiian women themselves viewed the tabus as onerous. While I dispute Valeri's (1985) characterization of Hawaiian women as symbolically "marginal," "passive," and distant from the gods, I nevertheless concur that the tabus devalued women in their own estimation and probably in the estimation of Hawaiian men. I will argue further that Hawaiian women's standing in the context of the sacrificial religion was at odds with their social efficacy and that the *kapu* system was an arena for gender politics. Women did not passively acquiesce in the constraints imposed by the male-dominated sacrificial religion.

The Hawaiian *kapu* system (see Malo 1951:27–28; Valeri 1985:109–29) forbade men and women from eating together. Each sex had a separate eating house. As elsewhere in Polynesia, cooking was men's work. A separate *imu* 'underground oven' had to be prepared for each sex (Dibble 1909:81; Malo 1951:27–29). Malo contradicts himself by mentioning a wife cooking her husband's food, but this may refer to the post-*kapu* period; in 1826 Paulding saw women cooking taro and making poi (1970:213). The women's eating house was not prohibited to men (Malo 1951:29), "but a decorous man will not enter it," according to Kotzebue (1921, 3:249). Men and women could associate freely in the sleeping house, where no eating was allowed (Malo 1951:29). Women were forbidden from entering *heiau* 'temples' or the men's house, which served as the domestic shrine, and were prohibited from the sea while priests were officiating in the temple (Corney 1896:100–101). Menstruating women were secluded in a separate house, the *hale pe'a*. A man was also prohibited from consorting with any other woman during his wife's menses, on pain of death (Malo 1951:29).

The food restrictions are perhaps the best known aspect of the Hawaiian *kapu* system. Pork, coconut, shark, some species of fish, sea turtle, porpoise, whale, and most varieties of banana were forbidden to women (for discussion see Valeri 1985:115–20). Several early observers attest that women (and, for that matter, commoner men) ate primarily fish and taro (Arago 1823:149; Beresford 1789:275; Campbell 1967:135; Ellis 1782:167; Macrae 1922:15; Samwell 1967:1163, 1184), although chickens were not forbidden them (Samwell 1967:1181; Vancouver, 1798, 3:53) and women could eat dog (Campbell 1967:135; Vancouver 1798, 3:53; "red dogs," Freycinet 1978:73; for discussion see Valeri 1985:115–17). Women and men, however, could not eat from the same individual animal or dish (Townsend 1921:15; Vancouver 1798, 3:53). The penalty for infraction in any of these areas was death (Malo 1951:29).

Kapu means both 'sacred' and 'forbidden' (Barrère 1959:180). Valeri (1985:90) adds that *kapu* means 'marked,' indicating "the need to pay attention." Valeri (1985) demonstrates that the gender prohibitions were part of the same logical system as the tabus surrounding the highest chiefs, but it can be argued that the differentiation of men and women indexed by the tabus was less salient than the rank distinction between chiefs and commoners. "In the ancient days there were many *kapus*," wrote Kamakau (1964:9), "and they were in the hands of chiefs." Significantly, Pukui's gloss for *kapu* in this passage is 'privileges.' Social rank was indexed by restrictions on the behavior of lesser-ranking persons in a chief's presence, and in Hawaiian literature high ranking men and women are referred to as *kapu* chiefs and chiefesses. The most critical fact for understanding Hawaiian chiefly politics is that rank was bilaterally determined; although men predominated as political rulers and conquerers, chiefly women were vessels of the highest *kapu* rank and were critical to the dynastic aspirations of their frequently lower-ranking husbands.

According to Kamakau (1964:4–5), chiefs of the two highest ranks, *pi'o* and *nī'aupi'o,* possessed the prostrating tabu or *kapu moe,* which required others immediately to lie face down upon the ground in their presence. Kamakau relates a famous episode in which the possession of this *kapu* stopped a battle and saved the losing side from certain destruction. Embroiled in an attempt to conquer Maui, the Hawai'i chief Kalani'ōpu'u sent his son Kīwala'ō, of *nī'aupi'o* rank, to beg the Maui chief Kahekili for their lives. When Kīwala'ō appeared, the soldiers on both sides had to prostrate themselves. He thus gained safe passage to Wailuku, where he successfully appealed to Kahekili (Kamakau 1961: 88). *Naha* chiefs, of the next highest rank, held the *kapu noho* requiring others only to sit in their presence. The *kapu* of *wohi* chiefs, who are described as being related in the junior line to the ruling chief, did not require others to lie down or sit but permitted the *wohi* chief to remain upright in the presence of a chief with the prostration *kapu* (Ii 1959:52; Kamakau 1964:5, 22 n. 6). The highest ranking person in the kingdom in 1819 was Keōpūolani, a *nī'aupi'o* chiefess and the mother of Kamehameha's children Liholiho (Kamehameha II), Nāhi'ena'ena, and Kauikeaouli (Kamehameha III). According to Kamakau (1961: 224), she was of such high rank that Kamehameha, a *wohi* chief, had to remove his loincloth in her presence.

The mythic origin of both the eating tabus (*'ai kapu*) and the *kapu* of the chiefs is a conflict between husband and wife: Wākea's deception of his wife Papa. Wākea instituted both *kapu* days, when male/female relations are restricted, and daily separate eating in order to conceal his incestuous relationship with their daughter Ho'ohōkūkalani (Ii 1959:160; Malo 1951:51–52; Valeri 1985:169–71). The child of this original consanguineous mating was the first *nī'aupi'o* chief. Papa, reincarnated in succeeding generations, in revenge took several husbands from among her own descendants (Kamakau 1964:25, 44 n. 1; Valeri 1985:169). Valeri (1985:169–70) points out that the Papa/Wākea story is a transformation of the Polynesian myth describing the separation of heaven and earth, but in the Hawaiian variant "the origin of the separation of heaven and earth has been transformed into the origin of the separation of the sexes and, correlatively, of the separation of the sacred ali'i from other men." Moreover, from the Papa/Wākea myth Valeri derives the requisites of the sacrificial system: "the separation of the pure and the impure and therefore the exclusion of women" (1985:171).

Valeri's interpretation, resting on the central opposition of sacred and profane, draws on Handy's classic study of Polynesian religion as well as on European intellectual traditions. According to Handy (1927:43), the concept of *kapu* embodies the separation of the common and the divine. The segregation of the sexes in Hawaii extends the dualistic principle of Polynesian religion, wherein sacredness, divinity, light, and strength are associated with maleness. "The inferior aspect of nature . . . is found to be the manifestation of the negative, female principle, to be the realm of darkness and death," of weakness and corruption (1927:37). According to Handy, Polynesian ideology links separate eating to the protection of the male from female pollution: "Since food was capable of acting as a medium to carry psychic influences into the body, it was considered safer for men not to eat in company with women, not to have their food prepared by them, or to employ the same fire or same utensils" (1927:49).

For his thesis regarding the categorical status of Hawaiian women, Valeri draws particular support from Malo's statement that a menstruating woman was "both unclean and unlucky" (Malo 1951:29). Kamakau (1961:3) too states that during menses "a woman was then defiled, for the god despised (*ho'o pailua*) all bloody things." He refers to the *hale pe'a* as "the defiled spot." And yet Hawaiians believed that a woman was particularly fertile in the waning days of her menses. Kamakau (1961:3) states that the tabu period lasted three to five days. A woman then ritually cleansed herself and could again sleep with her husband. This implies that sexual intercourse with a woman who might still be bleeding did not necessarily defile the man and was even thought most conducive to conception. Leaving the *hale pe'a* and ritually bathing appear to be the significant points in determining the woman's ritual state, not the presence or absence of blood per se. The paradigmatic legend of 'Umi, the famed ancestor of the Kamehameha line, is significant for the thesis of female pollution, for the narrative indicates that menstrual blood is not always dangerous and polluting to men.

In the account of 'Umi's conception the ruling chief Līloa seduces Akahiakuleana as she is bathing "in preparation for the ceremony of purification" after leaving the menstrual house (Malo 1951:259; cf. Kamakau 1961:9). In the version told to Jules Remy (1979:15) in 1853, Akahiakuleana "was then in her menses, so that the malo of the king was soiled with the discharge." I quote Malo's (1951:250; cf. Fornander 1916; 4:178–235) summary of what happened next:

> After the completion of the act, Liloa, perceiving that the woman was flowing, asked her if it was her time of impurity, to which she answered, "Yes, this is the continuation of it." "You will probably have a child then," said Liloa, and she answered that it was probable.

Līloa then gives Akahi tokens of their union: his feather cape, loincloth (see Stokes 1906:154), and whalebone pendant (*lei niho palaoa*). 'Umi displays these articles when he seeks out his father several years later, and they are accepted as proof of paternity.

The 'Umi story is paradigmatic on several levels, notably in its scenario of a usurping younger brother who recruits a following and uses his personal god to seize the chiefdom. The important point here is that the 'Umi legend also reveals Hawaiian premises about conception, paternity, and pollution. None of the available versions of the story offers an explanation for the apparent ritual contradiction in a high chief having intercourse with a menstruating woman. There is no mention that the blood was contaminating or that the act was polluting to Līloa. Rather, in the Remy (1979:15) version the show of blood is noted as sure confirmation of the child's paternity: "That would, indeed, be an unexceptionable testimony, for by the law of kapu a wife could not, under pain of death, approach her husband while in her courses. The soiled malo and the time of the child's birth would give certain indications."

The scenario of 'Umi's conception appears again in a chiefly life history recounted in a late nineteenth-century probate case. At issue in this case (P-805, AH) was the paternity of the deceased, William L. Moehonua, governor of Maui. Moehonua had inherited substantial lands from his chiefess wife, and King David Kalākaua sought to prove that he was a collateral heir through his grandfather, a warrior chief named 'Aikanaka. An elderly female retainer (*kahu*) was called to testify on behalf of the king's claim:

> I knew Moehonua, knew his father and mother. Keaweamahi was his real father because he was the kane ['man, husband'] of Napua, who was the

mother of Moehonua, but Aikanaka whom I knew cohabited with Napua. . . .
It was well known that Moehonua was a child of the chief Aikanaka. Kaaua
was Aikanaka's kahu. Aikanaka gave the child to be brought up by Kaaua and
also gave him a malo which was the one which he wore when he cohabited with
Napua and was smeared with blood. . . . Aikanaka knew that the child was his
and gave as a token of this a necklace with a bone. . . . Keaweamahi and
Kaaua were Kahus of Aikanaka, they prepared his food. Napua was their
wahine. (Testimony of Kawailiilii, October 10, 1878)

It appears that in the Hawaiian case the presence of blood on the chief's
loincloth is not interpreted as a sign of virginity as in Western cultures,
but as proof that the union took place at the most auspicious time for
conception. Both Akahi and Napua are specifically stated to have had
husbands when they had intercourse with the chiefly visitors.

Valeri's reconstruction of the ancient religion offers many brilliant
insights into Hawaiian society and politics. But symbolic material always
permits alternative interpretations. Other readings of Hawaiian gender
ideology are possible. The food taboos and separate eating can also be
interpreted as indicating special powers or capabilities possessed by
women. If women are dangerous to men in some contexts, is this because they are contaminating or because they have a special relationship
with the divine? The latter thesis has been developed by F. Allen Hanson (1982), and will be discussed further below. Leaving the issue of
pollution aside for the moment, it is worth considering the possibility of
contradictions or incongruities between male and female views of the
kapu system. We are treading here on speculative ground, but the
ethnohistorical literature provides evidence of gender conflict in the
observance and enforcement of the tabus.

Malo (1951:51) writes that because of the enforced segregation of the
sexes "the mutual love of the man and his wife was not kept warm." A
Christian convert, Malo lays many evils at the door of the indigenous
religion, but here he offers what may be an inadvertent insight: that the
tabus were the source of strain between men and women. Certainly in
the early postcontact period, as Sahlins (1981) documents, Hawaiian
women used their alliances with foreigners to defy the authority of Hawaiian men. Although tabu violations were theoretically punishable by
death, in practice the severity of the punishment depended on detection
and the disposition of particular male chiefs (cf. Sahlins 1981:47). Cook
and King (1784, 3:130; Beaglehole 1967:624) report that a girl was badly

beaten for having eaten the wrong type of banana on board ship. One of Lucy Thurston's (1921:71) pupils was a girl whose eye had been put out for eating a banana when a small child: "had she been of mature years," Thurston assures us, "her *life* would have been taken." But in 1820 another missionary, Lucia Holman (1931:24), was told that Kamehameha once encountered a group of women preparing to eat a stolen bunch of bananas. Upon hearing them pray on his behalf he pardoned them, but threatened them with death if they offended again (see Tyerman and Bennett 1832, 2:77 for a similar example). Kamehameha is said to have lessened generally the punishments for *kapu* breaking. Freycinet (1979:89) reports an interesting transformation of the penalty during Kamehameha's reign: women could in certain cases escape death by paying a fine of tapas or mats.

Yet Hawaiian women expressed dread of the ultimate punishment even as they broke the tabus in the company of Europeans (Campbell 1967:136; Vancouver 1798, 2:230). Beresford and Kotzebue offer the best attested examples of women being put to death for tabu infractions. At Oʻahu in 1786, Dixon (Beresford 1789:105) was told that a woman had "been offered as a sacrifice" for eating pork on board ship, and as a result the ships were placed under *kapu,* but the latter act was apparently motivated as much by Kahekili's desire to monopolize trade with the foreigners (1789:106). In 1815, Kotzebue (1821, 3:248–49) saw the floating corpse of a woman who had entered her husband's eating house (cf. von Chamisso 1981:437). Kotzebue also tells us that if a man participating in the *kapu pule,* the monthly days of prayer (see Valeri 1985:196), should touch a woman, she would be put to death (cf. Menzies 1920:24, 70ff.). But men could also be put to death for associating with women during this period. Campbell (1967:123) reports one such case: the man's eyes were put out, he was strangled, and his body exposed before the god.

Attempting to explain the vagaries of enforcement of the tabus, some of the early visitors to Hawaii state that the rules impinging on women applied less strictly at sea (Beresford 1789:105; Campbell 1967:135; von Chamisso 1981:143). The notion of a sea/land gradient in the force of the tabus is persuasive and could be supported in the context of Hawaiian ideology. But this conclusion may simply reflect the fact that most of the tabu violations witnessed by observers occurred on board ship, where Hawaiian women were abetted by foreigners who did not respect the rules. *Kapu* breaking by women was not solely a postcontact phenomenon, however. Cook's officers noted that Hawaiian women were not unacquainted with the forbidden foods and would eat them readily when unseen by Hawaiian men:

> while they were on board ships with us they would never touch any pork or ripe plantains except privately & by stealth, but then they would eat very hearty of both & seemed very fond of them. (Samwell 1967:1181)

> The women were not averse to eating with us, though the men were present, and would frequently indulge themselves with pork, plantains, and coco nuts, when secure from being seen by them. (Ellis 1782:169)

Lt. King (Cook and King 1784, 3:100) has a somewhat different version, attesting that they "would eat pork with us in private" but not turtle or plantains. Although the alimentary details vary, other early reports offer variations on the same theme. Campbell's observations, reflecting experiences in 1809–10, have been widely quoted:

> Notwithstanding the rigour with which these ceremonies are generally observed, the women very seldom scruple to break them, when it can be done in secret; they often swim out to ships at night during the taboo; and I have known them eat of the forbidden delicacies of pork and shark's flesh. (Campbell 1967:135; cf. von Chamisso 1981:437; Townsend 1921:115)

As early as 1779 Hawaiian women were also defying the tabus intended to prevent them from going out to the foreigners' ships (Samwell 1967:1171). Hawaiian women discovered in their relationships with foreigners a wedge to use against their men—or at least against *ali'i* men. On land, no women had the temerity to invade the tabu space set aside for Cook's expedition: "we were invariably answer'd that the Etooa [*akua* 'gods'] & Teree-oboo [Kalani'ōpu'u] would kill them" (King 1967:508). But within a decade the women's behavior toward indigenous male authorities graded into open defiance, at least from the haven of shipboard. At Kaua'i in 1788, a priest came out to James Colnett's ship to summon the women to shore because the *kapu pule* had been declared, "but few obeyed him" (Colnett ms.:160; cf. Menzies 1920:54; Sahlins 1981:48–50). During Vancouver's visit in 1793, a Hawai'i island chiefess found a way around the rule that during the prayer days no woman could be "afloat" (Vancouver 1798, 3:64): she would not ride in any Hawaiian canoe because of the tabu, but she would come out to the ship if they agreed to ferry her back to shore (Menzies 1920:57). Similarly, commoner women tabued from coming out in canoes swam to the ships "in great numbers." Menzies (1920:54) ingenuously concludes that "in the society of the honest tars, they found an asylum of freedom more congenial to their disposition and native simplicity."

Sahlins (1981:46) writes that "especially were the commoner women flaunting the sacred restrictions." But it is also true that the movements of commoner women were far less circumscribed and guarded than those of female chiefs, whose reproductive capacity was a crucial political asset for *ali'i* men. The high rank of Hawaiian chiefesses conflicted with their devaluation as women under the *'ai kapu*—a categorical "ambivalence" (Sahlins 1981:47) that adumbrated the instrumental role of certain female chiefs in the 1819 *kapu* abolition. The ambiguity of chiefly women's status is particularly evident in their immunity from severe punishment for tabu violations. Punishment fell lightly, if at all, on these women, who enjoyed *kapu* rank while having to submit (at least publicly) to the restrictions. The chiefess Kapi'olani told Lucia Holman (1931:76) that in her youth she and another high-ranking girl were discovered eating bananas: "they were tried for the ungodly deed and condemned to suffer the penalty, which was poverty, loss of rank, and to remain unmarried . . . unless suitable expiation could be made." However, as in similar reported cases, punishment was exacted upon a surrogate, a favorite boy servant who was put to death as an offering. When chiefly women were caught in liaisons with commoner men or lesser chiefs, the man would be punished but not the chiefess (Arago 1823:138; Freycinet 1978:89). In one well known instance, a nephew of Kamehameha was found with Ka'ahumanu and was subsequently "seized and strangled" for his dalliance (Laanui 1930:87; cf. Cox 1957:29; Kotzebue 1821, 3:250).

Were chiefly women more likely than commoners to defy the tabu restrictions because they were effectively immune from punishment by virtue of their rank? There is little evidence to suggest so. Female chiefs who broke the rules certainly feared discovery (Campbell 1967:136), and not all chiefly women appear to have chafed under the tabus. As the Cook expedition was leaving the islands in 1779, Kamakahelei, the "queen" of Kaua'i, conducted herself with decorum while visiting with Captain Clerke: "The old Lady . . . sits in the Cabin and Chats till about one O'clock when she begins to complain of Hunger, which as she will not eat with us carries her at that time onshore" (Clerke's log, in Beaglehole 1967:579). It is perhaps significant in this instance that Kamakahelei was a political ruler in her own right, not merely the consort of a male ruling chief. She may have had more of a direct interest in observing the restrictions for, as Valeri convincingly argues, the ancient religion with its system of tabus was very much about the maintenance of political power.

In less public contexts and when they could remain undetected, chiefly women seem to have been no less inclined to break the rules than commoner women. According to Beresford (1789:275), chiefly women were "sometimes indulged with" pork. Campbell (1967:136) witnessed Ka'ahumanu eating forbidden foods "and was strictly enjoined to secrecy, as she said it was as much as her life was worth." It is of course inconceivable that Ka'ahumanu, a cherished and politically pivotal wife often described as the key to Kamehameha's success, would have been killed for even the most flagrant transgression of the tabus.

Foreigners' accounts of tabu breaking suggest that Hawaiian men and women had differential views and interests in gender relations, differences that were heightened as contact with Europeans undermined the categorical logic of the *kapu* system (see Sahlins 1981:46–55). The entreaties and aggressive advances of Hawaiian women toward Cook's officers and crew are well documented. What is also extraordinary is how little the women's behavior altered in the time of hostility and distrust following Cook's death. According to Samwell (1967:1215) and Midshipman Trevenen (in Beaglehole 1967:559 n. 2), the women continued to swim out to the ships every night. Samwell (1967:1213) reports that when the ships' watering party burned Kealakekua in revenge, "we had two or three Girls on board all this Day, one of them looking on the Town burning said it was maitai or very fine." Perhaps the most remarkable example of Hawaiian women acting in opposition to the interests of their men is provided by James Colnett (ms.:160–61, 165–67), who visited the islands in 1788. A woman warned them of a planned attack by the Kaua'i chiefs, who hoped to gain the ships and arms for use in war. As Colnett kept the Hawaiians at bay with cannon and shot, "many women were onboard both Vessels for the night, & not at all alarm'd at what pass'd." Moreover, some of the women on board urged retaliation and pointed out particular men who should be targeted. In spite of their actions, most of the women who had informed eventually left the ship at Kaua'i; two were let off at Ni'ihau. While it is risky to interpret behavior at a vantage point of two hundred years, the incident indicates, minimally, an independence on the part of the women and a divergence between the goals of men and women. Colnett saw the women's actions as an attempt to settle old lovers' scores, and he may have been right. What is striking is the women's apparent freedom of action; for whatever reason, most of them seem to have had little fear of retribution.

Undeniably, myriad details in the everyday lives of Hawaiian women were shaped by the restrictions and categorical logic of the *kapu* system. But the evidence indicates that Hawaiian women did not submit to the tabus without resistance. Even a societywide normative system is subject to question or betrayal by those who do not benefit from its tenets; indeed, wihout making allowance for internal conflicts we would be led to assume a static, "cold" culture. Segments of Hawaiian society had different points of view and different interests in the system. The salient categories of Hawaiian society are formed by the intersection of four statuses: chiefly and commoner, male and female. The major temples where male chiefs worshiped were equally *kapu* to commoner men: "the common people have nothing to do in matters of religion" (Whitman 1979:23; cf. Kotzebue 1821, 3:248). Commoner men did, however, conduct worship at their domestic shrines, a worship from which women were excluded. As is clear from Valeri's reconstruction of the religion, those with the greatest stake in the system were society's paragons, *ali'i* men. Women—both chiefly and common—were a problematic term in the context of the male-dominated religion: powerful but devalued, hedged with restrictions but crucial to the aspirations of men.

Women's Worship

The Hawaiian religion documented in ethnohistorical sources is much concerned with conquest and the political conflicts of male chiefs. We know very little about the worship practices and beliefs of women insofar as they differed from those of men. Certainly no observer ever interviewed Hawaiian women on the subject. If women were excluded from participation in most phases of the major sacrificial rituals, does it follow that they "had no deities and just worshipped nothing," as Malo claimed? The Hawaiian ethnohistorical evidence—authored almost entirely by men—is insufficient to support a fully elaborated women's model of cosmology and beliefs, but there is enough to suggest that women did indeed have a religion. Malo's assertion seems a nonsequitur even in context, for it follows a long list of deities that includes numerous goddesses. The conceptual role of women and female deities in the indigenous religion appears more significant if we consider contexts other than the *luakini* war temple rites that are the subject of Valeri's book. There is also ample evidence that women had forms of worship parallel to but separate from those of men.

David Malo begins his discussion of the ancient religion by emphasizing the diversity of its worship forms, wherein allegiance to particular deities varied by social rank, gender, craft, and individual preference:

> There was a great diversity as to cult . . . for the reason that one man had one god and another had an entirely different god. The gods of the *alii* also differed one from another.
>
> The women were a further source of disagreement; they addressed their worship to female deities, and the god of one was different from the god of another. Then too the gods of the female chiefs of a high rank were different from the gods of those of a lower rank. (1951:81)

For female chiefs, as discussed above, high rank mediated to some extent the gender restrictions of the indigenous religion. Chiefly women played a role in the *luakini* ritual, but their activity in sacrifices was qualified. The case of the high *kapu* chiefess Keakealaniwahine is often cited to illustrate the limits of participation for a very high ranking woman (who was also a political ruler):

> Keakealaniwahine was once the ruler of all Hawaii. . . . As there was no other chiefess her equal, she was kept apart. . . . Though a woman, Keakealaniwahine was permitted to enter the heiaus to give her offerings and sacrifices. However, she was not allowed to eat any of the offerings and gifts with the priests and the men, who ate by themselves. . . . She participated only in the ceremonies. . . . Keakealaniwahine ate in her own house of the food permitted to women. (Ii 1959:159–60)

In Valeri's (1985:37) analysis Keakealaniwahine is the "sacrifier" (the one on whose behalf the ceremony is performed) but not the "sacrificer" (the ritual practitioner), because she is barred from consuming the offerings. Her participation in rites is explained by virtue of her rank. According to Kamakau (1964:10), when a temple was dedicated chiefesses of *nī'aupi'o* and *pi'o* rank "could enter the sacred place (*kahi kapu*) and eat of the bananas, the coconuts, and the pigs; no other chiefesses could enter." But it is important to note that it is not simply possession of the highest *kapu* rank that empowers a chief to take the lead in temple ceremonies. Keakealaniwahine is also described as a ruling chief, the highest political authority (Kamakau 1961:61–63).

In one phase of the *luakini* sequence, however, the "female relatives" (Valeri 1985:327) of the male ruling chief play a prominent part. The *hale o Papa* rites (Valeri 1985:327–30) that conclude the sacrificial ritual of Kū are significant for any interpretation of Hawaiian women's categorical status in the indigenous religion. The *hale o Papa* 'house of Papa," a temple dedicated to goddesses, is described as a separate structure located to the *hema* 'left' or 'south' of the *luakini* temple proper (Valeri 1985:237). Visiting Kauaʻi in 1778, Cook (1967:271) described the carved figures of goddesses on a *heiau:*

> These two images, which were about three feet high, they called Eatua no Veheina [*atua no wahine*], Goddess's. . . . they here make some kind of offerings, as several strips of the cloth before mentioned hung to and about them, and between them before the other piece of carving, lay a heap of a plant [called a fern in another account; 1967:271 n. 3].

Valeri, however, minimizes the importance of female deities in the Hawaiian pantheon on the grounds that "goddesses are few in comparison with the gods and are not as hierarchized as the latter" (1985:113). Although there are female images on the *luakini* temple, he writes, they "occupy spatially inferior positions" (1985:245).

It is significant for Valeri's thesis that the *hale o Papa* rite performs the function of *hoʻonoa,* of 'freeing' the *heiau* and its male celebrants from their *kapu* state for return to everyday life. Chiefly women—*na lii wahine* in Malo's account—figure prominently here as sacrifiers, offering tapa cloth and a pig to the góddess Papa. Moreover, according to one version, "prophets" (*kāula*) associated with the goddess Pele also come to offer (*mōhai*) pigs, chickens, and tapa cloth to "their goddesses" (Valeri 1985: 328, 401–2 n. 251). Although the account does not mention the gender of these celebrants, Valeri points out elsewhere (1985:112) that women have a special relationship with Pele and the sorcery goddesses and that *kāula* are often female. That women free men from a *kapu* state seems to support Valeri's contention that women are "polluting" and hinder male communication with the gods. In his interpretation, as men undergo a change in ritual status through the *hale o Papa* rite, their relationship with women is also altered: "by virtue of a transformation that men bring about in their own status, the value of women is correlatively transformed from negative to positive, from one in which they connote death to one in which they connote life" (Valeri 1985:332).

The interpretation of the *hale o Papa* rite depends crucially on one's analysis of the concept of *noa,* as does the more general evaluation of women's meaning within the Hawaiian religion. In their analysis of Maori ideology Hanson and Hanson (1983:72–73) offer an alternative interpretation of *noa,* as denoting the absence of tabu. The logic of Hawaiian women's capacity to free (*ho'onoa*) may be illuminated by a comparison with the similar Maori concept of *whakanoa.* For the Maori, the *tapu* state—reflecting "the presence of godly influence"—was clearly an inconvenience and under certain circumstances could be fatal (1983: 74–75). Certain agents had the capacity to remove tapu, the most important being "water, the latrine, female genitalia, and cooked food" (1983:75). As Hanson and Hanson (1983:87) point out, recent interpreters have seen the female capacity to *whakanoa* as reflecting the categorical disability of pollution: the prevailing view has been that the gods looked on female genitals as "repulsive," and would therefore vacate any place or object contacted by a woman. The Hansons (1983:88–94) argue, however, that Maori women were not seen as polluting, but that the vagina represented "a portal for the passage of influence of any sort from the world of *atuas* ['gods'] into this one." They cite a number of textual and ethnographic examples that are problematic for the notion of female pollution: that women could instill as well as dispel *tapu,* that menstruation was *tapu* and the menses were referred to as *atua* 'god.' The notion of female genitals as a portal is also persuasive in view of the evidence that Maori women did not merely contaminate but could effect a reversal of states.

The Hansons' interpretation regarding women as a conduit to the divine has the merit of explaining ambivalence and liminality in their categorical status. Godly influence, after all, may be positive or negative, beneficial or dangerous. Whether the Hansons' thesis is relevant to Hawaii can only be answered by a lengthy reanalysis of the materials relating to the Hawaiian religion, and that is beyond the scope of this book. For the present, suffice to say that the emphasis on female pollution as a categorical disability does not adequately explain some of the ethnohistorical evidence. It appears that Hawaiian women did indeed offer sacrifices, albeit not human beings and not to the same gods or in the same contexts as chiefly men.

The qualification on women's sacrifices at the *luakini heiau* may be logically related to evidence in chiefly myth-histories that women wielded ultimate political authority less frequently than men. Even women who possessed the highest *kapu* rank are less often found as military conquerers. Valeri demonstrates that competing chiefs vied not only in warfare but in temple building and sacrifice. If the ruling chief legitimizes his power by offering sacrifices—the preeminent offering being his defeated rival—then logically the limitation on women's sacrifice might hinder the ability of women to gain and hold political power. We must keep in mind, however, the contextual limits of the ethnohistorical materials. The sacrificial religion described in Valeri's book is the cult of male chiefs of Kona in the late precontact and early postcontact periods, a time of intensified political conflicts. This was a religion that legitimated conquest during an era of conquests. While one could expect the major premises and worship practices of the Hawaiian religion—particularly the practice of making offerings (*mōhai*)—to pertain to all levels and in other places, the worship of other gods on other islands may well have had a different ethos from that of the conquering god Kū. Ellis's discussion of the indigenous religion (1969:89–91) makes it clear that different deities were worshiped on different islands and gives further indication that the cult of Kū spread out from Hawai'i because of Kamehameha's conquest (see Valeri 1982 for consideration of the diachronic issues surrounding the worship of Kū). Ellis was told, for example, that "one of the ancient gods of Maui, prior to its subjugation by Tamehameha . . . was *Keoroeva.*" A "female idol" of Maui was Kiha, who "received nearly the same homage and offerings as Keoroeva."

The details of women's worship went largely unreported by Western and male Hawaiian observers. There was no major religious structure used only by women. The *hale o Papa,* the house of the goddesses adjacent to the men's sacrifical temple, is the only reported women's *heiau* (see Kamakau 1961:179). Women are reputed "to have a privileged relationship with the female deities of sorcery" (Valeri 1985:112), primarily Pele and her sisters, who are *kino* 'forms' of Haumea, goddess of childbirth and reproduction. As mentioned above, women are particularly likely to be *kāula* 'seers, prophets.' To this day Hawaiian women are particularly vulnerable to spirit possession, which some local people refer to as "the Hawaiian sickness." At Kaua'i in 1778, Samwell described a woman sacrificing pigs:

An old woman named Waratoi whom we supposed to be mad lived with our people all the time they were on shore; she performed daily some religious Ceremonies as we supposed them to be & offered Up some small pigs as Sacrifices for some purpose, and used many Extravagant Gestures . . . this woman had much Influence over the Indians. (Samwell 1967:1085)

Cook's expedition met Waratoi again a year later as they were leaving the islands. Of this occasion Samwell writes: "the Mad Woman . . . was dressed in the stile of a bedlamite with red & yellow rags flying about her" (1967:1226). Samwell also notes that Waratoi and her husband "both belong to the Priesthood" (1967:1229). Valeri interprets Waratoi as a seer or *kāula* (1985:112). Moreover, he views the *kāula*, like sorcerers, as outside the state religion and entirely marginal to it because, unlike "the king's sacrifice," their activities carry little import for society as a whole (1985:138–40). However, Valeri does offer an explanation for this report of a woman clearly sacrificing pigs: "the sex of the sacrificer depends less on that of the deity invoked than on his or her relative purity or impurity. Thus pure goddesses often require male sacrificers as mediators between them and women, while impure gods may in certain cases be approached by men through female mediators" (1985:112).

We have little other information about women's sacrifices. It is also unclear whether women were themselves acceptab le as sacrifices and, if so, to which deities. Reviewing the numerous accounts of Hawaiian women violating the tabus in early contacts with foreigners, Sahlins concludes that "the tabu did not sit upon Hawaiian women with the force it had for men. The sanction on women's violations, for one thing, was not a susceptibility to sacrifice" (1981:46). For the latter point Sahlins credits earlier drafts of Valeri's work (1985), which argues convincingly that sacrificial victims in the *luakini* war temple ritual were male. While women were not appropriate offerings for the god Kū, the accounts of Kotzebue and Dixon indicate that women were indeed liable to be killed—even "sacrificed," according to Beresford and Dixon—in other contexts (Beresford 1789:105). While observers have left us verbal and artistic renderings of the execution of sacrificial victims and criminals, we have no information about the conditions under which women tabu violators were put to death. Were they summarily dispatched and their bodies discarded, as is suggested by Kotzebue's report of the woman's body floating in the sea? What rituals were performed, if any?

It is possible that women were sacrificed to deities other than the major male gods. Some support for this suggestion may be found in Kēlou Kamakau's account of the *hale o Papa* rites, summarized in Valeri (1985:328). At one point the priest of the goddess Papa recites, "the women with guilty mouths (*waha hewa*) [i.e., tabu violators] will not have life from you; they will be killed by your goddess."

Evaluating the significance of Hawaiian women's worship hinges on the weighting of religious activities outside the *luakini heiau,* a ritual province that can be likened to a state religion. The salient formal and institutional contrast in the Hawaiian religion is not only male/female but also chiefly/common. Valeri acknowledges that women may sacrifice, but contends that they do so in marginal contexts and to "impure" or "marginal" deities—marginal, that is, to the sacrificial religion. I emphasize this point not so much to criticize Valeri as to underscore our different points of view—our different interests, in both senses of the word: Valeri's book is about a ritual complex in which women appear to have played at best a minor role, whereas I am drawing attention to the ethnohistorical evidence for a different, parallel realm of worship.

Malo (1951:81–83) emphasizes that female chiefs worshiped goddesses and lists "Kiha-wahine, Waka, Kalamaimu, Ahimu (or Wahimu), and Alimanoano." He specifically identifies Kū, Lono, Kane, Kanaloa, and their myriad forms as "the deities worshipped by the male chiefs." Malo also lists numerous patron gods and goddesses of various endeavors, noting some "that were worshipped by the people and not by the chiefs" (1951:82). Among the goddesses are Lea, who "was worshipped by women and canoe makers," Hinahele, who "was worshipped both by women and fisherman," Pele and Hiʻiaka, Papa and Hoʻohōkūkalani, as well as "female deities worshipped by women and practitioners of medicine" (cf. Kamakau 1961:179). Hula practitioners made sacrifices to their patron goddess Laka (Emerson 1909:23–25; see also Barrère, Pukui, and Kelly 1980). Chiefly women at least offered sacrifices to Haumea, the goddess of childbirth, for reproductive success, although Valeri (1985:111) contends that in these cases a man always acted as the sacrificer proper. Discussing medical experts (*kahuna* 'expert, priest'), Kamakau (1964:99–100) specifically contrasts the priesthoods of Kū, Lono, and Kāne with "the plant-using kahunas of Kū and Hina," who did not use the method of human sacrifice. A tantalizing passage by Whitman, who lived on Oʻahu from 1813 to 1815, offers another example of gender differentiation in religion: "The women also have their boxing matches and under similar regulations. They however do not box under the same Etour moco moco [*Akua mokomoko* 'fighting God'] as the men, it being necessary that theirs should be made especially for females, the mens being tarboo and the womens being nore [*noa*]" (1979:56).

Some goddesses were worshiped by male chiefs as well as by women. The image of Kihawahine, a lizard (*mo'o*) goddess (see also Kepelino 1977:50), was carried around the island with male gods during the annual Makahiki ritual (Kamakau 1961:180). According to Kamakau (1961: 166), the Maui chief Kahekili worshiped the goddesses Kihawahine, Haumea, and Walinu'u (see also Kamakau 1964:82–85). Kamakau adds: "These gods were deities whose heiaus were tabu and in which human sacrifices were offered." This statement seems to conflict with Valeri's ranking of Hawaiian deities, but one must add the qualifier that Kamakau was born in 1815 and had no firsthand knowledge of these rites. The worship of goddesses was evidently more prevalent outside the *luakini heiau* and among commoner men and women. This conclusion does not conflict with Valeri's analysis except in the weighting of such observances vis-à-vis the cult of Kū and would in part explain why certain forms of Hawaiian worship, such as of the volcano goddess Pele, not only survived the *kapu* abolition but continue in some form to the present.

In 1823 the missionary Ellis (1969:117) described coastal fishing shrines in Kona as "dedicated to *Kuura,* a male, and *Hina,* a female idol worshipped by fishermen. . . . The first of any kind of fish, taken in the season, was always presented to them." Traveling on O'ahu in 1825, Byron (1826:141) described a shrine at the foot of the Pali, a precipitous pass to the windward side of the island: "there are two large stones, on which, even now, offerings of flowers and fruit are laid to propitiate the Akua Wahini, or goddesses, who are supposed to have the power of granting a safe passage." While chiefs and commoners, men and women, and even individuals may have worshiped different deities, the practice of making offerings (*mōhai*) is basic to the Hawaiian religion. Even today Hawaiians often leave offerings at sacred places to express spiritual awe.

In light of Valeri's characterization of goddesses as marginal to the Hawaiian religion, it seems ironic that of all the major deities the goddess Pele (see Kamakau 1964:64–69) continues to be the focus of worship practices, although these are centered on Hawai'i where there is still active volcanism. The volcano was identified with Pele in precontact times, and Hawaiians made offerings to appease her wrath. The 'ōhelo berries that grow in the vicinity of the volcano were said to be sacred to her. In a famous incident in 1823, seen as a major victory by the missionaries, the chiefess Kapi'olani defiantly threw stones into the caldera and told Hawaiians not to worship Pele (see Byron 1826:186–88; Ellis 1969:277; Kamakau 1961:382). The French consular official Varigny visited the volcano around 1861; his Hawaiian guides "tied stones to a few small objects evidently carried for that purpose from Hilo—necklaces, glass beads, and so on" and, calling out a greeting to Pele, threw the offerings into the crater (1981:78). Varigny also gives an account of Cook's visit and death, allegedly based on a chant handed down from a chiefly retainer at Kealakekua (1981:15–18). Although the story is filled with inaccuracies, one detail is relevant to the present discussion. Varigny's Hawaiian informant is quoted as saying that Cook's crew "seized by force some of the sacred fish intended for Pele's altar," and to forestall this "sacrilege," the Hawaiians gave them their own fish supply (1981:17). Valeri (1985:140) also cites an anecdote in which Kamehameha summons "a priest of Pele" for counsel during an eruption. Ellis (1969:312–13) mentions the opposition of Pele's "priests and priestesses" to the tabu abolition. Unfortunately, we know little about how the ritual province and duties of these practitioners may have differed from the priests of Kū and Lono. In Ellis's (1969:275–76, 309–12) reports of two encounters with "priestesses" of Pele, their behavior resembles that of the woman Waratoi, that is, that of prophets. Indeed, Kamakau (1964:64–69) refers to them as *kāula Pele.*

The domestic worship of the *'aumākua* 'guardian gods' (see Kamakau 1964:28–32; Valeri 1985:19–30) and the practice of making offerings to them also did not end with the dramatic demise of the sacrificial religion in 1819, as the complaints of nineteenth-century missionaries attest. Identified with particular plant or animal species, the *'aumākua* were a family's ancestral spirits, and their worship was the predominant form of the Hawaiian religion practiced by commoners. Moreover, *'aumākua* beliefs persist among many Hawaiians today. *'Aumākua* were also associated with professional and specialist groups (Valeri 1985:19, 29). Malo (1951:82) mentions Lauhuki, who was worshiped by women who beat tapa, and La'ahana, patron goddess of those who stamped and printed the tapa. Differentiation by gender in religious worship was therefore also founded in the sexual division of labor, as women worshiped the particular deities of their crafts.

Pollution Revisited

I have suggested that an emphasis on the categorical and ritual status of women has obscured our understanding of women's power in Polynesian societies. The notion of female pollution as an "irreducible burden" (Valeri 1985:121) seems to preclude further inquiry (cf. Ralston 1988:79). The problematic notion here is the premise that women must be either symbolically valued or devalued, high or low, pure or impure, that "woman" is a static sign with unvarying meaning in a ritual system. Hanson's "affinity" or "attraction" thesis offers one escape from the apparent contradiction between Polynesian women's low ritual status and their efficacy in other social and cultural contexts. Before Hanson's (1982) essay challenging the notion of female pollution in Polynesian ideology, the prevailing interpretation was that women were seen as "dangerous, disruptive and polluting" (Hanson 1982:335–36; see, e.g., Handy 1927 and Valeri 1985), that they repelled the gods and were therefore globally inferior to men. Valeri, for example, interprets the Hawaiian *kapu* eating restrictions in terms of the following symbolic proportion:

men:women::sacred:profane::pure:impure

In Valeri's analysis men can appropriate the taboo foods because it is they who are responsible for the "symbolic preservation" of the gods, and the prohibited species are "considered manifestations of the deities" (1985:120). Valeri insightfully concludes that *kapu* eating demonstrates the functional complementarity of men and women rather than their opposition. Nevertheless, women's symbolic position is explicitly inferior, negative, and distant from the divine: "impure women are there to assume the burden of the irreducible reality of pollution, of the destruction of divine nature" (Valeri 1985:121). Women are excluded from a direct relationship with the gods because of the "global inferiority of women relative to men in the sacrificial system" (1985:113). While Valeri acknowledges that women are equal to men in the genealogical realm because of the bilateral determination of rank, he sees genealogy as an "indirect" and relatively "passive" link to the gods in comparison to sacrifice. Women's disability in sacrifice follows from their role in childbearing. As Valeri explains: "This is only natural. . . . [W]omen's role in reproduction involves the shedding of blood and therefore impurity, which also disqualifies them from a direct relationship with the gods" (1985:114).

Valeri's ambitious work offers many brilliant insights into the Hawaiian symbolic scheme. Particularly compelling is his exposition of the connection between the sacrificial religion and political conquest. But here I am concerned with women's ritual status primarily as it relates to women's roles in social organization and exchange, that is, women in praxis. This difference of goals and perspective leads inevitably to differences of interpretation. For example, in light of the accounts of intense politicking narrated in Hawaiian chiefly myth-histories, I find it difficult to agree that genealogy is "passive" in the making of Polynesian chiefly authority (see, e.g., Sahlins 1985 on Hawaiian "performative structures").

The contrast of purity and impurity may well underlie Hawaiian gender relations as conceptualized. But in view of other data regarding Hawaiian women's ethos and activities, I cannot help but question whether the sacred/profane dichotomy—so basic to Western religion and philosophy—has much relevance to Hawaiian gender relations as lived. Polynesian systems are characterized by a high degree of manipulability in the practical working through of status determination. For a politically complex and highly differentiated society such as Hawaii, I also have doubts about a model of indigenous ideology that postulates internal consistency and societywide norms. The logic of Valeri's model works well for society's paragons—*ali'i* men. But it is at least possible that women (and, for that matter, commoner men) construed the system quite differently from male chiefs.

Questioning the widely accepted thesis of female pollution in Polynesia, Hanson has argued that Polynesian women "had a special affinity with the gods and represented a conduit for the communication of influence between the physical and spiritual realms" (1982:363; see also Hanson and Hanson 1983). Hanson's interpretation does much to mitigate the apparent contradiction between women's ideological valuation and social efficacy in Polynesia. Nevertheless, I feel that there remains a degree of dissonance or tension in the standing of Hawaiian women within the *kapu* system that even the affinity thesis cannot resolve. It can be argued that the requirement of eating apart was actually more onerous for Hawaiian men, who had to build separate houses and prepare two ovens of food. But I still find it difficult to accept the argument that the tabus did not devalue women, if only in the context of eating.

The *'ai kapu* tabued the choicest foods of the society from women—"choicest," I would maintain, in Hawaiian terms. The foods prohibited to women were categorically high-status foods, the stuff of offerings to the chiefs and sacrifices to the gods. Even though, according to contemporary observers, commoner men also lived primarily on fish and poi, the eating interdictions emphasized male/female differentiation on a daily basis and there is evidence that Hawaiian women chafed under the restrictions. The enforcement of the *kapu* was also a mechanism by which men held life-and-death power over women. Commoner men, however, could be put to death for violating the tabus of female chiefs, while female chiefs were in practice exempt from punishment for infractions. Many aspects of the Hawaiian gender hierarchy can therefore be subsumed under the hierarchy of rank, a point I will return to below.

While I am persuaded by Hanson's reorienting of the notion of female pollution, I still feel that there is a discordant relationship between the valuation of Hawaiian women within the *kapu* system and their social and economic power—a power that, through the bilateral determination of rank, extended to the male-dominated arena of chiefly conquest. Likewise, the problem remains salient for Melanesia (e.g., Feil 1978; Weiner 1976) and for other ethnographic cases where men explicitly devalue women but women nonetheless have power in material and social exchanges (see, e.g., Friedl 1967 and Dubisch 1986, a volume stimulated by Friedl's article). Even if Valeri's characterization of women's semiotic value in the ritual context is correct, what does that have to do with their participation in political and familial affairs? The religion portrayed by Valeri functioned to effect and maintain chiefly authority, not merely the rule of a particular dynasty, but political authority in general; primarily, I would add, it was the authority of chiefs over commoners, and secondarily of men over women. This symbolic system was promulgated by the dominant group in society and might therefore be expected to have aspects of mystification. Nevertheless, the categorical devaluation of women did not go unchallenged on a day-to-day basis and, in any case, symbolic devaluation is not synonymous with subordination. Men needed women in order to effect conquest, but Hawaiian women had their own view of affairs and their own interests. Men's attempts to monopolize the sacrificial foods for their own gods through the eating *kapu* may have been the only domain in which women's efficacious power was more or less successfully negated.

Chapter 3

Women in Praxis

Women's status, in the holistic sense employed here, is never a simple matter of ritual valuation. My premise is that there are often incongruities between normative ideology and practical action. The divergence between cultural expectations and what Sahlins (1981) has called "human action in the world" may be heightened by refractory historical events or precipitated by contradictions internal to the system in place. The term "practical" as I use it here is not intended to connote economically rational or maximizing behavior, but neither is it identical to Sahlins's notion of "practical action" as situational adjustments to novel events. I invoke "praxis" to suggest material relations and to raise more general questions of control and authority, as played out in social action rather than as deduced from symbolic logic. This chapter examines Hawaiian women's roles in material production and exchanges as well as their participation in exchange more broadly defined. At issue here is women's control over people as well as things.

The Division of Labor

Throughout Polynesia, women's primary work is not food production. In Hawaii as in other island groups, women made mats and tapa cloth and personal ornaments while men did most of the agricultural work.[1] As Kamakau and Malo (1951:30) describe the division of labor, outdoor work was done by men, indoor work by women. Even so, the sources indicate that productive duties weighed lightly on young women. Macrae's (1922:61) statement is representative: "when the women get to a certain age, it is their duty to manufacture all the tapa cloths and mats" (cf. Corney 1896:105; Kotzebue 1821, 1:343; Samwell 1967:1181; see also Sahlins 1985). There is a difference, however, between a customary division of labor and a categorical prohibition or *kapu* on one gender performing a given task; while there is general agreement that men performed most of the outdoor labor, there is no evidence that women were categorically barred from working in the taro patches (for a recorded observation of them doing so before the *kapu* abolution, see Mathison 1825:450). Indeed, assuming an indigenous state of frequent warfare, there may have been times when they had to do so. Ebenezer Townsend, who visited the islands in 1798, leaves us the valuable observation that "the young women never work in the field but the old ones sometimes do" (1921:25). Kamakau's oft-cited characterization of the division of labor indicates that women were not prohibited from performing agricultural work:

> All the work outside the house was performed by the men, such as tilling the ground, fishing, cooking in the *imu*. . . . This was the common rule on Kauai, Oahu, and Molokai, but on Maui and Hawaii the women worked outside as hard as the men. . . . [I]t was not uncommon to see the women of Hawaii packing food on their backs, cooking it in the *imu,* and cultivating the land or even going fishing with the men. (1961:238–39)

It must be admitted, however, that the extent to which Hawaiian women participated in agriculture remains an open question. The issue is further complicated by the possible impact of the *kapu* abolition on the division of labor: customary strictures could have been relaxed when the tabus were removed. Kamakau's statement regarding Maui and Hawai'i seems to indicate that different parts of the archipelago could sustain quite different customs regarding the sexual division of labor. Handy and Handy (1972:75) have suggested that the differentiation was by crop, with women allowed to plant sweet potato, a "common" food, but men predominating in the production of taro, a "high" food and the preferred staple (Malo 1951:67). Taking a cue from this distinction, Kirch (1985:224–25) has offered an explanation for Kamakau's remarks: the leeward sides of Maui and Hawai'i supported "intensive dryland field systems" where sweet potato was the dominant crop. "On those islands," Kirch writes, "the role of women in agriculture reflected the increased labor required in the vast dryland field systems, for weeding and crop-tending" (1985:2). Still, I have never found a statement that wetland taro cultivation was tabu to women.

Kirch (1985:224) notes quite rightly that ethnologists have underplayed the importance of the dryland field systems and have tended to treat irrigated taro cultivation as the quintessential Hawaiian subsistence mode. The contrast between Kirch's discussion of women in Hawaiian agriculture and Valeri's characterization is revealing in this light. In a passage cited earlier, Valeri states that, in accordance with their symbolic status, women could appropriate secondary or "residual" foods, including the sweet potato, "a little-prized tuber reserved for marginal land" (1985:123). In the intensely cultivated fields of Kohala and Kona men would also have tended sweet potatoes, of course, and Kirch (1985:225) notes that these dryland field systems "provided the economic base for the powerful chiefdoms descended from Līloa and 'Umi," the dynasty that ultimately prevailed in the conquest of the islands.

Later nineteenth-century sources must be approached cautiously for insight into the sexual division of labor. Barrot, who visited O'ahu in 1836, wrote that "the women share the cares of agriculture with the men, prepare the food of the family, and make cloth for its garments" (1978:77). Traveling on O'ahu in 1853, Bates (1854:115–16) described several women cleaning out a taro patch to convert it into a fishpond. Hawaiian women gathered shellfish, seaweed, and other products of the reef. Arago (1823:130) noted that women did most of the fishing from shore. As in the rest of Polynesia, deep-sea fishing was the job of men. The 1841 "Law Respecting the Labor of Criminals" gives a list of women's proper occupations:

> Females shall not be made to serve at labor appropriate only to males, nor at any labor inappropriate to females. The beating of tapa, the braiding of mats, braiding of hats, sewing, twisting fish lines, weaving nets, and such like labor as is appropriate to females. Those are the works at which females shall be employed. (Hawaii 1894:95–97)

While this law does list several of the customary pursuits of Hawaiian women, it cannot be interpreted as revealing an indigenous prohibition on women's participation in other activities. Hawaiian laws during this period were heavily influenced and often directly authored by white men (Gething 1977; Silverman 1982), and this particular section seems to have a normative cast reflecting a Western view of women's roles (for a discussion of which see Grimshaw 1985). Nevertheless, the fact that in the 1840s widows were sometimes evicted because there was no man present to work the land suggests that at midcentury agriculture was still primarily men's work. In the 1866 census of Lāhaina, 50 percent of Hawaiian men but only 14 percent of Hawaiian women reported their occupation as *mahi'ai* 'farmer' (compiled from census enumeration sheets, originals in AH).

The 1866 census certainly does not reflect the precontact or pre-*kapu* abolition state, but neither does it present a radically anomalous picture of the sexual division of labor among Hawaiians. The other occupations listed by women are seamstress, matmaker, washerwoman, and hatmaker, with *mālama hale* 'housekeeper' the most frequently cited. My interpretation is that women participated increasingly in cultivation after the *kapu* abolition, particularly as proletarianization and emigration removed family members from the local group. Marion Kelly has suggested (personal communication, 1987) that after the coverture law of 1845 women refused to marry (or remarry) in order to protect their property. Some, if not most, of the women listed as *mahi'ai* in the 1866 Lāhaina census were probably landholders and heads of households. If so, these figures may offer an indication of the minimum extent of female landholding at this time, at least in the Lāhaina area. I will return to this point in chapter 7.

Westerners and some male Hawaiian writers have tended to see women's role in primary subsistence activities as an index of their overall social valuation. After Cook's visit, most Western ships stopped at Hawaii because they wanted provisions. Although the chiefs frequently made prestations of mats and tapas (women's goods), ship captains were for the most part little interested in these "curiosities," although they admired their ingenuity of manufacture. There is no evidence, however, that Hawaiians shared Western utilitarian values, either viewing agriculture as an intrinsically more worthy activity than weaving mats and beating cloth, or seeing taro as something "higher" than a fine mat or tapa. If anything, judging from other Polynesian cultures, the reverse is more likely to have been true. In Tonga, for example, women's products were categorically superior to men's, which were seen as impermanent and consumable (Gailey 1987:107; for Samoa see Weiner 1982, 1985). Male and female goods represent different and complementary kinds of productivity, and the Hawaiian evidence does not support the inferiority of the female set. In Samoa, where fine mats and tapas are still a crucial component of ceremonial exchanges, women have considerable say in the distribution of their manufactures. In Hawaii we will find that the products of women were high cultural valuables as well.

High Goods: Mats and Tapas

Hawaiians, like Samoans, made a qualitative range of mats and tapas. The finest of these articles were high valuables, suitable for use only by chiefs and gods. This is a well documented fact but one that has been strikingly underemphasized by contemporary writers. The prevailing assumption has been that these articles primarily served domestic, utilitarian needs and are therefore not worthy of attention (although visitors from Captain Cook onward were frequently presented with fine mats and tapas by chiefs). Malo (1951:75) emphasizes the usefulness of women's products but gives little indication that they were seen as valuables. But the use of fine mats and tapas in offerings and rituals and as high gifts belies the notion that Hawaiian women's products were relegated to the domestic domain. If such goods served as tributary and ceremonial objects, then they are no more domestic than are the foods that men produce.

The surgeon Ellis (1782:176) noted that Hawaiian mats varied greatly in size and decorative patterns, "some of them are twenty-four feet long, and eight feet wide, others not above five feet long and eighteen inches wide." The missionary Stewart (1970:150) describes some as reminiscent of the fine mats of Samoa: "These . . . are generally small; finished with a deep fringe at the ends; and carried on the arm of a servant, after his chief, to be spread on other mats, on which he may choose to sit." Stewart (1970:150) also mentions the fine rush *makaloa* mats made on Kaua'i and Ni'ihau, which "for the purpose of sleeping on, the chiefs in all the islands prefer to any others" (Ellis 1969:20; see also Brigham 1906).

In Hawaii fine mats and tapas were markers of high chiefly status. Their abundance within chiefly dwellings categorically distinguished the houses of chiefs from the commoners' unadorned huts, which contained but a few coarse mats and tapas. In a letter of June, 1820, missionary Lucia Holman (1931:27) described the qualitative and quantitative gradation of mats as domestic furnishings:

> The floor of the houses of the nobility are first paved with small pebble stones, then a layer of hay, next a coarse mat made of the cocoanut leaf . . . next a finer mat made of the rush. . . . Next a straw mat, and so on. . . . The richer or higher the Chief, the more mats he walks and sleeps upon. I have counted 20 or 30 upon one floor. (Cf. Campbell 1967:130–31; Colnett ms.:84–85; Beresford 1789:272, 274; Judd 1928:8)

The chief's raised bed, or *hikie'e,* consisted of a stack of fine mats, up to thirty or forty in number, each eight to ten feet square (Stewart 1970:149; cf. Barrot 1978:21, 65; Tyerman and Bennett 1832, 2:46). As late as 1849 a missionary in a remote district reported that a commoner family had to dismantle a built-up bed of mats because such was *kapu,* reserved only for the chiefs on pain of death (Lorenzo Lyons, in Doyle 1953:151).

Western observers have sometimes characterized the customary chores of Hawaiian women as undemanding because men did most of the agricultural and heavy labor (e.g., Samwell 1967:1181; Valeri 1985:123). But judging from descriptions of chiefly houses and accounts of the numbers of mats and tapas that went into tributary prestations, Hawaiian women must have been busy indeed. They not only had to manufacture mats and tapas for chiefly tribute and sumptuary display but also for the domestic use and clothing of their own households. Stewart (1970:146) underscores the perishability of tapa: some tapas were saturated with coconut oil for durability, "but even these quickly wear out, and require to be renewed every few weeks. That which is not oiled does not allow of being washed; and a new suit is necessary once a month. An immense deal of time and labour must therefore be requisite, to meet the demands of the whole population." Pandanus mats were, incidentally, also used for sails, shields in war (Samwell 1967:1187, 1202) and canoe covers (Brigham 1906:54), as well as for wrapping corpses (Colnett ms.:88; Thurston 1921:79). Old mats were used to cover the underground oven to keep in the steam (Colnett ms.:85; Whitman 1979:38).

Kapa, the Hawaiian bark cloth, also had a variety of uses, and early visitors to Hawaii were impressed by its beauty and ingenuity of design. There were numerous kinds, from fine to coarse, with a variety of dyed colors and decorative motifs: "some White, black, red, yellow, green and gray & they have some striped in an infinite Variety of patterns & some of them exceedingly beautiful" (Samwell 1967:1186; for types of tapa see also Ellis 1969:111–12; Kamakau 1976:105–6, 108–16; Stewart 1970:148–49). Thin tapas were used for *malo* and for *pā'ū,* the women's sarong; tapa for men's cloaks and sleeping covers was somewhat thicker (Stewart 1970:148). Kamakau (1976:112) also describes a type of "ribbed tapa" called *hamo'ula* or *kua'ula* that was made by men, but he does not indicate whether this was more highly valued than those made by women. The finest sorts of tapa were reserved for chiefly and ritual use; Beresford (1789:272), for example, describes a white variety worn by chiefly women (on chiefly tapas see also Kepelino 1977:62–63; Doyle 1953:62–63; Whitman 1979:47). John Iʻī mentions two fine white tapa varieties, *ʻoloa* (1959:39, 56) and *ninikea* (1959:44–45), that were used in the *luakini* temple ritual. A white tapa called *kopiliʻoloa* was used in the ceremonial blessing of a new house (Kamakau 1976:105–6). Interestingly, the term *ʻoloa* also denotes ceremonial valuables in Samoa, but there *ʻoloa* refers to categorically male gifts—formerly men's manufactures but now largely Western goods and money—presented to the woman's family at marriage.

The size of Hawaiian bark-cloth garments and furnishings, in conjunction with the fact that great numbers of them went into the people's regular tribute to the chiefs, may be taken as an indicator of the duration and significance of women's daily work. According to Colcord (ms.:86), a sleeping tapa might be from twelve to twenty feet long by eight to fifteen feet wide. Westerners may have an image of a loincloth as something scanty, but the Hawaiian *malo* consisted of "a piece of cloth, six or eight inches wide, and about nine feet in length" (Whitman 1979:18). In addition, Whitman continues, "suits of tarpers, consisting of five or ten sheets, from four to six feet square, are sometimes worn like a mantle." And the women's *pāʻū* was "composed of five pieces of cloth, each about nine feet long, and about two feet wide, sewed together like so many leaves of a book, this they wind two or three times around the body, and fasten it in front" (1979:18).

I have stated that mats and tapas were not only utilitarian items but cultural valuables. While it is difficult to impute from the Hawaiian evidence a system of circulating valuables or formal prestations such as is found in Samoa, it is striking that chiefs' gifts to visiting Europeans tend to conform to a standard format, typically including mats, tapa cloth, and coconuts (examples include Clerke 1967:572; Colnett ms.:159; Cox 1957:29; King 1967:517; Lapérouse 1799, 1:351; Samwell 1967:1165, 1170; Vancouver 1798, 1:179, 2:128; see also Dampier 1971:64; Conrad 1973:260; Tyerman and Bennett 1832, 2:93). Nor were the valuables always presented by male chiefs; in 1778 Kamakahelei, the ruling chiefess of Kauaʻi, gave Captain Cook a quantity of mats, feather ruffs, and tapa cloth (Ellis 1782:133, 136). Although we have scant data on internal exchanges in Hawaii, Kamakau (1976:105–6) provides rich details of a house-opening ceremony strikingly similar to analogous ceremonies in Samoa, in that men's things and women's things are exchanged. Making the house was the work of men, but women furnished the interior with myriad kinds of mats and tapas. Kamakau lists nine different types of "tapa skirts" (*pā'ū*) for women alone. While the "valuable things" made by "the relatives of the women" were displayed inside, other gifts—most of them the work of men—were assembled outside the house, "such as a canoe, *ōlona* cordage, nets of various sizes of mesh . . . bag nets, fishlines, feathers, pearls . . . and other treasures." According to Kamakau, both commoners and chiefs held house-opening ceremonies; the chiefly event would of course have been more elaborate.

Descriptions of tributary prestations and tax payments suggest that men's and women's products were equally valued in Hawaii. William Richards (1973:24) reported that an annual tax on an *'ili* land section included twenty tapas, "a part of these last were nearly square for bed-clothes, and a part narrow and long for female dresses." Bloxam, who was with Lord Byron in 1825, reported that after one such presentation of gifts from the people of Hilo on the island of Hawai'i, Kamehameha's widow Ka'ahumanu took away two thousand pieces of tapa (Bloxam 1925:55–57, 71). Perhaps the best account is from Stewart (1970:199–200), who described a procession of people presenting their district's annual tax to the king:

> The procession consisted of one hundred and fifty persons . . . the first twenty men bearing each a baked pig or dog . . . followed by fifty others, bearing thirty immense calabashes of poe. . . . Then came females, to the number of seventy or eighty, each bearing on her shoulder a large package of tapa. . . . The whole was deposited in front of the royal tent, and the company . . . seated themselves in a circle . . . apparently with the expectation that the king would present himself.

The value of women's goods is also strikingly evident in a report from Freycinet (1978:89):

> During the last years of Tamehameha's reign . . . it became possible to avoid the death penalty for tabou infraction—in cases of small importance—by paying a fine. Thus a young girl caught eating a coconut, a banana, turtle meat, etc. . . . could hope to save her life by contributing armfuls of cloth, several mats, etc.

Tapa also figured importantly in the Hawaiian religion as a wrapping for idols and offerings (see Bloxam 1925:76; Ellis 1782:180, 182; Emerson 1909:23; Tyerman and Bennett 1832, 2:55, 74; see Kirch 1985:151–52 for an archaeological example). Valeri (1985:244, 267, 269, 300–301, 318) documents numerous examples where tapa is used ritually to wrap or to adorn images. Kepelino (1977:50–51) reports that the goddess Kihawahine was worshiped with "offerings of tapa [*me na mohai, na tapa*]" and other things. Tapa and mats also figured in rites outside the context of the sacrificial *heiau*. Stewart (1970:264) encountered a sorcerer praying before "a small mat covered with several thicknesses of tapa . . . on the top of which were placed two very large trees" (the latter possibly corms of the mountain taro). Ellis (1969:435) and Mathison (1825:474–75) report that the marriage ceremony was effected by throwing a piece of tapa around the woman. Similarly, at the marriage of Ka'ahumanu and Kaumuali'i in 1822, Thurston (1921:64) reports that the couple "reclined on a low platform, eight foot square, consisting of between twenty and thirty beautiful mats of the finest texture. Then a black *kapa* was spread over them."

Tapa figures prominently in the *hale o Papa* rites that conclude the *luakini* temple ritual (see Valeri 1985:327–32). As discussed earlier, this is the one part of the *luakini* sequence, as reconstructed by Valeri, in which women participate. In this rite chiefly women bear a long loincloth of the '*oloa* tapa cloth as their sacrifice (*mōhai* 'offering' in the Hawaiian accounts), with the male ruling chief holding one end of the *malo*. The ruling chief's favorite wife offers cloth and a pig to the goddess (in Valeri's analysis she is the "sacrifier" but not the "sacrificer"). According to the Kēlou Kamakau account (1919–20:27–31; Valeri 1985:328) numerous other sacrifices are also made to the goddesses. For the present context, the significant point is that the priest's dedicatory chant suggests the complementary valuation of male and female offerings: "Here is your cloth and your pig, my husband and myself will have life by you, O goddess; and give us a male child, to fetch *pala* [fern] for you (*i ki'i pala nou*), O goddess; if not, a daughter who will beat '*oloa* cloth for you."

The use of women's products in religious rites may or may not conflict with the notion of female pollution as a fixed, contaminating state. As Valeri (1985:300–301) notes, wrapping constitutes consecration. Tapa was used to wrap "objects regarded as manifestations of the gods" (Valeri 1985:300). Valeri explains that wrapping has this function because it (*a*) removes the object from mortal sight and (*b*) immobilizes, binds, and constrains and "can thus represent man's control of the divine" (1985:301). While the symbolism of wrapping thus seems obvious enough, the symbolic valuation of women as manufacturers of the cloth and sometimes as the wrapped objects themselves is not unequivocal in this context. It was the custom of chiefly women to wrap themselves in enormous lengths of tapa on significant occasions. Valeri (1985:301) recounts the famous incident when, at a feast to commemorate Kameha-meha's death, Liholiho's favorite wife Kamāmalu rolled herself into a *pā'ū* "according to court ceremony . . . as to be enveloped round the middle with seventy thicknesses" (Thurston 1921:41; cf. Tyerman and Bennett 1832, 2:64). After presenting herself to her royal husband, Kamāmalu then lay upon the floor and unrolled herself. Valeri's interpretation of this act is that "Liholiho controls his wife and the divine rank of the children she can engender . . . she thus represents a wild potentiality that has been tamed and made productive by her husband." Yet this incident might equally well be interpreted as a challenge to Valeri's portrayal of Hawaiian women as symbolically impure and distant from the divine. The ceremonial wrapping could also support Hanson's thesis that women in Polynesia are thought to have a special relationship with the gods. Minimally, the wrapping episode suggests that women embody a certain power, but the valence of that power is ambiguous—women may be "wild," but not repellent to the gods.

A counter to my emphasis on the manufactures of women might be that women's products are appropriated by men for their own uses and women do not control the goods they make. But even among the Enga of the Papua New Guinea Highlands, where the ideology of sexual asymmetry is held to be developed to an extreme, women exert control over goods for which they are responsible (Feil 1978). Certainly in other Polynesian societies, such as Tonga (Gailey 1987) and Samoa (Weiner 1982), women had authority over the cloth wealth they produced. There is little evidence that Hawaiian women were subservient to or dominated by men in interpersonal relations; their behavior vis-à-vis Europeans certainly exhibited a high degree of independence, even aggression, in varying sorts of exchanges (see Sahlins 1981, 1985 for discussion). In brief, the evidence indicates that the products of men and women were equally valued in Hawaii. One other recorded incident attests that Hawaiian women, like their Tongan and Samoan counterparts, could indeed use their productivity to assert their will over their men: at the island of Hawai'i in 1823, a merchant picked up a Hawaiian man seeking passage to O'ahu on the grounds that his wife did not treat him well;

specifically, he complained, "She gives me only one marro in two or three months" (Hammatt ms., May 8, 1823).

Who Made the Feather Cloaks?

The point of the preceding discussion is that many of the highest valuables of Hawaiian culture were made by women. Fine mats and tapas were used in exchange and in ritual and served as markers of chiefly status. But what of other high valuables? Perhaps the best known and most distinctive artifacts of Hawaiian culture are the feather cloaks (*'ahu'ula*), which are as impressive to modern observers as they were to Cook, Vancouver, and Portlock. Fashioned of thousands of feathers in vibrant red, yellow, and black, these artifacts are unique to Hawaii (see Brigham 1899, 1903; Kaeppler 1970, 1978:50–78, 1985). Although early visitors to the islands received many featherwork articles as gifts or in exchange, apparently no non-Hawaiian ever saw them being made. At least there is no extant eyewitness account of their manufacture.

It is surprising then that the most detailed statement about the making of feathered garments is found not in the early observers' accounts but in Peter Buck's (1957) *Arts and Crafts of Hawaii*. Buck (1957:217) states that the capes and cloaks "were prohibited to commoners and to women. To further mark the distinction against women, the garments were made entirely by men." While Malo (1951:76–77) and other writers (e.g. Cook and King 1784, 3:136–37) affirm the association of feather cloaks with chiefs, Buck gives no reference for the bar against women, nor have I been able to find any corroborating statement in early ethnohistorical sources. Concurring with Buck's thesis, Adrienne Kaeppler (1970:92) has written that "though the feathers might be sorted and cleaned by women, the fabrication of the feather cloaks was done only by men of rank, surrounded by sacred tabus." Arguing from the internal logic of Hawaiian ideology, Kaeppler still supports the conclusion that the cloaks were made by men under conditions of tabu (1985:110). But my own reading of the early materials suggests that women may well have made these valuables or, at least, were not categorically barred from a role in their manufacture.

To view the feathered garments in their proper context, one must first consider the circulation and uses of feathers in Hawaiian society. The cloaks, capes, and helmets were only one species of article involving featherwork (see Kaeppler 1978:50–78; Rose 1980:18–27, 191–96). The chiefs had feather standards or *kāhili* (called "fly flaps" by early European visitors), which were carried by their attendants as insignia of rank (see, e.g., Cook and King 1784, 3:135; Kamakau 1961:183). Hawaiian women were found of feather ruffs or leis, worn in the hair or around the neck (Ellis 1782:156–57; Kaeppler 1978:74–75; King 1967:626 n. 3; Stewart 1970:150). The other significant use of featherwork was in movable idols of the gods (*akua hulu manu*), fashioned of wickerwork to which red and yellow feathers were attached (for a discussion of these see Valeri 1985:246–47). There is also no account of the manufacture of these items, although it is more likely that these would have been made under conditions of tabu, given the customary exclusion of women and commoner men from the sacrificial rites of male chiefs (Valeri 1985).

Feathers were collected and reserved specifically for chiefly and ritual uses. They went in one direction only in the social hierarchy—up. While chiefs might distribute food and tapa clothing to their retainers and to commoners (Kamakau 1961:180, 190; King 1967:518; Laanui 1930:86, 90; Mathison 1825:451), there is no account of feathers being redistributed downward. Feathers were a part of tributary prestations (*ho'okupu*) to the chiefs (Campbell 1967:98, 139; King 1967:517–18; Judd 1928:23; Malo 1951:77; Menzies 1920:82; Stewart 1970:130; Whitman 1979:55). When Captain Cook's remains were returned to his officers, the bundle was "coverd with a spott'd cloke of black & White feathers, which we understood to be a mourning Colour" (King 1967:566). Kamehameha's supporter Isaac Davis, a *konohiki* in his own right with large estates and several hundred commoners living under him, "frequently made the king presents of feather cloaks, and other valuable articles" (Campbell 1967:98). In 1845 in Waimea, Hawai'i, the missionary Lorenzo Lyons received as contributions one yellow feather each from two members of his flock (Doyle 1953:138).

As befitting high-status visitors, feather garments were formally presented to Cook, Vancouver, and on at least one occasion to missionaries (Tyerman and Bennett 1832, 2:93). We have little information on the extent to which feathered garments were exchanged among the Hawaiian chiefs themselves, but in conjunction with the fact that Hawaiian chiefs presented these articles as gifts to the early Europeans, there is enough to suggest that feathered cloaks were customary gifts of alliance, respect, and gratitude (see Brigham 1918:33 for the history of a *malo* given by Kamehameha to the king of Kaua'i).

Kaeppler (1985:115) suggests that in precontact times feather cloaks and capes "were worn only in battle and other dangerous and sacred situations" (cf. Malo 1951:38, 77; Sahlins 1985:130–35). The ethnohistorical evidence certainly supports the association of these garments with *ali'i* men, although women were apparently not barred from controlling them; Brigham (1903:449) describes one feather cloak, made in the time of Ke'eaumoku and finished in 1782, that according to legend was owned by women: "Keeaumoku's wife gave it to Peleioholani's grandmother." In August, 1819, Liholiho's queen Kamāmalu presented Freycinet (1978:28) with "a small feather cape." Kamakau (1961:183) describes a great feast that Kamehameha gave in honor of Ka'ahumanu, where feathered articles served to celebrate this politically powerful woman: "Many beautiful ornamental objects were made for this feast, such as a huge *kahili* . . . and a feather lei of great value. Ka-'ahu-manu was borne by the chiefs upon a litter . . . spread with feather cloaks and cushions."

Brigham (1899:59), however, refers to the feather *pā'ū* of the princess Nāhi'ena'ena as "the only known example of a feather robe made for a woman." Presented to her by her retainers in 1825, when she was ten years old, the garment was twenty feet eight inches long and thirty inches wide, but she was reluctant to wear it at the time because it would leave her breasts exposed (for a description of this incident see Byron 1826:113–14; Stewart 1970:343–44). Kaeppler (1985:115) argues convincingly that in the early postcontact period the design and function of the feather capes was transformed. From "sacred protection devices" they became prestige symbols, "appropriate for status verification and ceremonial occasions." Brigham (1899:59 n. 34) presaged this point when he suggested that Nāhi'ena'ena's unusual feather *pā'ū*, made in the early 1820s, "perhaps marks the transition from a war-robe . . . to a state decoration and mark of high rank."

The feather cloaks' protective function in warfare and, by extension, their role in conquest also provide logical support for the notion that they were worn exclusively by chiefly men. If women were barred from offering sacrifices on the *luakini* war temple, they would have been at a disadvantage in the politics of conquest, which was also a politics of *heiau* building and sacrifice (Valeri 1985). The monopolization of the feather capes and cloaks by *ali'i* men would then make sense in view of the less frequent occurrence of women as ruling chiefs. It should be noted, however, that *ali'i* women could own another feathered symbol of conquest, the standards or *kāhili,* some of which were made with the long bones of defeated rivals (Cook and King 1784, 3:135). At Kaua'i in March, 1779, Captain Clerke was visited by the ruling chiefess Kamakahelei and her daughter, who carried "a curious Fan or Fly flapper compos'd of a bunch of Feathers made to adhere to a Human Bone as a Handle" (Beaglehole 1967:576–77). The handle, he was told, was the arm bone of an O'ahu chief killed in battle by the queen's war leader, the Kaua'i chief Ka'eo.

The sexual division of labor in societies is frequently painted with broad strokes, but it must be noted that any productive or manufacturing process is almost infinitely divisible into subtasks that may be customarily assigned to men or women (see Linnekin 1988). Making a feather garment consisted of several steps and required the collection and processing of different sorts of raw materials (see Brigham 1899; Kaeppler 1985:118–20). Malo (1951:20, 37) and Kamakau (1961:38–40) mention a class of bird catchers who were male (Judd 1928:23) and had their own patron deities, notably Kūhuluhulumanu (Emerson 1894:105; Malo 1951:82). Emerson characterizes these specialists as solitary hunters who followed migrating birds from upland to lowland and suggests that the bird catchers were a special class of chiefly retainers. But it is unclear whether the bird catchers were residents of the *ahupua'a* or followers in the chief's personal retinue. The fact that feathers also made up a part of the annual tributary offering demanded of every land district (see Menzies 1920:82) suggests that there were *ahupua'a* residents skilled in this craft. All in all, the evidence suggests that bird catching may not have been a full-time specialization, but was practiced by certain people, evidently commoners, who lived in a land section belonging to their chief.

The sources indicate that bird catching was a male activity. This is further supported by the fact that the bird catchers' patron deity was a form of Kū, the preeminently male god of conquest (Valeri 1985). In the preceding chapter I argued that men and women prayed to different gods, with women primarily worshiping goddesses. But it was not tabu for women to handle feathers. Emerson (1894:105–6) states that in the forests the bird catchers were accompanied by their wives, who sometimes plucked and sorted the feathers. Once collected, the feathers were tied to sennit fiber for storage (King 1967:517). Stewart (1970:150) also attests that women in chiefly households worked at sorting and trimming feathers. The backing of the feather cloaks was a netting of *olonā* fiber

(*Touchardia latifolia;* see Brigham 1899:50; Stokes 1906), to which the feathers were tied by a special knot (Buck 1957:224).[2] Strips of *olonā* cord were also the structural basis of feather leis (Brigham 1899:26). The primary steps in the manufacture of the feather garments were the processing of the *olonā,* making the cord, weaving the backing, and tying the feathers to the netting.

As noted above, weaving *lau hala* (pandanus) mats was one of the primary productive tasks of Hawaiian women. But the division of labor in the manufacture of basketry and cordage is less certain, for there were tasks that could be performed appropriately by either gender. Furthermore, there is a conceptual and practical difference between a customary division of labor and the categorical barring of one sex from performing a particular kind of work or handling a certain material. The ethnohistorical evidence, as we will see, suggests that women may have figured prominently in the manufacture of feathered goods.

Freycinet (1978:85) unambiguously states that women made baskets as well as mats, although he is specifically referring to baskets of ti leaves. Kamakau (1976:44–45) gives a detailed description of the cultivation and processing of *olonā,* but says only that "men, women and children" did the scraping of the fiber. Brigham's photographs of Hawaiians demonstrating the processing and spinning of *olonā* show only men (1899:50–51). For the making of cordage, Stokes (1906:106) describes the following division of labor: "The spinning of cord, *hilo,* was always done on the bare thigh by women. . . . Men generally attended to the braiding."

Stewart (1970:150) writes that women, especially retainers in chiefly households, "spend much time in making articles of ornament; in the braiding of human hair for necklaces; trimming and arranging feathers for wreaths and kahiles; polishing tortoise shell and the ivory of whale's teeth, for finger rings, and the handles of feathered staffs. &c." (cf. Ellis 1782:156; Malo 1951:77). The feather leis made by women used a base of *olonā.* One of Cook's officers, however, stated that Hawaiian women used the nails and hatchets they procured from Cook's men to "purchase" feather leis, though it is not stated from whom (James Trevenen, in King 1967:626 n. 3), suggesting that their manufacture was an area of specialization. In the missionary period, Hawaiian women became expert makers of woven hats, using such materials as fern stems and horsehair (Brigham 1906:72). Another clue may be found in the 1841 "Law Respecting the Labor of Criminals," which lists the kinds of work appropriate to females as "the beating of tapa, the braiding of mats, braiding of hats, sewing, twisting fish lines, weaving nets, and such like labor" (Thurston 1904:79–80). Even though such laws were heavily influenced and sometimes directly authored by male foreigners, the list of women's tasks does resonate with the customary division of labor in Hawaii.

Brigham (1899:55), who had firsthand knowledge of other Hawaiian manufactures in the late nineteenth century, believed that the feather cloaks were made by chiefly women. Freycinet (1978:85), who was in Hawaii in 1819, offers the clearest statement by an early visitor that women made the feather cloaks and helmets: "In producing the feather cloaks and helmets worn by the chiefs at special ceremonies, it is again women who demonstrate their industrious skill." Perhaps the most important reference for the making of the feather cloaks—because it is the earliest—is Lt. King's account of 1779:

> Their Labours are as far as we saw, properly divided, to the Women falls the care of Manufacturing their Cloath, making ornamental dresses &c, To the men the more laborious parts of cultivating the land, building their houses & Canoes, making their War instruments, & whatever related to Wood works. . . . Their Cloathing divides itself into three branches, The Manufactoring of Cloth for common Wear, their Matts for Sleeping & for battle, & their Ornamental dresses. . . .
>
> Their feathered Cloaks . . . with their Caps are perhaps the most Splendid & Striking dresses in the South Seas. . . . (King 1967:625–26)

One other issue is important for the question of whether women made the feather cloaks. Were the feather garments, in and of themselves, dangerous, sanctified, or *kapu?* If they were, at what point in their manufacture and history did they acquire their *mana?* If they were intimately identified by *kapu* with their chiefly wearers, when did this association begin? The earliest contacts between Hawaiians and Europeans may offer some insight here. There seem to have been two kinds of transactions in which feather garments were transferred to Europeans. On several occasions, ruling chiefs presented cloaks and helmets as gifts to those Europeans whom they perceived as the highest-ranking members of their party. These gifts can be likened to formal prestations between chiefs, and the many documented examples involve the best-known early European visitors: Cook, Clerke, Vancouver, and Portlock (Ellis 1782:91; Cook and King 1967:499, 512; Samwell 1967:1151; Vancouver 1798, 2:127, 129, 159–60; Portlock 1789:176). Vancouver's description of one of these presentations supports the cloaks' association with warfare and corroborates the supposition that once worn they were *kapu* to their chiefly owners. Kamehameha, on giving Vancouver a cloak to be presented to King George, showed him

> the two holes made in different parts of it by the enemy's spears the first day he wore it, in his last battle for the sovereignty of this island. . . . as it had never been worn by any person but himself, he strictly enjoined me not to permit any person whatever to throw it over their shoulders, saying, that it was the most valuable thing in the island of Owhyhee. (Vancouver 1798, 2:160)

In contrast, however, there were transactions that, as described by the European participants, can only be characterized as outright barter. Off Kaua'i early in 1778, in one of the first encounters between Hawaiians and Europeans, canoes ventured out to Cook's ships offering "to sell" (Samwell 1967:1084) produce, necklaces, bracelets, fans, feather cloaks and caps, and spears (Ellis 1782:171). At Maui later that year, the crew found the Hawaiians "very extravagant in their demands," but they were able to scale the prices down; on this occasion Hawaiians brought "some of the largest and best feathered cloaks we ever saw, and likewise some of the caps" (Ellis 1782:69). Similar examples are reported by Samwell (1967:1084), Portlock (1789:78), and Lapérouse (1799, 1:351). By the early 1820s the *Blonde* expedition encountered a flourishing market in Hawaiian curiosities, including cloaks and "tippets" (Dampier 1971:47); it can be argued, of course, that by that time—namely, after the abolition of *kapu*—the feathered garments had been devalued.

It can be argued that the distinction between gift and barter is blurred in these examples since no gift comes unencumbered; even those who offered the feather garments "freely" expected some material return. But the early sources support a gradient of reciprocities, from formal presentations by high-ranking chiefs, who gave the articles on board ship or on land, to the bartering of feathered cloaks by Hawaiians (apparently of lesser rank) who approached the ships in canoes along with others bringing things to trade. It would seem axiomatic that only chiefs could control feather garments (Malo 1951:77; Kaeppler 1978:51), but then who were these Hawaiians offering them rather unceremoniously in trade? They were not all high chiefs; they may have been lesser chiefs, but even lesser chiefs in the service of rulers such as Kalaniʻōpuʻu were usually identifiable as such to the early voyagers.

The way in which some feather garments are described as being bartered in the early sources suggests that these articles were not in themselves particularly sanctified, dangerous to handle, or *kapu* until worn by the chief for whom they were made (perhaps not until they were worn in battle), at which point they acquired and symbolized the wearer's *mana*. It should also be kept in mind that there were different types of cloaks, and these indexed social rank. King (Cook and King 1784, 3:136–37) and Beresford (1789:271–72) contrast the cloaks of the highest chiefs with an "inferior kind" belonging to lesser chiefs. According to King, the length of the cloak was proportional to the wearer's rank. The shorter capes of lesser chiefs were constructed primarily of the feathers of cocks and the tropic and frigate birds, with only a narrow border of red and yellow feathers.

Malo (1951:77) states that feather cloaks were "conferred upon warriors" who distinguished themselves in battle and were highly prized objects of plunder from defeated enemies. Those bartering them to the early voyagers may have been warriors who were not necessarily of high birth. It seems, in other words, that ownership rights over the feather cloaks could be earned as well as ascribed. It is also possible that the Hawaiians bringing feather garments to the ships were chiefly retainers. Since commoners gave feathers as tribute, the garments were made in chiefly households. Female chiefs may have worked on them, as Brigham thought, but it is likely that skilled female retainers accomplished most of the work. A connection may be drawn here to reports that when male and female chiefs worked, they supervised parties of attendants and commoners (Bloxam 1925:38; Ellis 1969:109).

In 1819 the chiefs wore Western military and formal dress as well as feather cloaks to mark their high status (Freycinet 1978:14), but by the 1820s feathered garments were scarce (Freycinet 1978:28) and, as Kaeppler (1985) argues, their significance to Hawaiians had altered. In 1825 Dampier (1971:47) wrote that the chiefs had forsaken the feather cloaks and helmets for European dress: "They however form a very excellent article of traffic, and the Islanders can hardly be induced to part with them, except at a very high price" (cf. Byron 1826:137). On high ceremonial occasions some chiefs still wore feather helmets (Stewart 1970:117), and several cloaks were in evidence at the funeral of Liholiho and Kamāmalu (Stewart 1970:348). But for chiefly *pāʻū* and *malo,* "scarlet silk" and other imported cloth had become the material of choice (Stewart 1970:117–19).

My conclusion is that women made feather cloaks. The encounter between Kamehameha and Vancouver suggests that after they had become identified with particular wearers the garments were *kapu* to anyone else, but the same was true of any garment worn by a high chief, male or female (Kamakau 1964:10). Prior to this point, I see no evidence that the feather garments were treated with marked reverence, avoidance, or caution, even in the earliest reports; there are no accounts, for example, of commoners or women being put to death for touching them, as there are for infringements of other *kapu* prohibitions. Two early ethnohistorical sources (King and Freycinet) and one reliable turn-of-the-century scholar (Brigham) state that women made these articles, as they did other high cultural valuables, even those that were to be used and exchanged primarily by men; women also made fine tapas that were used in *heiau* rituals where men were the central actors. Women were not limited to producing valuable goods, however. In the next section we will see that women also controlled and exchanged goods in their own right.

Women as Exchangers

Ethnohistorical evidence of women participating in exchanges on their own behalf in the early postcontact period suggests that Hawaiian women not only manufactured cultural valuables but also had authority over the distribution of these products. The logic of the tabu system, under which men and women did not eat together and for the most part lived apart, allowed women considerable freedom of action in practice. The evidence indicates that Hawaiian women, both chiefly and common, owned movable property—personal items reserved for their own use, which they could distribute as they wished. Moreover, Hawaiian women could and did use material and sexual gifts as instruments to influence the behavior of others.

In their early liaisons with foreigners Hawaiian women aggressively used their sexual favors in hopes of acquiring higher status for their children and a secure future for themselves (see Sahlins 1985). The women were by and large not coerced into these unions by Hawaiian men but were acting in their own interests. As Sahlins so eloquently explains, the cultural logic behind this well-documented sexual aggressiveness is hypergamy: among both chiefly and common Hawaiians the goal was to marry up. Since rank was bilaterally determined, having children by someone of higher status effectively raised the rank of one's descendants and held the promise that in old age one would be well cared for. Hence Hawaiian women flocked to the ships by the hundreds, eager to make alliances with the high and powerful strangers (for admiring comments see especially Samwell 1967). Men *and women* brought their daughters and female relatives out to the ships (Cox 1957:30; Samwell 1967:1182), a point that will be discussed further in the next section.

As might be expected, the nature of exchanges with foreigners differed for chiefly and common women. Chiefly women gave material gifts to the ships' officers, but the women who consorted sexually with the seamen were commoners (Cook and King 1784, 3:130). Kamakahelei, ruling chiefess of Kaua'i, exchanged valuables with Captains Cook and Clerke over the course of several days (Ellis 1782:133–34; Clerke 1967:576–77, 578; Samwell 1967:1226; for a gift from another chiefess see Samwell 1967:1160). In 1778 Kamakahelei, whom Ellis and Clerke refer to as the "queen" of Kaua'i, was embroiled in a war with a rival chief, and her gifts were in part aimed at recruiting supporters from among the foreigners: "She was very desirous for some of our people to stay and fight for her, promising them every good thing the island produced in the greatest abundance" (Ellis 1782:133).

In control over resources as in other contexts, rank appears to have been far more salient than gender as a basis of social differentiation in Hawaii. Except in the ritual sphere, male and female chiefs enjoyed the same prerogatives of rank. Chiefly women had rights in personal property just as they controlled use rights in land sections and received their own tribute from the commoners (Stewart 1970:132; Tyerman and Bennett 1832, 2:75). Powerful women such as Ka'ahumanu and Liliha made their own deals with traders and kept separate accounts (Conrad 1973:220, 258). Long after the abolition of the tabus Hoapili, governor of O'ahu, and his wife Kalakua Kaniu, widow of Kamehameha, kept separate houses and separate possessions (Andrews 1836): "No man ever uses his wife's book, and vice versa; and so of a slate and other property." Again, residential segregation under the *kapu* system actually enhanced Hawaiian women's ability to control their own possessions.

With their own households and retainers, female chiefs especially seem to have maintained a separate but equal domain of authority.

Like their male counterparts, female chiefs presented high goods to early visitors—not to ordinary seamen, but to those whom they perceived as having a status comparable to their own. But Europeans receiving gifts from chiefly women usually reciprocated with the stereotypic female articles of their own society, items which they regarded as "trinkets" or "trifles." Colnett (ms.:159), for example, gave the *ali'i* women of Kaua'i "Scissors, Beads, & many Baubles for Ornaments which highly pleas'd them" (see also Ellis 1782:173–74). Seamen gave similar presents to commoner women. According to Samwell (1967:1151), the women especially liked "bracelets" made with metal buttons from the crew's clothing sewn to pieces of red cloth (cf. Ellis 1782:158). While the European men viewed these favors as quintessentially feminine gifts, Hawaiian women also sought practical articles such as nails and hatchets. In a famous example, Samwell (1967:1164) tells of the crew pulling out the ships' sheathing nails to give to the women for sexual favors.

Women did trade for Western items on their own account quite outside the context of sexual liaisons (see Lapérouse 1799, 1:351). Although the women were swayed by articles such as the cloth-and-button bracelets, Ellis (1782:158) reports that these made up only part of the price for traded provisions: "So much did they at first value them, that a small hatchet and one of these would purchase a hog, which without it could not have been bought for three hatchets." An intriguing observation by Midshipman James Trevenen (Beaglehole 1967:626 n. 3) suggests further that Hawaiian women used the Western goods they procured to acquire indigenous specialty items such as feather leis:

> The fondness of the women for these ornaments was very great even to supersede that which they had for the different articles of our trade, so precious amongst the Men, Whenever a Woman had acquired a large nail or Hatchet she carefully concealed it from the knowledge of her male friends till an opportunity offered of purchasing one of these beautiful ruffs in the number & variety of which they placed their chief pretensions to finery and ornament.

Unfortunately, Trevenen does not say from whom the feather leis were purchased—what sort of specialist, male or female. Samwell (1967:1221) reports a similar example of women from Hawai'i island using iron and other Western articles to "buy" cloth on Oʻahu. Trevenen's comment on women concealing goods from men parallels reports of women surreptitiously breaking the tabus and lends support to the thesis that there was relative sexual egalitarianism in early Hawaii, that Hawaiian women were by no means submissive, passive, or obedient to their men (or to foreign male representatives of the lord; cf. Grimshaw 1985 on missionary attempts to teach "femininity" to Hawaiian women). Once again, there is an indication of gender politics, of men and women vying for control of resources and jockeying for relative status.

Women as Wife Givers

Though women produced and controlled many kinds of goods, perhaps the most important product of Hawaiian women was children. In marriage choices, Hawaiian women exercised control over their own reproductive potential and that of their daughters and granddaughters. This was particularly true of commoner women, whose unions did not carry dynastic import. For the vast majority of the Hawaiian population, marriage took the form of cohabitation. Unions were by and large easily formed and easily broken and were unmarked by material exchanges; not all unions were transient, however, and I will say more about Hawaiian marriage in chapter 5. But for the present discussion one important implication of this flexible marriage custom is that women were free to leave men when it suited them.

Among commoners, who were not concerned with rank and dynastic succession, there is no evidence of family pressure on a woman to remain with a man who displeased her. And in local-level social organization, the solidarity of the kindred—particularly sibling relationships—was privileged over the marital tie (this point too will be developed further in chapter 5). While there was a patrilineal bias in authority over land, Hawaiian social organization was thoroughly bilateral and was characterized by a wide range of options for residence and affiliation.

For chiefly women, however, freedom of action was constrained by the dynastic implications of their sexuality. The bilateral determination of rank made it imperative for an aspiring ruler to produce children by the highest-ranking woman and, further, to prevent rivals from having children by her. Affiliation with a higher-ranking woman—marrying up—was one way for an ambitious junior collateral to effectively raise his social rank. Finding a successful chief to serve—the custom of *'imi haku* 'to seek a lord'—was also a culturally recognized path to higher status. Matrilocality and *'imi haku* are frequently associated with each other in Hawaiian chiefly myth-histories (e.g. Fornander 1916–19). A common theme is the success of a younger brother who marries a higher-ranking women and, with his father-in-law's support, usurps the power of his elder sibling. In Hawaiian literature matrilocality represents the mythic encoding of female power, but it was always a pragmatic alternative among both commoners and chiefs.

Despite the negative associations of women with danger or pollution in the ritual sphere, Hawaiian ideology embodies a high regard for women in certain statuses, particularly that of mother. Like the potentially negative connotations of the tabus, this positive symbology is derivable from premises fundamental to Polynesian religions, where "everything has a female of its kind, which acts as a 'house' (receptacle), in which and through which things have life, growth, and reproduction" (Handy 1927:38). In myths, proverbs, and chiefly legends, the mother/ son relationship is consistently characterized as solidary, supportive, and affectionate, while the father/son tie is portrayed as respectful and often tense. In the legend of Kūapaka'a (Fornander 1918–19, 5:72–135), for example, the protagonist's father Paka'a is a retainer of the ruling chief of Hawai'i. Despite his relatively low rank, Paka'a possesses great *mana,* symbolized in the narrative by his magical wind gourd. Through his wind gourd Paka'a becomes the chief's favorite and receives gifts of land. As a receptacle, the wind gourd invokes femaleness; this association is also suggested by the narrative detail that the gourd is named after Paka'a's mother. By marrying a high chiefess "belonging to the land," Paka'a raises the rank of his child through a hypergamous alliance. His son Kūapaka'a later invokes his mother's high rank in defeating the chiefs of Hawai'i.

In the legend of Palila (Fornander 1918–19, 5:136–54), the hero's maternal grandmother saves him from a rubbish heap and rears him among the spirits. Indeed, Palila is "partly spirit, being so by the influence of Mahinui, his mother." In the story of Puniakaia (Fornander 1918–19, 5:156–70), mother/son solidarity is contrasted with tension between affines. Puniakaia's mother advises him: "You are going to the home of your wife to live, but you will be insulted and you will return here in a very short time." In myth and, arguably, in Hawaiian sentiment "mother" is a substantive for the land and home to which the hero always returns. In John ʻĪʻī's account of his own childhood, his mother dominates the narrative and determines his destiny: he first "knew by the words of his mother that she was determined to make him a member of the court" (1959:17–32). His mother instructs him in the chiefly tabus, commands his obedience to her brother, his namesake, and brings him to Honolulu. Twelve years later, on the occasion of Kamehameha's return to Hawaiʻi, ʻĪʻī is suddenly "seized with a longing for his mother . . . this longing came to him and prompted him to say to his companion, 'I have a yearning for my mother.' " Other notable mother/son relationships exhibiting affection and obedience could be cited, such as Kamehameha and his mother (Ii 1959:4), Liholiho and his "mothers" Kaʻahumanu and Keōpuolani, who pressed him to abolish the tabus (Ii 1959:157; Kamakau 1961:318).

If, as Lévi-Strauss has said, myths tell us something about internal contradictions in a social system, then the Hawaiian chiefly histories reveal the essential ambivalence of women's genealogical power from the male perspective: women are both the means to power and a potential means of losing power. Chiefly women did have liaisons and secondary unions, but women with high *kapu* rank or politically critical relatives could not do so with impunity; they may have been freer after giving birth to their first (and therefore senior in rank) children (see Malo 1951:55). At least some male chiefs jealously guarded the sexuality of their consorts (for an example see King 1967:624), but not without resistance on the part of the women. Most vivid are the anecdotes detailing the stormy relationship between Kamehameha and his politically pivotal wife, Kaʻahumanu (see Kamakau 1961:189, 194, 386–87; Vancouver 1794, 3:28). Kamehameha placed his favorite and highest-ranking wives such as Kaheiheimalie under tabu. Kaʻahumanu was under a tabu "whose infringement meant death" (Kamakau 1961:386). Kamehameha's daughter Nāhiʻenaʻena was similarly guarded by attendants, "she being tabooed by her father, who says she is to marry some great chief" (Townsend 1921:8).

That women also have some authority over their children's destiny is suggested by the bilaterality of Hawaiian social organization. The absence of corporate lineages in Hawaii (Sahlins 1985:24–25) meant that neither the father's nor the mother's people had an a priori right over their offspring. A child's social affiliation was a matter of politics, negotiation, and situational factors and would likely shift several times as an individual passed through different stages of life. But grandparents are said to have a "claim" (*kuleana*) on the children of their offspring (Kamakau 1964:26), and Hawaiian ideology associates girl children particularly with the mother's family. In the story of 'Umi, after Līloa lies with Akahi he instructs her, "This is my command: when our child is born if it be a girl, name her for your side of the family; but if it be a boy, name him for mine" (Kamakau 1961:3). An adoption norm recorded in early postcontact sources states that boys were taken by the father's family, and girls by the mother's (Kamakau 1964:26; Boit ms.:28), a statement that, while not borne out statistically in my nineteenth-century data on adoptions, indicates minimally that a woman's family was perceived to have a privileged right over girl children.

Reports by early visitors also indicate that women were not simply sexually aggressive on their own account, but sought to enhance the *mana* of their children. Elderly women often brought their daughters out to the ships (Cox 1957:30; Samwell 1967:1182). On Kaua'i there is a sacred site of fissured stones said to be a place where chiefly women once gave birth. After birth the umbilical cord was inserted into the boulders in order to imbibe the power of the gods or goddesses of that place. As Cook's ships were preparing to leave Kaua'i in March, 1779, Hawaiian women came out to the ships to insert their infants' umbilical cords into cracks in the ships. As told in Samwell's famous account (1967:1225), women took the lead in this activity:

> These people bring their Children's Navels tyed up in little slips of Cloth and hide them in any little holes they can find about the Ship, but they do not mind whether they are observed by us or not. . . . The Women seemed to have the chief hand in this mystic Affair, they staid in their Canoes & sent in a Man with them on board the Ship and directed him where to place them.

The period of first European contact in Hawaii was a time of intensified warfare and political conflict, culminating in Kamehameha's conquest of the windward isles in 1795. The military actors—those who led armies and sacrificed defeated rivals on the *heiau*—were for the most part male. One aspect of the politics of conquest during this period is that male chiefs attempted to monopolize the sexuality of high-ranking women. But female chiefs were equally concerned with the alliances of their daughters and female relatives, and their acquiescence in the unions was not a trivial matter. The tale of Kamehameha and Keōpūolani lends

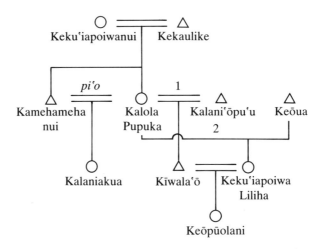

Fig. 2. Kalola *ma*

support to this thesis. Keōpūolani was the daughter of Kamehameha's senior collateral and rival Kīwala'ō and eventual mother of his highest ranking children, including Kamehameha II and III. After the defeat of Kīwala'ō and the conquest of Maui, Kamehameha went to Moloka'i, where Keōpūlani had been taken by her maternal grandmother Kalola Pupuka, daughter of the Maui chief Kekaulike. Ill and near death, Kalola had fled to Moloka'i, Kamakau tells us (1961:149), "with her daughters and granddaughters." In other words, Kaloka Pupuka's matriline was present on Moloka'i at this time (fig. 2). Kamehameha sued for the women with these words:

> "Since you are so ill and perhaps about to die, will you permit me to take my royal daughter [referring here to Keōpūolani, his classificatory daughter] and my sisters [referring to Kalola's daughters, Keōpūolani's mother and aunt] to Hawaii to rule as chiefs?" . . . Kalola answered, "If I die, the girl and the sisters are yours." Then Kamehameha and all the chiefs waited until the death of Kalola. They wailed and chanted dirges . . . and the chiefs tattooed themselves and knocked out their teeth. Kamehameha was also tattooed and had his eyeteeth knocked out. . . . (Kamakau 1961:149)

While Valeri (1985:168) calls this incident a "capture" of these women by Kamehameha, I also see a conquering chief asking a high-ranking chiefess for her daughter and granddaughter and going to great lengths to pay respect to her. Granted that it was politically important for a conquering chief to take the widow and female relatives of his defeated rival and that these women effectively had little recourse but to accede, he evidently could not or should not do so by outright coercion. Instead, Kamehameha asks the permission of the female head of the matriline. One possible outcome of "capturing" chiefly women against their will is exemplified by the action of Keōpūolani's aunt Kalaniakua. Herself a chiefess of the highest *kapu* rank, Kalaniakua detested Kamehameha and his lineage as low-born usurpers and killed herself with poison (Kamakau 1961:260).

The authority of matriarchs and grandmothers such as Kalola Pupuka over their female descendants may in part account for the appearance of matrilines in Hawaiian chiefly genealogies. Sahlins (1981, 1985) and Valeri (1972) have insightfully discussed the political dimension of chiefly marriage during the conquest period, particularly the pivotal role of the Maui chiefs, Ka'ahumanu's male relatives, in Kamehameha's success (Sahlins 1981:55–64). In these political/structural analyses of Hawaiian chiefly genealogies, island dynasties and senior/junior lines are the wife givers. In the Kamehameha period, for example, the Hawai'i island chiefs take wives from Maui and O'ahu. I will return to the political aspects of Hawaiian chiefly marriage in the following chapter, but for now I want to consider the issue of women's control over women, another structural level, if you will, that is as much "in" the genealogies as are male collateral lines.

Hawaiian chiefly genealogies trace upward through both male and female links to an ancestor and are susceptible to innumerable readings. Hawaiians could and did trace their relationships in a variety of ways, invoking particular ties, lines, and ancestors according to context and situational advantage. As Sahlins has felicitously phrased it, "Hawaiians . . . do not trace *descent* so much as *ascent,* selectively choosing their way upward, by a path that notably includes female ancestors, to a connection with some ancient ruling line" (1985:20; emphasis in original). By virtue of the multiple matings of male and female chiefs, lines differentiate and branch through both affinity and descent. Figure 3 shows the relationships between the Ka'ū and Kona chiefs, from Keawe down. These are the male links in Kamehameha's immediate lineage (cf. Sahlins 1981:59). Figure 4 shows the most prominent wives of Kamehameha; he is said to have had twenty-one (Thurston 1921:88), but not all of these unions were politically consequent.

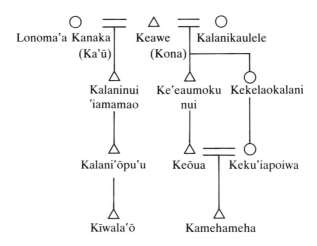

Fig. 3. Collateral relations of the Hawai'i chiefs

Hawaiian chiefly marriages must be understood in their political context, particularly in the case of Kamehameha, a usurping junior collateral of *wohi* rank. At least eight of his wives could trace their descent to the Maui chief Kekaulike: Keōpūolani, Ka'ahumanu, Keku'iapoiwa Liliha (widow of Kīwala'ō), Kaheiheimalie Kaniu, Kahakuha'akoi (also known as Wahinepio), Lilia Nāmāhana (also known as Pi'ia or Keku-aipi'ia), Kekāuluohi, and Manono. What is striking, however, is the degree to which the tracings to Kekaulike are matrilineal, even consistently so (see fig. 4). If one highlights female ancestors in these genealogies rather than males, a pattern appears: lines of women, three to five generations long, give wives to lines of men. In this case, a line of women descended from one women, Keakealani, gives its daughters to a line of men descended from Keawe. The pattern continues in the next generation when Liholiho inherits his father's wives and also marries Kamāmalu and Kīna'u.

Is a pattern of matrilines unique to this dynasty and this era? I suggest that it is not. But it remains to be seen how these matrilines are constituted and how they should be interpreted. As shown in figure 5, Keakealani can trace to a brother/sister pair: matrilineally to Kaikilani and through males to Makakauali'i. Brother and sister lines are also evident in further ascending generations (fig. 6). Iwikauaikaua can trace to 'Umi through a line of women and a line of men, both originating in a

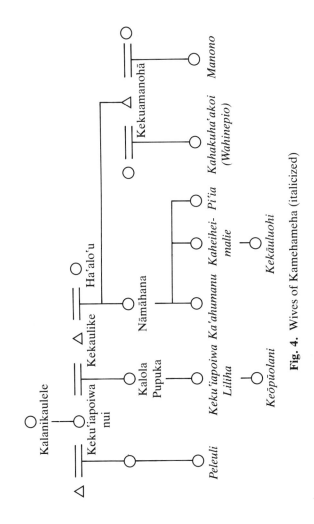

Fig. 4. Wives of Kamehameha (italicized)

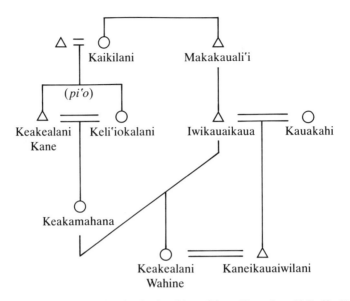

Fig. 5. Genealogy of Keakealani wahine. (From Kamakau 1961:60–62.)

union of paternal half-siblings. These examples suggest that what I have called matrilines are ultimately sister lines, whose women marry into lines of men related to them through a half-sibling tie. I wish to stress once again that this is only one of several dimensions of the Hawaiian chiefly genealogies, and I do not offer this interpretation in order to dispute other analyses. Because of cognatic tracing, the absence of descent groups, the lack of a positive marriage rule, and the political import of marriage choices, it is impossible to substantiate a unitary model of Hawaiian chiefly marriage. This is no "elementary structure" in Lévi-Strauss's terms. But even in complex marriage systems, pragmatically motivated choices are constrained by a limited set of structurally defined strategies and alternatives. The possibilities are finite, and in Hawaii women figure crucially in their realization.

Matrilines—or, more precisely, lines of women descended from a sister in a sibling set—occur in the Hawaiian chiefly genealogies because of the conjunction of several factors: the bilateral determination of rank, the multiple matings of the chiefs, and the complementary strategies of senior (ruling) and junior (usurper) lines. In Hawaiian genealogies women are points of segmentation; different lines may trace not only to an elder or younger brother, but to a sister, or to one spouse of a ruling

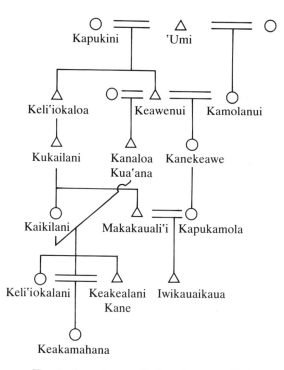

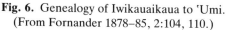

Fig. 6. Genealogy of Iwikauaikaua to 'Umi.
(From Fornander 1878–85, 2:104, 110.)

chief. In general, the ideal in Hawaiian marriage is hypergamy. Male ruling chiefs attempt to monopolize the reproductive potential of high-ranking women in order to produce heirs. But junior collaterals, always potential usurpers in the Hawaiian chieftainship, also seek to marry up. The ruling line must therefore guard its high-ranking sisters by marrying them—or at least by marrying them first. There is a high frequency of consanguineous marriages among the ruling chiefs—male chiefs with their classificatory "sisters" (usually half-sisters) and "daughters" (siblings' daughters). Brother/sister unions conserve high rank in the sibling set and produce children of the highest tabus, of *pi'o* and *nī'aupi'o* rank (Kamakau 1964:4). Correlatively, such unions are explicitly forbidden to all but the highest chiefs (Malo 1951:54).

It can be argued that descent lines through women in Hawaiian chiefly genealogies are merely the artifact of the cognatic, opportunistic reckoning of descent: a pattern without singular meaning or content. But I suggest that in tracing descent through women Hawaiians recognized the transmission of female power. I have attempted to show that women exercised autonomy in their own and their daughters' marriage choices. Genealogies are not formed solely from male interests, in other words, but also reflect the strategies and preferences of women. Moreover, the lines of women may have had institutional correlates. While men predominate as paramount political rulers, women are associated with the inheritance of certain intangible, spiritual property, a theme that emerges also in the comparative literature on Polynesia (see Goldman 1970:291; Rogers 1977: 171, 180). Some early postcontact sources state that women predominate in the hula (Colcord ms.:89). Chants and genealogies are often passed down through women (Malo 1951:67; Varigny 1981:10; cf. Linnekin 1985:188–91; Valeri 1985:123).

The pivotal role of women in the Hawaiian chiefly myth-histories suggests an importance even exceeding their theoretical half-share in determining rank. Some foreign observers thought that a child's rank was determined primarily or even solely by the mother's (Jarves 1843:33; Kotzebue 1821, 3:247; Olmstead 1841:194). Because of their crucial political importance as points of access to rank and power, women are in a sense more equal than men in Hawaiian genealogical mathematics (cf., for Tonga, Herda 1987 and Rogers 1977, and for Samoa, Schoeffel 1978). The highest *kapu* tend to be vested in women, so that the matrilines in the chiefly genealogies are lines whereby the highest tabus are transmitted. Again I stress that this is an underlying pattern, one that is not explicit in Hawaiian ideology and chiefly traditions. Nonetheless the matrilineal descent lines represent a dimension of the genealogies that corresponds to women's personal and structural power in Hawaiian thought and society.

There is, of course, no necessary correlation between the genealogical importance of women and female authority. Nevertheless, I submit that where women *count* in a genealogical sense, they are less likely to be treated as chattels or pawns. The ethnohistorical evidence amply supports the independent ethos and personal authority of Hawaiian women. We have few details on the interpersonal negotiations involved in Hawaiian marriage arrangements, but this may be a red herring. Excepting certain chiefly marriages, sexual unions were for the most part not a matter for formal negotiation among Hawaiians. In contrast to the Western formal concept of marriage, a rich indigenous literature chants of "the political economy of love" (Sahlins 1985) in which women were the initiators at least as often as men. The early seamen's reports may actually be the most revealing sources about how Hawaiian women experienced control over their own and their daughters' sexuality.

The *Kapu* Abolition

In October, 1819, the young king Liholiho sat and ate with the women. In a few days' time the Hawaiians destroyed their indigenous religion, before the first Christian missionaries had even arrived. When the latter disembarked a few months later, they saw this circumstance as a certain act of divine providence. If the practices and enforcement of the tabus did devalue women—at least from the perspective of Hawaiian men— then their elimination may have served to enhance female authority. (I already noted in chapter 1 that a statistical shift in land relations appeared to signal greater jural authority on the part of women.) Indeed, Sahlins (1981:66) argues that through the *kapu* abolition and subsequent events "king and affines, men and women, foreign and indigenous, tabu and *noa* all exchanged their places." The *kapu* abolition has few parallels in ethnography and has fascinated anthropologists for decades. I will not recapitulate here the events surrounding the overthrow, nor the arguments of the many authors who have written on one or more aspects of the event (Davenport 1969; Kroeber 1948:403; Levin 1968; Sahlins 1981; Webb 1965). Each has insights to offer. I will instead highlight a few points that are particularly salient for understanding nineteenth-century changes in the status of Hawaiian women.

As Sahlins (1981:55–56) and others have noted, the *kapu* abolition was not as abrupt an occurrence as it appeared to Kroeber. Rather, the event represented the "final crisis" of the tabu system, a crisis set in motion by interactions between foreign men and Hawaiian men and women, chiefs and commoners. And although formal emissaries of Christianity had not yet arrived, it is not true that Hawaiians knew of no competing cult. Cook himself, revered as Lono, initially embodied the challenge of a returning god to the order in place (Sahlins 1981). The Hawaiians soon recognized that the European gods were different from their own; it was evident enough that the foreigners did not subscribe to the tabus. Vancouver, for one, vigorously attempted to convert Kamehameha to his own cult (Sahlins 1981:9–10).

There was also a more immediate and specific precedent to the free eating of October. Collective *kapu* breaking had an established place in the indigenous religion as part of the mourning custom for high chiefs. For several days following a chief's death "every restraint"—sexual and alimentary—"was cast off" (Stewart 1970:216). During the mourning time women could also enter the temples (Kamakau 1961:222). Significantly, Stewart also claims that chiefly authority held no sway over the people during this period, after which it was the duty of the new ruler to proclaim "a new tabu following old lines" (Kamakau 1961:222). Campbell (1967:101) reports that at the death of a high chief in 1809 "a general, I believe I may say universal, public prostitution of the women took place." Kamehameha died in May of 1819, and according to Marin, "the women ate pork and cocoa nuts . . . all the women and men, even to the royal family went to commit fornication one with another" (Conrad 1973:230). Kamakau (1961:222), Davenport (1969), and Sahlins (1981:65) all point out that the *kapu* abolition merely continued the suspension of tabus after Kamehameha's death. By encouraging Liholiho to eat publicly with his father's wives "Ka'ahumanu had simply tried to prolong the ritual license" (Sahlins 1981:65).

For my present purpose, the most salient aspect of the *kapu* abolition is that it was instigated by women: specifically, Liholiho's own and classificatory "mothers," the high chiefess Keōpūolani and the politically powerful Ka'ahumanu. Kaheiheimalie, another of Kamehameha's widows, and Kekuaipi'ia, sister of Ka'ahumanu, also supported the free eating. According to Kamakau (1961:224), Keōpūolani—"the only remaining high tabu chiefess"—was particularly responsible: "it was through her influence alone that the eating tabu was freed." When Liholiho was to return to Kona to be installed as king—a time when by custom he should reinstate the tabu—Keōpūolani ate with his younger brother Kauikeaouli, the future Kamehameha III. After two days of tacking offshore, periodically sending for rum, Liholiho landed at Kailua and entered the house of the chiefess. The free eating was declared: "Then pork to be eaten free was taken to the country districts and given to commoners, both men and women" (Kamakau 1961:225).

That women should play a major role in this event is predictable from the categorical implications of being both female and high-ranking. The tabu eating restrictions were most in conflict with the status of chiefly women, who had high *kapu* rank but were at least theoretically susceptible to death at the hands of men for eating certain foods or entering certain places. Commoner men and women alike seldom had opportu-

nity to eat the ritually high foods. Although chiefly women were effectively immune from the ultimate punishment for transgressions, they
were enjoined from eating delicacies that were the stuff of tributary and
religious offerings. Interaction with powerful tabu-breaking foreigners
intensified the contradictions inherent in the system, but even before
Cook's arrival Hawaiian women—particularly chiefly women—had cultivated some disdain for the tabus.

In the *kapu* abolition female chiefs were pursuing their own personal
and political interests. But this is only one of many causes. Davenport
(1969) stresses that the event was a political act by which the fledgling
monarchy reorganized and consolidated itself, and notes that Ka'ahumanu particularly sought to preserve her own power and authority as de
facto head of state by supporting the abolition. Sahlins (1981) has also
explored political circumstances and effects that are pertinent to women's
personal authority and political importance. In his reliance on the Maui
chiefs related through Ka'ahumanu, Kamehameha effectively replaced
junior collaterals with affines as his primary source of support. This
"affinal strategy" was an innovative variation on a traditional theme
(Sahlins 1981:57ff.), but with the conquest of the islands and the overthrow of the indigenous religion it became the basis of Hawaiian political
power. The sacrificial religion was both a source of legitimacy for the
ruling chiefs and, through the assignment of religious guardianship to
junior collaterals, a potential basis for rebellion.

Like 'Umi, the apical figure of his dynasty, Kamehameha lived the
paradigmatic scenario wherein a usurping younger brother uses the
power of his god to overthrow his senior, the rightful ruler. And at his
death, following the precedent of 'Umi's father Līloa and Kīwala'ō's
father Kalani'ōpu'u, Kamehameha gave rule over the land to Liholiho
and the god Kūkā'ilimoku to a junior relative, Kekuaokalani, his sister's
son. Lest the myth-historical scenario be repeated, Liholiho destroyed
the gods. Appropriately, Kekuaokalani opposed the *kapu* abolition and
was eventually killed in battle by one of Ka'ahumanu's collaterals.
Kekuaokalani's death both exemplifies and symbolizes a related political effect of the abolition. The overthrow of the religion broke the
traditional power base of the priesthoods (Davenport 1969). The structural effect of giving guardianship of the gods to younger brothers was
that priests were related to the ruling chief as junior collaterals. Nullify-
ing the tabus effectively disenfranchised the younger brother, priestly
lines. Ellis (1969:31) reports that when the missionaries arrived they

found "priests no longer existing as a distinct body, but merged in the other classes of the community." Even the power of the "priests and priestesses" of Pele was undermined (Ellis 1969:313).

With the defeat of Kekuaokalani and the political strategy he symbolized, women became more important than ever as points of access to power and as politically powerful figures in their own right. By all accounts, as premier (*kuhina nui*) and regent Ka'ahumanu was the de facto ruler of the Hawaiian kingdom until she died in 1832. Her successor Kīna'u was said to exercise "an absolute control" over the young King Kamehameha III: "she rules in his name" (Barrot 1978:39, 42). After her, the *kuhina nui* Kekāuluohi was "second only to the King" (*Polynesian* 10/23/1841:78); the *Polynesian* called her "the Big-Mouthed Queen." The increasing influence, however, of Euro-American jural models on the Hawaiian government in the 1840s was a countervailing trend to women's enhanced political authority, a point that will be developed further in subsequent chapters.

In the struggle following Liholiho's rejection of the tabus, Kekuaokalani was a traditionalist, defending the Hawaiian religion and by extension the old strategies of succession against Ka'ahumanu's proforeign faction. If the religion of Kū was particularly a cult of male chiefs, then by relative contrast the religion that succeeded it can be identified with women. High-ranking women—notably the widows of Kamehameha—adopted and promoted Christianity in Hawaii. Liholiho, and Kauikeaouli after him, resisted and rebelled against the strictures of the new faith, but Ka'ahumanu and her faction adopted the missionary Hiram Bingham as their own high priest (Sahlins 1981:65). Those who mark the victories of Christianity in the islands cite prominent chiefly women—including the very women who had promoted free eating—as their earliest patrons. Liholiho's queen Kamāmalu was an early convert (Ellis 1969:452–53). The Kona chiefess Kapi'olani defied Pele in 1823 and advised the people not to worship her (Kamakau 1961:382). Stewart (1970:197–98) describes Keōpūolani remonstrating with Liholiho over the worth of the *palapala*, the teachings of the missionaries. She was baptized moments before her death (Stewart 1970:218), and left instructions that the people should not indulge in the traditional mourning practices. Afterward Kaheiheimalie became a devout Christian, "and Ka'ahumanu followed" (Kamakau 1961:387). She was baptized in 1826 as Elizabeth Ka'ahumanu and the following year made a celebrated tour of O'ahu spreading the gospel.

Sahlins (1981) interprets Kaʻahumanu's conversion after Liholiho's death as a restoration of the tabus, but with new rules reflecting a stern Calvinist orthodoxy. As Sahlins (1981:66) points out, Kaʻahumanu undertook her journey on Oʻahu in the ritually correct direction for restoring the tabu. It is significant that the new tabus were particularly espoused, if not defined, by women. In the aftermath of the *kapu* abolition women replaced men as the active, focal figures in the state religion. And perhaps correlatively, with the demise of the sacrificial cult that legitimated conquest, male Hawaiian *aliʻi* seem to have lost some of their *mana,* their efficacy and directedness. In the nineteenth-century monarchy one sees fewer personally powerful and effective male chiefs, at least in the ruling line, and more of a tendency to psychological conflict, depression, and dissipation. By several accounts, Kauikeaouli—a boy of eleven when he became king—was thoroughly dominated by his several mothers through most of his reign. And the powerful women who served as *kuhina nui*—premier and regent—were all devout Christians under the influence of the American missionaries (Kamakau 1961:334; Barrot 1978:40). The fall of the indigenous religion is only one of many factors in the demoralization of male chiefs. But if, as I have suggested, the tabus were a way in which men exerted some control over women, then *aliʻi* men may well have suffered differentially from the loss of that ritual system.

Chapter 4

Chiefs and Commoners

The intersecting categories male and female, chiefly and common, produced the matrix of Hawaiian society. In Hawaii social rank was the most crucial determinant of a man or woman's life situation. The chiefly/common distinction defined prerogatives or liabilities in the sorts of food one ate, the type of tapa one wore, and the way one worshiped. Chiefly women, like their male counterparts, received tributary offerings (*ho'okupu*) from commoner men and women. Hierarchy pervaded land relations especially. Female chiefs were superordinate land givers in their right, standing "above" their local *konohiki* and commoners "below." High-ranking women, while exercising considerable personal authority, were also structurally pivotal figures in chiefly politics. Despite the ideology of unambiguous ascription there was considerable room for maneuver in the Hawaiian status system. Women had rank differentiating power and were thus crucial in the status ambitions and strategies of male chiefs. This chapter elaborates political and exchange relations between chiefs and commoners, and explores the possibilities of status manipulation in the Hawaiian rank gradient. The focus here is on women's structural and symbolic significance at the top of society, among the chiefs. The following chapter will consider women's position in the local group of *maka'āinana*.

Chiefdom and State

The relationship between chiefs and commoners is the most salient fact for understanding how Hawaiian society was structured indigenously and how the polity and economy were transformed in the nineteenth century. Accounts by Westerners have perennially likened the Hawaiian chiefdom to European feudalism. This is a distortion, but an understandable one. Foreign observers judged Hawaii according to their own cultural referents, and the people's tenancy under the chiefs seemed feudal to them, as did the chiefs' apparent tyranny toward the commoners. Marion Kelly (1967:402–8) has also made the point that Kamehameha, heavily influenced by his discussions with Vancouver, patterned his government in part after Western feudal forms. But there are important differences between early Hawaiian society and a feudal state. There has been much debate over whether Hawaii was or was not a state at the time of contact, but most of the dialogue has been carried on in the archaeological literature and centers on interpretation of archaeological evidence (see Kirch 1984, 1985). The ethnohistorical data, however, suggest that Hawaii in 1778 was a complex and populous chiefdom on the verge of state formation, but still lacked the important criterion of political centralization. The fact remains that only after foreign contact could one chief, Kamehameha I, establish and maintain military hegemony over more than one island. And Kamehameha's campaign was decisively aided by firearms and European military advisers. The Battle of Nu'uanu in 1795, which sealed the conquest of O'ahu and unified the windward islands under Kamehameha, is often cited as the decisive event in the birth of the Hawaiian kingdom, marking Hawaii's transition from a chiefdom to a state.

The Hawaiian chiefs were a floating class, tenuously related to the people on the land but dependent on them for support. Indisputably, there was a wide social gap between chiefs and people in the pre-European society. Nevertheless, in both tributary and land tenure relationships there was also reciprocity—mutual obligations and expectations, even mutual checks on behavior. Chiefly oppression was not a historical constant but represented a postcontact distortion of the chiefs' relationship to the people. Under the indigenous chieftainship chiefly exaction "had a moral limit consistent with the kinship configuration of the society" (Sahlins 1972:147). Exploitation of the commoners worsened particularly during the excesses of the sandalwood era and through the period of the Māhele. The "aloha" between chiefs and commoners was not indigenously an empty ideological mystification, although the chiefs' behavior from the 1820s through the 1850s mocked the concept of mutuality. At issue here is not simply the normative ethic, but the material and political balance in Hawaiian society.

Care and Service

Kamehameha cultivated land at Waikiki, Honolulu, and Kapalama, and fed the people. He fished, made huge hauls, and gave food to the chiefs and people. Thus he cared for both chiefs and commoners.

—Kamakau (1961:190)

Accounts by nineteenth-century writers, both haole and Hawaiian, amply document chiefly oppression of the commoners. Anecdote after anecdote recounts the chiefs' conspicuous consumption, excessive material and labor demands, arbitrary seizure of property, unwarranted eviction, and general disregard for the people's welfare. Such behavior was a transformation of the indigenous relationship between chiefs and people, a change precipitated by exogenous factors but one that played upon native structural tensions. There is a tendency for chiefs to lean on their people to produce too much, particularly in a chiefdom such as Hawaii, which was continually flirting with political centralization (Sahlins 1972:144–45). Yet, paradoxically to a Westerner, the Hawaiian commoners appear to have loved the chiefs through the worst of times. They chanted and danced hula in their honor, even when they had to do so in secret (see Barrère, Pukui, and Kelly 1980); most of the ancient style (*kahiko*) hulas performed today celebrate particular chiefs of old. This aloha of the people for the chiefs is clearly evident in an anecdote recorded by Edwin Locke (ms.), who taught school in Waialua on the north shore of O'ahu in the 1830s. One of Locke's more troublesome students was the daughter of the local chief, Gideon La'anui. In his journal Locke dubbed her "Miss chief." On one occasion in 1837, he sentenced her to bring a half-bushel of sand to school as punishment for some misbehavior. She told him that others would bring it, and came to school the next day with her foster mother and about twenty men and women, the latter bearing calabashes of sand. The people told the incredulous teacher that "it was *love* that made them bring it." Similarly, the girl's nurse offered her own bottom to be struck instead of the girl's.

The prerogatives of chiefly status included not only the personal tabus surrounding the chief's body and personal articles, the finest mats and tapas, and the high foods, but also the right to place *kapu* on particular crops, lands, or species, thereby reserving the proceeds for themselves.

Through their tributary prestations, the commoners fed the chiefs. Every land section included *kō'ele* patches, worked by the commoners specifically for the chief's support. During the annual Makahiki festival and at other ritually prescribed times of the year, commoners in every land section presented offerings (*ho'okupu*) to the gods and the chiefs (in this context the two are equivalent; for explication see Valeri 1985): pigs, dogs, fish, chickens, yams, taro, bananas, tapa cloth, mats, fishing line and nets, feathers, cordage, sometimes canoes (Campbell 1967:118; Ellis 1969:416; Kamakau 1961:177, 1964:20–21; Malo 1951:145–46; Menzies 1920:82; Richards 1973:24; Stewart 1970:130, 199). After the god, the chief received the first fish caught and the first fruits of the land (Ellis 1969:417; Whitman 1979:75–76). The impressive Hawaiian fishponds of the coastal wall type (*loko kuapā;* see Kikuchi 1976) were reserved for chiefly use (Bloxam 1925:26, 36; Byron 1826:169; Dampier 1971:53–54; Stewart 1970:365; Whitman 1979:78). They appear to have served as a "bank" for chiefly largesse or provisioning; Marin's journal (Conrad 1973), for example, contains numerous references to high chiefs making gifts of fish.

In general, chiefs were entitled to the first, best, and biggest of everything, and they had the absolute right to confiscate goods that were qualitatively or quantitatively inappropriate to commoners. In 1841 William Richards (1973:26) wrote: "none of the lower orders even if they were able ever dared to live in a large house, cook a large hog, fish with a large net, or wear the finest quality of dress." Several early observers corroborate the chiefs' right of seizure (cf. Dampier 1971:47; Ellis 1969:418; Stewart 1970:116, 131, 152). Mathison's (1825:385) statement is representative:

> whenever an industrious person brought more land into cultivation than was necessary for his subsistence, or reared a good breed of pigs and poultry, the Chief, on hearing of it, had no hesitation in making the property his own.

Granted, these accounts all date from 1820s or later, but nothing suggests that the chiefs' right of expropriation was an innovation; on the contrary, this mechanism of social control was simply an extension of the chiefs' right to tabu goods, lands, species of fish, or other resources for themselves. In 1793 members of the Vancouver expedition saw a Hawaiian friend seized and their gifts to him confiscated. Worse yet, the chiefs asked Kamehameha for leave to kill him. According to resident foreigners John Young and Isaac Davis, this was customary "when any of the lower rank became wealthy without power or any connection among the chiefs" (Menzies 1920:99–100). Menzies (1920:170) also reports that when members of the expedition hiked up Mount Huālalai in Kona, Kamehameha himself distributed their gifts to the servants who had accompanied them: iron chisels, nails, beads, knives, scissors, mirrors, and tapa. But the retainers gave up the tapa to the king. A chief in the party received the same sorts of items, plus enough red cloth to make a cloak; but this last he had to surrender to Kamehameha.

At the level of ideal types, the economic mode characteristic of chiefdoms is redistribution: goods flow into a political center and then are given out again. Alternately, a chiefdom can be conceptualized as a pyramid: tribute from the common people travels upward to the chiefs, who redistribute goods as gifts to their followers and occasionally to their rivals. One of the "paramount" ethics of chiefly behavior is that chiefs are generous to their people (Sahlins 1965; 1972:139–48). The underlying political imperative is that for all their prerogatives of rank, chiefs still lack a monopoly of force and their authority ultimately rests on the loyalty of their followers. Bad chiefs, warns Malo (1951:195) "have been put to death by the people because of their oppression of the *makaainana*." Rebellion would take the form not of a popular revolt, but a challenge by a junior collateral successfully marshaling support from among the dissatisfied. A representative tale is that of 'Umi's younger son Keawenui, who deposed his elder brother Keli'iokaloa (Kamakau 1961:34–46). The contrast between the two brothers is stereotypic: Keawenui "was a kind ruler who looked after the welfare of chiefs and commoners." The unfortunate Keli'iokaloa was "righteous" but "did not mind his father's advice to take care" of the people:

> He deserted the god and oppressed the people. . . . He seized the property of the chiefs . . . and the food for the commoners, their pigs, dogs, chickens, and other property. The coconut trees that were planted were hewn down. . . . Their canoes and fish were seized; and people were compelled to do burdensome tasks such as diving for *'ina* sea urchins and *wana* sea urchins, and sea weeds at night. (Kamakau 1961:35)

Because of Keli'iokaloa's "unjust rule . . . and the burdening of the common people," some of his chiefs and commoners went to Keawenui and offered the chiefdom to him.

After European contact and particularly from the 1820s on, the actions of the Hawaiian chiefs toward their people increasingly approached the stereotypic behavior of the "bad chiefs" of legendary histories. But even in the earliest ethnohistorical accounts it is difficult to find evidence of goods moving downward in the social hierarchy. Did the chiefs give back to the people? Were there material correlates to the ideology of chiefly aloha? Indisputably, the material flow between chiefs and commoners in Hawaii was unbalanced even before foreign contact—the imbalance, indeed, was an index of the Hawaiian tendency to political centralization and of the incipient structural breach between chiefs and people. But the tendency to characterize the Hawaiian system as "feudal" distorts the nature of the political relationship, which was structured by stipulated kinship and founded on an exchange of service for care. The commoners owed service to the chiefs as their superiors and senior kin; in turn the good chief was supposed to care for the people, an obligation not to press too much and to give back at least occasionally.

Complementary obligations such as these are more or less explicit throughout Polynesia in the context of senior/junior relations within the family. The concept of *mālama* 'care' is central to Hawaiian familial role expectations, as evidenced both in the early materials and in normative statements made by modern Hawaiians. As testified by nineteenth-century Hawaiians and by the twentieth-century ethnologist Mary Kawena Pukui (Handy and Pukui 1972), household members are said to live "under" the land giver in the family, to whom they owe obedience and respect. Similarly in Samoa, the young and untitled owe *tautua* 'service' to their *matai*, the titled family head. Moreover, the quality of their service is considered the principal measure of their personal character. A famous Samoan proverb states that "the way to power is service" (*O le ala i le pule o le tautua.*). In other words, one can also further one's own ambitions by serving well, a theme that emerges clearly in the story of the Hawai'i chief Lonoikamakahiki (Kamakau 1961:53–54). A visiting Maui chief attempts to shame Lono by demonstrating his servants' alacrity. When Lono calls for his own food, it is not ready, and in anger he strikes his steward Puapuakea. But Puapuakea still manages to ready Lono's food and kava before that of the Maui chief: "The chiefs and commoners praised Puapua-kea greatly because the chief of Maui had planned to humiliate the chief of Hawaii" (Kamakau 1961:53). The Maui chief requests Puapuakea for his own servant, but Lono replies that Puapuakea is the heir to the chieftainship: " 'This is not my servant, but an important person in my court. He is my younger brother, a protector of my land. I am the chief, and he comes next to me as chief of the island of Hawaii and its people' " (Kamakau 1961:54).

Hawaiian traditions explicitly apply kinship norms to the behavior of political superiors toward the commoners: "The land agent was like a parent over the people of his district" (Kamakau 1961:378). Statements about the qualities of a good chief stress generosity, fairness, and caring for the commoners:

> That was their appropriate business, to seek the comfort and welfare of the people, for a chief was called great in proportion to the number of his people . . . wherefore it behooved the chiefs to look well to their people against the time of war. (Malo 1839:125–26)

Of a famous ruler of Hawai'i, Kamakau (1961:75) writes: "Alapa'i was a good ruler, one who loved the common people. . . . He did not take lands from the chiefs or the commoners. He honored his wives, made feasts for them, and gave them ornaments." (That good chiefs respect their wives is a cautionary note for those who would stay in power.) Praising Kamehameha, Kamakau (1961:181) writes that many of the goods collected for the gods during the annual Makahiki festival were subsequently distributed "to all the people," who were thus suitably reminded that their chief was worthy of their allegiance: "Men said, 'Our needs will be supplied if we live under this chief; here is food, fish, tapa, loin cloths, skirts, mats, *olona* fiber, nets, and feathers, all to be had in one day.' " (For other descriptions of Makahiki distributions see Kamakau 1964:21; Ii 1959:76; Valeri 1985:209–10.) Further, the legends of good chiefs recount instances of their spontaneous largesse. Kamehameha was known above all as "a good provider" (Kamakau 1961:178). According to Kamakau (1961:182), he "loved pious people." He and a companion once spied on an old man and saw him use up the last of his kava (*'awa*) in prayers for Kamehameha. Kamehameha then approached him, saying:

> "Is all your 'awa gone? . . . let my man bring you some." After they had gone away he said to his companion, "Bring him forty 'awa stocks . . . twenty bundles of *pa'i'ai* [dried, pounded taro] . . . five tuna fish (*ahi*), forty *aku* fish, forty *mamaki* tapas, and twenty heavy loin cloths (*malo uaua*)." When the things were given to the old man he said, "It must have been Kamehameha and his man who came here last night." (Kamakau 1961:182)

It is important to stress that before the formation of the Hawaiian state there were palpable sanctions inducing chiefs to approach the ideal. The moral charter of stipulated kinship between chiefs and people was backed by the real threats of desertion and rebellion. "It was a wise thing," Malo writes (1951:194), "for the king to invite all of the people to partake of the food, that they might not go away fasting." Even in Hawaii, chiefs garnered support through the power of the gift. Malo explicitly links chiefly generosity to maintaining the allegiance of one's followers:

> It was well for the king to gather many people about him and for him and his queen to deal out food and meat, as well as *tapa* and *malo* with a liberal hand. Thus he would dispose the men to be as a shield to him in the day of battle.

Similarly, Kamakau (1961:197, see also 178) reports that when Kamehameha observed the chiefs on Oʻahu "increasing their households and cultivating large tracts . . . to feed their followers," he interpreted their actions as a sign of impending rebellion.

Although retainers in the chief's immediate party would have been the primary beneficiaries of her or his generosity, ethnohistorical accounts also document distributions to commoners. In a parting prestation to Cook in 1779, the Kona chief Kalaniʻōpuʻu gave out cloth, feathers, and provisions. Cook selected only the large hogs for the ship. As King (1967:518) reports, "I believe more than 30 pigs were given to the Common People, as well as the great part of the breadfruit, Coco nuts & sweet Potatoes, as they would not keep." Mathison (1825:451) reports the chiefs "if kindly disposed . . . distributing supplies of maros, tappers, cloth, etc, gratuitously among them." King Kamehameha V's response to the 1868 eruption and tidal wave on Hawaiʻi further attests that, even in this late period, the commoners could expect chiefly care to translate into material aid in times of crisis. The king's actions after the disaster epitomize the normative response of a good chief. As recorded by Varigny (1981:216–26), who accompanied the king on his inspection tour, the monarch apportioned small lots from his own estates to be given to victims of the disaster, that they might have land to support their families. The king heard the people's requests for immediate assistance and then distributed food, money, and supplies to them. He also gave them permission to cut bamboo and wood "from his royal lands" and to take cows and sheep from his herds. "As for orphans," reports

Varigny (1981:219), then a cabinet officer, "the king generously announced that he would look after them . . . [and] he would see that they were well brought up by his own relatives and retainers, or perhaps else he would simply provide homes for them on one of his royal estates."

There is little evidence, however, to suggest regular potlatch-type redistributive events in Hawaii. Neither is there evidence of a system of formal exchanges in Hawaii such as still flourishes in Samoa, although the prestations made to Cook, Vancouver, and other early visitors suggest a customary, and characteristically Polynesian, etiquette of gift giving among high-status individuals. But it is clear that chiefs regularly redistributed their *ho'okupu* among their retainers, with the commoners receiving less frequently. Most vivid are the reminiscences of Gideon La'anui (1930), a lesser chief who lived with Kamehameha's train from the age of five. La'anui describes the series of prestations to the king as he made his rounds of the islands: A "prostration hookupu" on O'ahu, a "royal hookupu" at Lāhaina "to which Lanai [island] contributed." After the latter, clothing was distributed "till the stock of malos gave out." La'anui's own share was two dogs and forty tapas "for children" (1930:90). The island of Maui "held a hookupu that gratified the heart of [the Maui chief] Keeaumoku; kapa, paus, nets, food and fish. Our share was two forty's of kapa, ten paus, ten dogs" (1930:91). Moloka'i islanders too offered their *ho'okupu,* after which La'anui received more tapas, *pā'ū,* and dogs. La'anui only mentions one distribution that may have been to the common people: at Lāhaina "food was distributed to men and women, consisting of wailau (bundled hard poi)" (1930:86).

Many of the tributary goods that the chiefs received went to feed, clothe, and ingratiate their immediate retainers. But many others—especially the fine mats and tapas produced by women—were used specifically to index chiefly rank and reify social distance. Without potlatch-type events where fine goods would be distributed to actual or potential rivals, the primary function of stacks of fine mats and tapas was sumptuary display. In other words, the chiefs commanded and flaunted these articles in order to demonstrate that they were chiefs. In obvious fashion, this way of manifesting social rank provided the precedent for the later chiefly conspicuous consumption and oppression of the people. When high status came to be indexed not by fine mats and white tapas but by silver service and Western military garb, the "price" of the chieftainship inflated geometrically. The people could no longer directly satisfy chiefly sumptuary requirements; they became instead a tool used to satisfy chiefly material wants, which the foreign market could stimulate and supply almost indefinitely. It was the commoners who then had to make up the merchants' profit factor with increased labor and intensified production.

But I am getting ahead of the story. The process just described became acute late in Kamehameha's reign, and chiefly oppression was chronic thereafter. The issue of the precontact relationship between chiefs and people must be kept separate from these later developments. Through the mechanism of tribute the Hawaiian chiefs clearly siphoned off domestic produce (Sahlins 1972:139ff.), but Hawaiian commoners appear to have perceived their own consumption needs as correspondingly modest. Western visitors, particularly missionaries, frequently judged Hawaiian commoners to be miserable because of their lack of possessions and the "hovels" that they lived in. But the people are nowhere described as starving, and several accounts allege that they were essentially content. Dampier's comment (1971:47) may be an accurate summary of the commoners' welfare: "Notwithstanding this arbitrary mode of government, I should say that these people are perfectly happy, their wants are very few." Although Westerners saw Hawaiian hierarchy as inherently oppressive, the people's aloha for the chiefs appears to have diminished remarkably little even through the middle of the nineteenth century.

Access to Resources

Largely because of the paucity of the ethnohistorical record on ordinary Hawaiian women, much of the preceding analysis has focused on women of rank, women "of some consequence" in Samwell's (1967:1160) words, but any examination of Hawaiian women's "status" must take into account the differentials of rank, the contrasting positions and experiences of chiefly and commoner women. As we will see in the remainder of this book, the social position of commoner women through the economic and political upheavals of the nineteenth century is bound up with kinship roles and land relations—both political and familial.

Pre-Māhele Hawaiian land tenure can be conceived of as a hierarchy of distribution rights. The paramount chief allocated *ahupua'a* to lesser chiefs, who entrusted the land's administration to their local agents, the *konohiki*. The latter gave out lands to the commoners and saw that the chief's labor and tributary demands were met. In Māhele records the chief of the *ahupua'a* is frequently referred to as the "owner" of the land, but ultimately there were no owners in the Western sense. Land could not be alienated permanently and, with the exception of the highest ruling chief, everyone in the hierarchy held the land at the discretion of some higher ranking landlord. Theoretically, the paramount could take away lands from the *ahupua'a* chiefs, but it is almost inconceivable that this right would be exercised except in case of rebellion. Arbitrary takings from allies and supporters would be risky indeed for a ruler; in the histories of the conquest era and through the reign of Kamehameha II, land redistribution appears as a frequent source of conflict between paramount and lesser chiefs.

Hawaiian land tenure was thus highly contingent and entailed a succession of caretakers; against this view the question of "ultimate" control seems a peculiarly Western fetish. Abstract statements of principle such as are required in Western law seem out of place in the Hawaiian context. Kamakau's (1961:376) irresolute attempt at a generalization suggests that ownership as an abstract issue was not a source of concern to the Hawaiians: "Before the constitution was established [1840] all property rights for both chiefs and commoners were unstable; the entire control over the land was vested in the king. According to the opinion of learned men the land belongs to the common people." Defending the latter contention, Kamakau again contrasts the transience of the chiefs with the commoners' continuity, invoking the people's knowledge of secret burial sites in their natal locality: "The rule of kings and chiefs and their land agents might change, but the burial rights of families survived on their lands. Here is one proof of the people's right to the land." Significantly, Kamakau (1961:376–77) traces "land irregularities"—meaning particularly the displacement of local populations—to the period of intensified warfare preceding Kamehameha's conquest:

> The land belonging to the old chiefs was given to strange chiefs and that of old residents on the land to their companies of soldiers, leaving the old settled families destitute. During that period they left the lands of their birth and settled on other lands. But for the most part the common people remained on the lands inherited from their ancestors. Strangers move about but native sons remain.

Kamakau's summary stands as an insightful description of the late eighteenth-century political developments in Hawaii; it has a particular historical correlate in Kamehameha's occupation of Oʻahu (ca. 1804–12), when an army of perhaps seven thousand—mostly lesser chiefs and commoners from Hawaiʻi island—was settled in over the local population (see Kamakau 1961:148; Kirch 1985:223, 235–36, 311–14; Kirch and Sahlins ms.).

Whether the right conveyed was to an *ahupuaʻa* or a taro patch, the Hawaiian land relation was definitively hierarchical. It is inaccurate to characterize Hawaiian land tenure as 'communal,' for there is no evidence to suggest that all members of a familial group had equal say over the destiny of land or produce. Rather, in characteristically Polynesian fashion, land giver was in a superordinate position to land taker; the terms "over" (*maluna*) and "under" (*malalo*) are commonly used to describe the relationship. When the younger brother of Kalaniʻōpuʻu urged his nephew Kīwalaʻō to divide the lands among the chiefs, he described a gradient of rank that would materialize as strata of *konohiki:* " 'You are chief over the island, I am under you, and the chiefs under us' " (Kamakau 1961:119). Similarly in Māhele testimony, a witness describes transferences of a *kuleana:* "Kahuna above, he beneath, when he died it came to Kalua; I was beneath him; when he was removed, it came to Palemo, and we are under him" (NT 3:555).

Even though political land-giving relationships are most in evidence in Māhele testimony, the legitimacy of the commoners' tenure had a dual basis. Chiefly and *konohiki* donors allocated use rights, while particular plots were for the most part passed on from parents to children, as long as the holder met the chief's tributary and labor requirements. As phrased by a visitor to the islands in 1836: "although upon the death of an occupant of a land, that land by right reverts to the king, yet he almost always permits the son of the deceased to inherit the hut and field of his father" (Barrot 1978:104). It would be wholly wrong to conclude from Māhele testimony that commoners were a mobile and rootless class, continually moving to new lands at the will of some *konohiki* or other. Nonetheless, the commoners were not bound to the land, but were free to move to other localities if they wished (Campbell 1967:122; Dampier 1971:47; Ellis 1969:417; Kotzebue 1821, 3:246). Commoners too, in other words, could *ʻimi haku* 'seek a lord.' The extent to which they availed themselves of this alternative is addressed in the following chapter.

The meaning and function of Hawaiian land categories reveal much about the productive system, and the nature of chiefly control. As in other

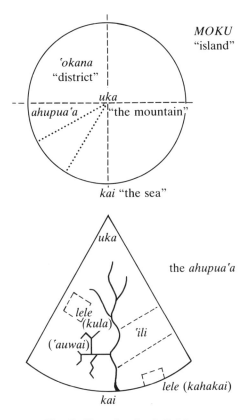

Fig. 7. Hawaiian land divisions

Polynesian high-island societies, the major Hawaiian land categories embody a radial symmetry based on the opposition of mountains and sea, *mauka* and *makai* signifying the contrasting directions, inland and seaward. Figure 7 is a schematic diagram of native land divisions. The island (*moku*) was subdivided into several districts (variously called *moku* or *'okana;* see Kamakau 1961:180; Malo 1951:16; Hawaii 1929:ix), of which there were six on Hawai'i. Functionally, the most important land section was the *ahupua'a,* ideally a valley running from the mountains (*uka*) to the sea (*kai*). In its typical form the *ahupua'a* was a naturally bounded unit containing a full range of ecological and productive zones: a beach section, irrigated taro flats, dry open or cultivated land (*kula*), and upland forests (Hawaii 1929:ix). Not all *ahupua'a* conform to the ideal in shape and composition, however; in some politically significant areas such as

North Kohala, *ahupua'a* appear to have been subdivided in the past so that ruling chiefs could accommodate loyal followers, perhaps the Hawaiian equivalent of gerrymandering. Usually the province of a single chiefly "owner," the *ahupua'a* was a unit of tributary collection and conquest land redistribution through Kamehameha's time. Under the monarchy the *ahupua'a* was a unit of tax collection.

In Māhele records Hawaiians use a bewildering variety of terms for land divisions smaller than the *ahupua'a* (see Lyons 1875; Malo 1951:16; Territory of Hawaii 1929:ix–x). These differed regionally both in meaning and in frequency of usage. The most common of these is the *'ili* or *'ili 'āina,* a named section of the *ahupua'a.* In some areas the *'ili* in turn claimed several subsections, also named and located in different productive zones:

> one, for instance, would be on the sea shore, another in dry, open land or *kula,* another in the regularly terraced and watered taro patch section, and still another in the forest section. (Hawaii 1929:x)

On O'ahu, these discontiguous parcels belonging to a single *'ili* were called *lele* 'to fly' or 'to jump.' Some claimants cited *lo'i lele* 'patches that jump,' apparently meaning taro *lo'i* scattered in different locations. The allocation of dispersed rights in varied microenvironments indicates that each landholder was assured of access to different productive zones and suggests that local organization and solidarity were not based on symbiotic specialization.

In the Māhele Kalaiheana, a *konohiki* in Mānoa Valley, Honolulu, claimed taro lands, *kula,* a houselot, as well as "the trees of the forest at Kolowalu, and the fish in the sea" (NR 5:466). He testified that these rights were given him by the Maui chief Ke'eaumoku at the time of the battle of Nu'uanu. Kolowalu was an *'ili* located upland of Kalaiheana's lands, which lay perhaps a mile and a half from the ocean. Kalaiheana also received a *lele* at the beach in Kahala to preserve his rights in the sea. Other claimants speak of *kula lele* and *paukū lele*—scattered 'pieces.' A Hawaiian surveyor's testimony in a nineteenth-century court case further corroborates the conclusion that chiefs and *konohiki* customarily gave different types of land and use rights to a household: "Waikalulu is lele—that is the lele makai. The kumu ['source'] of this land is mauka—the kalo land. . . . a lele is an outlying land. . . . it is the old custom so as to give a variety of sorts of land to a person" (testimony of Makalena, L-542, 1871).

Since the time of the Māhele Westerners have interpreted the Hawaiian land divisions as nested subsets of one another (see, e.g., Hawaii 1929:ix–x). But Hawaiian land terms such as *mo'o* 'strip' and *kīhāpai* 'a dryland garden' point to qualitative rather than spatial distinctions; relative size was at most a secondary component of their meaning. Hawaiian land terms were not well suited to the exclusive demarcation required in the Māhele and posed irresolvable difficulties to those charged with defining individual claims. Artemas Bishop, assigned to survey claims in a rural *ahupua'a* on Oahu, wrote: "My greatest trial everywhere is the extreme indefiniteness of boundaries, and the consequent warm contentions between opposite claimants" (letter to William L. Lee, March, 1852, AH).

There were of course other discrepancies between Western categories and the indigenous system. Private landed property had no precedent in Hawaiian land tenure. An underlying principle was that objects not made by the human hand could not be owned, that is they could not be set aside for the exclusive or perpetual use of any individual. Moreover, Hawaiians recognized not only rights in land parcels, but use rights in a range of dispersed resources from the forests to the sea. Campbell (1967:142–43) gives perhaps the most detailed description of *ahupua'a* residents' rights in the sea, though this reflects observations made in 1809: "The occupiers or proprietors of land are entitled to the privilege of fishing upon their own shores as far as the tallest man in the island can wade at low water," excepting tabu periods.

Nearly all early observers comment on the intensiveness and beauty of Hawaiian agricultural production (e.g., Beresford 1789:88, 264–65; Campbell 1967:103–4; Freycinet 1978:8; Kotzebue 1821, 1:340–41, 3:236; Menzies 1920:75–76). Even the banks between the taro patches were planted in sugar cane and bananas. Campbell's admiring description of Ewa, near Honolulu, is representative:

> . . . an extensive and fertile plain, the whole of which is in the highest state of cultivation. Every stream was carefully embanked, to supply water for the taro beds. Where there was no water, the land was under crops of yams and sweet potatoes.

Although wetland taro cultivation is usually portrayed as the archetype of Hawaiian agriculture, the chiefdoms of Kona and Kohala were supported by vast dryland field systems of breadfruit, sweet potatoes, yams, bananas, and dryland taro (King 1967:521; see Kirch 1985:223–36). Beresford (1789:92, 264–65) even judged Hawai'i to be more fertile and "plentiful" than O'ahu and Kaua'i, a measure not so much of the land's innate fertility as of the Hawai'i chiefs' political dominance at the time. There is general agreement that the Hawaiian productive system was capable of supporting a large population and that agricultural intensification was at least in part stimulated by chiefly ambitions (for other discussions see Kirch 1985:231–36; Sahlins 1972:101–48). William Ladd estimated that "forty feet square" of taro would support a man for one year, while a square mile would, according to his calculations, feed 15,151 souls. Yet "not more than one twenty-fifth of that number would be required to cultivate it" (quoted in the *Friend*, July 7, 1844:62). The accuracy of Ladd's numbers aside, the commoners' labor requirements appear in any case to have been moderate, at least they were so before chiefly conspicuous consumption and introduced diseases combined to place increasing demands on an ever-dwindling population of *maka'āinana*.

Kalo 'taro' and *kula*, wet and dry land, were contrasting categories in Hawaiian land use. Irrigated taro lands were usually located in the valley bottoms and were fed by a reticulated network of irrigation ditches (*'auwai;* Kirch 1985:218–27). The *kula* was unirrigated, open land, either inaccessible to water or temporarily let fallow. Crops grown on *kula* land included dryland taro, sweet potatoes, yams, *wauke* (for tapa cloth), gourds (*ipu*), bananas, and sugar cane (Malo 1951:205). Māhele claims from leeward and upland areas do include some references to irrigated *kula*, and archaeological study of the Lālāmilo field system, Hawai'i island, has revealed irrigation ditches leading to dryland fields. Nevertheless, most *kula* land was unirrigated, and the productive contrast between wetland taro and the mixed dryland *kula* crops still holds. By the time of the Māhele *kula* land was also used for pasturing the Hawaiians' goats, horses, and cattle. In wetland taro-growing areas *kula* and *kalo* were reversible categories, as attested by this witness to the Land Commission:

> I know this loi . . . my older brother came there, when it was just kula, with no loi on it. We made the loi and planted the taro . . . when the loi dried up we abandoned it. (NT 10:171)

One of the great injustices of the Māhele was the alienation of the *kula*. By the terms of the Kuleana Act commoners could claim only houselots and lands actually cultivated in food crops. In claim after claim, taro patches previously planted but in weeds (*nāhelehele*) at the time of the testimony were not awarded. This limitation on the people's *kuleana* seems especially cruel when one considers that during the period of the Māhele most Hawaiian families suffered some loss during the epidemics of measles and smallpox, and many households were decimated. By long-established precedent "waste" lands and the uplands and forests were the province of the *konohiki* of the *ahupua'a,* but the commoners had access to these lands as a manifestation of the chief's aloha for them. Although the Kuleana Act included a provision for the people's gathering rights, the Hawaiian government failed to protect *kuleana* holders from large landowners after the Māhele (Linnekin 1987).

Chiefly ownership of the *kula* after the Māhele illustrates how, in the changed economic and political context of the middle nineteenth century, ostensibly using Hawaiian cultural precedent as the basis for law simply provided a blueprint for oppression. The injustice continues to this day in the implementation of other laws dating back to the Māhele. In the indigenous system the land of a householder evicted or deceased reverted to the *konohiki.* Until 1987 Hawaii state law allowed abandoned or unclaimed Land Commission awards to "escheat" to the surrounding landowner; thus for over a century many plantations, ranches, and large estates were given carte blanche to absorb old *kuleana* lands. Another example is, of course, the vast discrepancy in the acreages awarded to the king and chiefs in comparison to the commoners. Instead of instituting a "reform," the Māhele effectively sedimented the existing social hierarchy. Those who were low before the Māhele were merely awarded rights commensurate with their status.

A Hawaiian Ramage?

A symbolic opposition between "stranger-kings" and "the people of the land" pervades Hawaiian and Polynesian ideology (Sahlins 1981, 1985). Yet Hawaiian myth-histories also stipulate a common ancestry of chiefs and people: "There is not a commoner on Hawaii who can say, 'Umi-a-Liloa was not our ancestor" (Kamakau 1961:19). Earlier comparative studies of Polynesian societies, notably Goldman (1970) and Sahlins (1958), analyzed Hawaiian social and political organization as a variant of the conical clan (Kirchhoff 1959) or ramage (*ramage* is French for a branchlike pattern; see Firth 1957:298–329). This model posits a gradient of rank encompassing the entire society. The polity is the territorial arm of a status lineage, and political units are identified with genealogical segments. As Sahlins explained in *Social Stratification in Polynesia* (1958:141), the entire society "can usually be analyzed as composed of sections of a single genealogical system at the apex of which stands the paramount chief."

In recent scholarship, however, the trend has been to point out how the ramage model is at variance with the empirical realities of status ascription in Polynesian societies. Earlier writers overemphasized the inflexibility of social boundaries and rank ascriptions, giving primary weight to patrilineality as a principle of recruitment. Ethnographers continue to correct these portrayals with studies showing that manipulability and the active negotiation of social rank are characteristic of Polynesian societies (see, e.g., Sahlins 1985 on the Hawaiian "performative structure"). Most significantly for my purposes, recent Polynesian ethnology has paid increasing attention to women. In revising our assumptions about Hawaiian political organization, we must also revise our evaluation of the structural efficacy of Hawaiian women.

Many earlier assumptions about Polynesian societies do not fit Hawaii. The ramage model implies that an entire chiefdom can be assimilated to a single genealogical grid; similar ideas, such as the Kamakau statement quoted above, can indeed be found in the Hawaiian materials. In the *Kumulipo,* the Hawaiian creation chant, chiefs, commoners, and the taro are all descended from Papa and Wākea, the original couple. Good (male) chiefs are stereotypically praised for their polygyny and their progeny, of both high and low status: "Keawe-nui . . . was a kind ruler who looked after the welfare of chiefs and commoners, and increased the number of chiefly children. . . . Many sons and daughters were born to him, and these became the ancestors of chiefs and commoners." Yet Hawaiian traditions also contrast the indigenous right of the *maka'āinana* with the itineracy of the chiefs, who were not intrinsically identified with any one land but roamed through the areas under their control accompanied by a retinue of followers: "numberless were the people that came into the train of the chiefs" (Malo 1839:122). Even the birthplace of the chief was usually apocryphal.

Without a territorial base, the ruling chief was obliged to move continually over subject lands, living off the tributary offerings of each in turn. Menzies (1920:86) was told that a cluster of tabued houses was kept in each village for such chiefly visitations, "which he once occupies or eats in, cannot afterwards be used by any other." This comment, incidentally, has repercussions for archaeological population estimates based on counting housesites (see, e.g., Kirch 1982). Documentation of chiefly wanderings in a later period is offered by La'anui (1930), who describes Kamehameha traveling from one island to another during the "hookupu season." According to the missionaries Tyerman and Bennett (1832, 2:47), his successor Liholiho likewise "has no fixed residence, but moves about from place to place, and island to island, as humor prompts." The land ultimately belonged to the commoners, writes Kamakau (1961:376): "it was they [the chiefs] who were the wanderers."

The transience of the chiefs has a historical correlate in the practice of conquest land redistribution, whereby a ruling chief reallocated conquered lands to supporters as reward for their loyalty. By Kamehameha's time it was also customary for the lands to be redistributed after a ruling chief's death by his successor. In a seminal analysis of Hawaiian chiefly histories, Stokes (1932:14) points out that land redistribution was a relatively late phenomenon associated with intensified warfare and expanded conquests. He traces the first reference to land redistribution to the first reported sacrifice of a king; reallocating the lands at the death of a ruler "is said to have begun after the reign of Keawenui," a son of 'Umi. Stokes (1932:15) calls this disturbance of titles "distinctly un-Polynesian." The spoils system affected particularly lesser chiefs and local *konohiki,* who might shift through warfare, while the *maka'āinana* "are generally considered as attached to the soil, and are transferred with the land from one chief to another" (Ellis 1969:417). Thus in spite of the theoretical sanction of eviction, insecurity of title plagued not the commoners but the chiefs. In the political system "the *makaainana* were the fixed residents of the land; the chiefs were the ones who moved about from place to place" (Malo 1951:61).

This social distance between the chiefs and the commoners is not necessarily incompatible with the ramage model. One can always argue that Hawaii had a purer form of the conical clan in earlier periods and that late precontact developments widened the breach between chiefs and people, consistent with the increasing complexity of the Hawaiian chieftainship. Such reconstruction must remain speculative, however. The fact remains that all the ethnohistorical evidence available for Hawaii serves to refute the notion of bounded descent groups associated with land (cf. chap. 5 below; Sahlins 1985:20–25). But neither were there clans or "segments" among the chiefs. Since rank was bilaterally determined, descent could be traced upward in myriad ways, the details varying contextually depending on what was advantageous in a given situation. To fix group boundaries in such a system would be clearly dysfunctional, a limitation of possibilities. As Sahlins (1985:20) has phrased it, "in this genealogical game . . . lineage is not so much a structure as it is an argument." Likewise did the chiefs vie with their genealogies: "The strife between the chiefs took the form of denying each other's pure descent from a line of high chiefs. . . . Both sides . . . had composers of meles who chanted the names of ancestors, the high and godlike rank of their own chief, and the mean ancestry of the other" (Kamakau 1961:152–53).

In the ramage model, segmentation commonly occurs along the lines of brothers, descendants of an older and younger brother forming senior and junior branches. Social rank is then a measure of genealogical distance from the senior line. But in Hawaii, differentiation occurs between brother lines, between descendants of primary and secondary spouses, and between descendants of brother and sister in a sibling set. In the matrilines or sister lines discussed in the last chapter, we may see echoes of the Samoan *tama fafine* or sister line, which has formal authority in the selection of a successor to the family's title. The Hawaiian genealogies do not recognize exclusive boundaries between defined sets of relatives; there are no groups. Indeed, chiefs are great in proportion to the number of ancestral lines to which they can trace. Thus relations among the chiefs are multiplex and tangled. As Kamakau (1961:86) poetically phrases it: "Kalani'ōpu'u turned to his defenders, the chiefs of Hawaii— to Keawe-ma'u-hili, the Keawe tabu was doubly twisted, twisted into knots, woven in and out, broken from the topmost branch of the expanding I family with the Mahi and the Ahu under his feet."

Correlatively, Hawaiian kinship terminology does not distinguish male and female lines: siblings, half-siblings, and collaterals on both sides are equally called brother (*kaikunane,* female speaker), sister (*kaikuahine,* male speaker), older sibling of the same sex (*kaikua'ana*), or younger sibling of the same sex (*kaikaina*). In the Hawaiian conception overlapping relationships are praiseworthy; such ties can be invoked to make peace between warring chiefs (Kamakau 1961:70–71). But the multitude of genealogical possibilities also constitutes the structural instability of the Hawaiian chieftainship. Just as ruling chiefs can legitimize their claim through a multiplicity of links, so can ambitious junior collaterals justify rebellion by tracing to high-ranking ancestors, male or female.

Achieving Status

In the wisdom we typically impart to introductory anthropology classes, rank in a chiefdom is ascribed rather than achieved. One is a chief or a commoner by birth, and that status is unchanging through life. In Hawaii there was a classlike separation of chiefs and commoners. In Hawaii, unlike some other Polynesian societies, the people could not trace immediate kinship to their chiefs, nor could they carry on face-to-face relationships with them because of chiefly tabus. In myth-histories commoners are often said not to be able to recognize their chiefs, who lived apart in compounds surrounded by rail fences (see Kamakau 1961:7). Nevertheless, rank in Hawaii had both achieved and ascribed aspects, and women figured crucially in the strategies by which men effectively raised their own status and ensured higher rank for their children.

The breach between Hawaiian chiefs and their people was, arguably, never decisive—largely because chiefs and commoners were never wholly endogamous classes. There was, moreover, a finely gradated hierarchy of chiefs (Kamakau 1964:4–6), from those possessing the highest tabus to lesser chiefs (*kaukauali'i*) who were destined to serve. Commoners too might distinguish themselves in war or through loyal service, thus raising their effective status by association with a patron chief; and if this association led to hypergamous marriage, even a commoner's descendants might become *kaukauali'i*. For ambitious junior relatives or secondary children of a high chief there were ample ways to elevate oneself. Social status in Hawaii could be earned, one's birthright adjusted; it was possible either to rise or fall. Indeed, Hawaiian traditions are obsessed with those who achieve—or suffer—changes in status: lowborn individuals who make good through hypergamy and service, bad chiefs whose genealogies "fall low" (see Kamakau 1961:4) because of unchiefly behavior and unwise marriages.

Hawaiian genealogical reckoning, with its myriad possibilities and entwining paths, in itself carries considerable potential for play. Ambiguity of parentage can powerfully enhance genealogical claims—another instance where the Western and the Hawaiian logic are neatly at variance. In Western families ambiguity of ancestry is shameful and discrediting, but in Hawaii it vastly increases possible lines of attachment: the result is geometric enhancement of a pedigree rather than diminution. It is not unusual in chiefly histories to find claims that a ruling chief was "really" the son of some other great chief, rather than the one cited in accepted genealogies. In the Hawai'i dynasty, Kalani'ōpu'u and Keōua (see fig. 3) are said to have been the "sons of Pele-io-holani through their mother," an O'ahu chiefess (Kamakau 1961:75; cf. Kelly 1978:129). Pele'ioholani was a famous chief linked to the Kaua'i and O'ahu lines, and ruler of O'ahu at the time of European contact. Kalani'ōpu'u is said to have been conceived in central O'ahu and was named after the characteristic neck ornament of the O'ahu chiefs; Keōua "he probably begot after he became ruling chief." With this version the Hawai'i line of Keawe can trace more kin links to the O'ahu and Kaua'i chiefs, an important source of legitimacy. Similarly, "it is said . . . that Kamehameha was the real son of Kahekili, king of Maui, and that Kahekili gave him the name of his brother, which was Kamehameha" (Dibble 1909:41; cf. Kamakau 1961: 68, 188). Kahekili later used this link as a pretext in appealing to Kamehameha not to conquer East Maui.

The potency of ambiguous parentage in Hawaiian chiefly genealogies is formally recognized in the concept of *po'olua* 'two heads,' which refers not so much to ambiguity as an acceptance of dual paternity. The child who was an *ali'i po'olua* 'two-headed chief' was acknowledged by two fathers (Kamakau 1964:4–5). This did not imply a dispute, but an enhancement of the child's lineage. As explained by Pukui and Elbert (1971:315), the child was "sired by other than the husband but accepted by both husband and sire, thus increasing the number of relatives of the child who give their loyalty as kinsmen; it thus fostered the prestige of children of chiefs." The best known *ali'i po'olua* is probably Princess Ruth Ke'elikōlani (see Kelly 1978:128). Kamehameha's first child, Ka'oleiokū, born of Kalani'ōpu'u's wife Kānekapolei, is said to have been recognized both by Kamehameha and Kalani'ōpu'u (Kelly 1978:128); he would thereby link the usurping junior line of Kamehameha to the legitimate senior line of Kalani'ōpu'u.

In Hawaiian chiefly histories, however, genealogy is not the only way in which *mana* is transmitted; here one can point to a cultural contrast with Western notions of genetically based abilities and biologically transmitted substance. The tokens of paternity that chiefs give to *maka'āinana* women are accepted as proofs of the child's link to a chiefly line. Like the giving of tokens, the giving of names is a way for chiefs to transmit the *mana* of their line (Dorton 1986). Hawaiian names are not gender-typed, and one analyzes recurring names in chiefly genealogics in vain for a prescribed pattern or rule. Chiefly names were apparently bestowed (and requested) in order to enhance the destiny of a chosen child. Ka'ahumanu was the namesake of Kahekilinui'ahumanu, thus receiving the *mana* of the Maui lineage, similar to the case of Kamehameha cited above. Like a genealogical relationship, the name establishes a set of possibilities as a potential claim or *kuleana* that can be tapped as needed in the future.

Hawaiian culture also recognizes more active ways to achieve *mana*, and most of these can be subsumed under the celebrated custom *'imi haku* (see Sahlins 1985). As Kamakau (1961:207) describes *'imi haku*, the search for a lord had reciprocal benefits for patron and servant:

> The search for a superior and the finding of a chief . . . was a custom considered high and honorable in old days and one which might carry the seeker from one end of the group to the other. On the other hand chiefs of rank sought trustworthy followers, generally among those of their own kin, to hold their *kahili* and cut their hair. . . . It was thought a great and worthy object in life to go in search of a chief or for a chief to seek a trustworthy follower, and it was through the faithful care of such servants that chiefs grew strong and multiplied.

Again the 'Umi story (Kamakau 1961:1–21; Fornander 1916–19, 4:178–235) is paradigmatic, both in 'Umi's strategies and in the actions of those associated with him. Kamakau attributes 'Umi's success to "his humbleness and . . . the prowess of his adopted (*ho'okama*) sons and his care of the god Ku-ka'ili-moku." Recall that 'Umi is the child of the high chief Līloa by a commoner woman, who raises him as the child of her own husband. Even in boyhood, before his true rank is revealed, 'Umi is generous and gives away "food, fish, tapa, and loin cloths." He also recruits followers—"adopted sons"—one of whom sees 'Umi wearing the *lei niho palaoa* on his journey to Līloa and offers himself on the spot. The boy's parents "saw that 'Umi was a chief and gave him Pi'i-mai-wa'a, to live or to die in his service" (Kamakau 1961:6). Līloa sees 'Umi's patronage of others as a clear sign that the boy is destined to be a great chief: "Although he is still a child, he has made himself like a father and mother to his people. His descendants cannot fail to become rulers" (Kamakau 1961:8).

Despite the enmity of Līloa's elder son and heir Hakau, 'Umi distinguishes himself by service to his lord. When Līloa dies, he leaves the kingdom to Hakau and the war god Kūkāʻilimoku to ʻUmi. At first a good ruler, Hakau later becomes abusive and ʻUmi and his adopted sons take up residence in the neighboring district. In this exile ʻUmi takes four wives; his adopted sons marry and their in-laws also serve ʻUmi, who is notably handsome, strong, and especially solicitous in caring for his god. A lesser chief, seeing rainbows over ʻUmi's canoe—a sign of chiefly status—offers a pig to him and becomes his personal attendant (*kahu hānai*). ʻUmi now begins to build up his forces in earnest, and it is specifically by giving food that he is said to have recruited men: his attendants built many eating houses, and visitors were given the high food pork to eat. ʻUmi's fame spreads as one "who cared for the big men, the little men, the old men, the old women, children, the poor, and the sick. One thing he did was to give food to people" (Kamakau 1961:12).

In contrast, Hakau's downfall is precipitated, in equally paradigmatic fashion, by a failure to be generous: two old men—who are described as priests (*kāhuna*) of Lono (Kamakau 1961:13–14)—ask Hakau for food, but he "answered with insulting words, reviling them." It is then that the two conspire to offer the chiefdom to ʻUmi, who attacks at a ritually fitting time, the tabu period of Kū. ʻUmi offers the bodies of Hakau and his followers in sacrifice to his god (for a discussion of the significance of this custom, see Valeri 1985), but it is left to him to sediment his rule. He rewards his followers with land (Kamakau 1961:15) and takes charge of Hakau's daughter Pinea "in order to preserve the rank in which there was no mixed blood." He also takes a high-ranking woman, Kapukini, his half-sister by Līloa, to bear his heirs. ʻUmi eventually unites the island of Hawaiʻi under his rule and takes other chiefly women as his wives, including a daughter of Piʻilani, the famed ruling chief of Maui. As a result of this marriage there is peace between Maui and Hawaiʻi during ʻUmi's lifetime (Kamakau 1961:21).

ʻUmi's story narrates the fatal flaw of Hawaiian chiefly authority: a chronic threat of rebellion founded on the dialectical relationship between ascribed and achieved status. Child of a chief by a liaison "in the bush," ʻUmi is at best an inferior chief by birthright (Kamakau 1964:6). But ʻUmi seeks his lord and proves himself by tendering proper service to his superior and by caring well for his own followers. His guardianship of the god instantiates the tendency for the Hawaiian priests or *kāhuna* to be related to the ruling line as junior collaterals. ʻUmi embodies the potential danger of the *kahuna* lines, who may invoke the *mana* of the gods against a ruling chief. *Kapu*—the observance of formal tabus indexing rank—is clearly a matter of birthright and cannot be lost in one's lifetime. A deposed tabu chief is customarily sacrificed; his high-status wives are taken and guarded by the successor in a manner resembling house arrest. *Mana* is associated with tabu because of the semidivine stature of the highest chiefs. But continued possession of this power is ultimately contingent on one's actions; a ruling chief demonstrates *mana* by warding off challenges, and remaining in place is possible only if the chief cares for the people properly. *Mana* can be acquired or lost. A chief who fails to demonstrate *mana* may be overthrown; retrospectively, of course, a chief who is overthrown is one whose *mana* was inferior.

The message of the 'Umi story is also that women are crucial to the ambitions of men. 'Umi accomplishes his victory over Hakau through *'imi haku,* devotion to his god, and caring for the people, but hypergamy is the key to sedimenting the destiny of his line. Other chiefly myth-histories associate marrying up with uxorilocality as an instance of *'imi haku.* 'Umi's "adopted sons" were also "seeking a lord" by linking their fortunes to one whom they saw as a rising star. The successful rebel's followers would in turn be rewarded with land and might even stand to marry up through their association with the chief. An old chant (Kekoa 1865) brought to light by Marshall Sahlins suggests that certain "favorite" children (*punahele*) were consecrated for a future liaison with a chief (Sahlins 1981:40). The chant dedicating a boy to the goddess Lilinoe makes explicit the dual hopes invested in a child who would marry up: protect us your parents and raise the rank of your descendants: "But join your body with a chiefess daughter, beloved (*punahele*) that the lives of your parents be preserved, also to preserve your offspring to give birth to chiefs to dwell as lords." The corresponding invocation for a girl asks: "Devote her to the man that will rule the land, a husband with an *ahupua'a,* a chief, to preserve us the parents, and your offspring" (Kekoa 1865:41).

There were several established roles for would-be retainers who hoped to attach themselves to a chief. According to Kamakau (1961:178), "Kamehameha took the children of commoners and trained them to be warriors or to learn other arts. He called these 'adopted children' (*ho'okama*), 'friends' (*aikane*), 'favorites' (*punahele*), or 'companions' (*hoa-'ai*)." The 'Umi story names "adopted sons" (*keiki ho'okama;* for other examples see Fornander 1916–19, 4:178, 5:56–58, 302) and *kahu hānai*, a personal attendant or 'guardian who feeds'; the latter term is also used for the personal caretakers and nursemaids of chiefly children (e.g., Hammatt ms., June 17, 1823). It is said that the *ali'i* seldom raised their own offspring but gave them to be reared by retainers—*hānai* 'feeding' or adoptive parents—who often vied for the privilege, a potential guarantee of comfort and safety in old age (Kamakau 1961:68, 260; Stewart 1970:138). According to legend Kamehameha was stolen at birth by a Kohala chief who wanted to be appointed his *kahu*. He was brought up in Kohala until the age of five, when the ruling chief Alapa'i gave the child to his sister to rear; Kamehameha's two "fathers," Kalani'ōpu'u and Keōua, had themselves been brought up in Alapa'i's train to serve as war chiefs (Kamakau 1961:66–69).

Punahele can also refer to the chiefs' chosen "favorites," pampered children or "bosum friends" who received the best and did no work (Stewart 1970:137). *Aikane* 'intimate companion' or 'intimate friend' may have been a homosexual relationship. Sahlins (1985:10) speculates that many chiefs were bisexual; in any case intimate association with a chief, whether homosexual or heterosexual, was a recognized route to higher status. Malo explicitly states (1951:56) that an *aikane* or a *punahele* of a chief might marry an *ali'i* woman, and his children would be called *kaukauali'i*, lesser chiefs but nonetheless "*alii maoli* (real *alii*)." Gideon La'anui (1930:88), who served Kamehameha, describes himself as the *aikane* of Kekūanaō'a, an important government figure in the middle nineteenth century and father of the future Kamehamehas IV and V. La'anui also married up (to one of Kamehameha's widows, Pi'ia) and held Waialua district, O'ahu, after her death.

The compelling advantages of following a successful chief—immediate material benefits, the promise of receiving land, the elevation of one's family—explain the numerous ethnohistorical accounts of bloated chiefly retinues, although it must be remembered that the drain on subject lands intensified after the formation of the monarchy. Stewart (1970:137) estimated that every chief had from thirty to a hundred "personal attendants, friends and servants . . . who always live and move with him, and share in the provisions of his house." According to William Richards (1973:25), Kamehameha's retinue numbered a thousand persons "entirely supported in their travels by the presents of the people." Shaler's (1935:82) observation of Kamehameha's train in 1804 is perhaps the most vivid: "it is well understood that no chief of the least consequence can reside any where but near the person of the monarch, and, as he migrates through his dominions, he draws after him a train more destructive than locusts."

To Stewart's (1970:138) missionary sensibilities, the revels of the chiefly party resembled "a perpetual *saturnalia*" (emphasis in original). For the ruler, keeping lesser chiefs in his immediate company had a certain advantage. According to Turnbull (1805, 2:24) and others, it was Kamehameha's policy that "all those who possess any authority or influence in the country, should accompany him in his progress through his dominions, that he may have them constantly under his eye, and not leave them exposed to the seductions and conspiracies of his rival chiefs" (cf. Kotzebue 1821, 1:316; Shaler 1935:82). Kamakau (1961:178) tells us further that when Kamehameha "saw any chief collecting a number of retainers about him, he would summon the chief to him at Kawaihae or some such place; when the provisions ran short the hangers-on had to go back to the country, but the chief was always well provided with food, fish, tapa. . . ." However, this policy may well have been one of Kamehameha's innovations, part of the strategy of centralizing political control and placing his own loyalists over conquered lands.

Chiefly Marriage: A Reprise

Keawe-nui-a-'Umi . . . was fond of women. He took his nieces and the daughters of his cousins to be his wives, and from his many wives were born sons and daughters. They became the ancestors of chiefs and commoners.

—Kamakau (1961:45)

Why are great chiefs routinely praised in Hawaiian literature for their sexual conquests? Why this stereotypic litany about the multiple matings of successful rulers? Sahlins (1985) has argued that in the Hawaiian "performative structure" love was the key to a family's destiny: through love might an ambitious lesser chief achieve higher status or a ruler recruit allies and consolidate authority. A unitary model such as one of Lévi-Strauss's "elementary structures" will not explain Hawaiian chiefly marriage because chiefly unions were multidirectional: 'Umi "had many wives of chiefly blood and he became an ancestor for the people. . . . As to his children by the country women, he had many of them" (Kamakau 1961:19). To use Lévi-Strauss's phraseology, neither wife giver nor wife taker was categorically superior or inferior. David Schneider (1965:58) once pointed out that it is unclear in alliance theory whether marriage *creates* alliance or is an *expression* of alliance, and he posed the question: "What is marriage for a system without 'a positive marriage rule?'" Schneider's answer is particularly appropriate to Hawaii: "This is the innovative, inaugurative relationship which 'creates.'" Hawaiian chiefly marriage creates political alliances, destinies, and opportunities.

At the top of society, the ruling chiefs of all the islands were linked by repeated, reciprocal marriages (see Valeri 1972:46), thus tending to form (imperfectly, however) an endogamous class with multiple overlapping kin and affinal connections. Kamehameha's political success is often attributed to his alliance—marital and military—with the Maui chiefs. But the strategy of forging ties among the chiefs of the different islands is common in Hawaiian chiefly histories. Such ties were seen as advantageous precisely because they could be invoked in times of crisis to recruit allies, prompt negotiations, or induce an opponent to halt an attack: "It was the custom, when blood relatives went to war with each other and both sides suffered reverses, for some expert in genealogies to suggest a conference to end the war; then a meeting of both sides would take place" (Kamakau 1961:72). The Hawai'i chief Alapa'i, brother-in-law to the ruler of Maui, was dissuaded from attacking Maui because "he had no desire to make war upon his sister's child" (Kamakau 1961:70).

Because of the tangled genealogical relationships among the high chiefs, it was always possible to use—or discover (Valeri 1972:48)—a tie retrospectively, as a pretext for politically motivated action. Alapa'i came to the rescue of the Moloka'i chiefs, under attack from O'ahu, because "most of the chiefs of Molokai . . . were of Hawaii, children and grandchildren of Keawe. . . . Alapa'i's sympathy was aroused, for these were his own brothers and children" (Kamakau 1961:70). This interconnectedness of the highest chiefs is, incidentally, another factor underlying their classlike separation from the people and their relative lack of native ties to any particular land. When Alapa'i made war on O'ahu the Kaua'i chief Pele'ioholani was "sent for" to assume the rule (he ruled on O'ahu around the time of the first European contact). A "wise counselor" induced Pele'ioholani to make peace with Alapa'i on account of their relationship:

"You can stop this war if you will, for the chiefs of Maui and Hawaii are related to you and that not distantly, for they are your own cousins." "Is

Alapaʻi related to me?" asked Pele-io-holani. "You are a god, and on one side you are related." (Kamekau 1961:71; for a similar example, concerning Kīwalaʻō and Kahekili, see 1961:88–89)

If Hawaiian chiefly marriage can be said to have a unitary function, it is the capacity to innovate, to create possibilities. Strategies in the Hawaiian "political economy of love" vary according to structural position and context (see Valeri 1972). Male ruling chiefs seek to monopolize women of the highest tabus, at least for their primary unions—that is, until the birth of an heir (Malo 1951:54–55). Indeed, as Valeri (1972:61) has pointed out, a union with a higher-ranking chiefess is by definition a "principal" marriage. The mother's rank takes precedence over chronological birth order in determining a child's rank; Liholiho, Kamehameha's heir, was not his firstborn child. Before his rise to power he fathered Pauli Kaʻoleiokū by Kalaniʻōpuʻu's wife Kānekapolei (Kamakau 1961:79, 127, 156–57, 206–7). Yet Kaʻoleiokū, "born while [Kamehameha] was still a beardless youth," was never considered in line to inherit the rule because his mother was not of the highest rank. The ideal dynastic unions of ruling chiefs are with their sisters or "nieces" (classificatory daughters). Successful chiefs are praised particularly for these rank-conserving consanguineous matings, which are explicitly forbidden to their subordinates (Malo 1951:54). Correlatively, the usurper seeks to marry up, and once successful must guard his defeated rival's high-ranking wives: "Umi-a-Liloa cared for the daughter of Hakau, the chief" (Kamakau 1961:15), as did Kamehameha the widows of Kīwalaʻō.

Since unions are both hypergamous and hypogamous, Hawaiian chiefly marriage creates senior/junior relations more than it is structured by them. In a broader sense, the chiefs' serial polygamy creates Hawaiian society by generating a hierarchy of rank. By marrying up, the chiefs produce successors; by taking spouses from below, they produce retainers. *Kaikaina* 'younger sibling of the same sex' also refers to the children of a ruling chief's secondary unions (Sahlins 1981:57). In a nineteenth-century probate case a witness calls a female's chief junior male relative and retainer *kaikaina* rather than *kaikunane* 'brother, female speaker' (P-805, AH). *Kaikaina* implies a hierarchical relationship where *kaikunane* does not. Thus *kaikaina* is not only a familial kin term but also a status category that may refer to juniors related through either descent or affinity.

The logic of Lévi-Straussian myth interpretation suggests that Hawaiian chiefly histories are preoccupied with rebellion precisely because the normative expectation for a lesser-ranking relative or *kaikaina* is not rebellion but service. Why did Līloa give tokens of paternity to Akahi and instruct her that a boy child should be named after his line, thus creating the possibility that the child might someday activate the link? The chief's child by a commoner should be the perfect retainer, destined to serve by virtue of low birth and enjoined to loyalty by close kinship. Through hypogamous unions ruling chiefs attempt to constitute their retinue as a kindred. Children of secondary matings are therefore recruited to serve as *kahu* of the chief: "And if children were thus begotten they were called *kaikaina,* younger brothers or sisters of the great chief, and would become the backbone (*iwi-kua-moo*), executive officers (*ilamuku*) of the chief, the ministers (*kuhina*) of his government" (Malo 1951:55).

Sahlins (1981:57) has pointed out that Kamehameha's political genius lay particularly in his "affinal strategy," whereby he chose to rely on affinally related *kaikaina* as his closest supporters and the "backbone" of his rule, rather than on junior collaterals by descent, who were potential rivals. The nineteenth-century materials offer other examples of *kaikaina* lines created through marriage. In the probate case of William L. Moehonua, governor of Maui (P-805, AH), the issue of his paternity figured prominently (see chap. 1). King Kalākaua sought to sustain a claim as collateral relative through his grandfather 'Aikanaka, who had a liaison with Moehonua's mother and gave her tokens of the meeting, including an ivory pendant and his bloody loincloth, with the words, "Here is your child." According to testimony, Moehonua's mother Napua (see fig. 8) lived with two men, Kaaua and Keaweamahi. These co-husbands (*punalua*) were *kahu* of 'Aikanaka: "They prepared his food. Napua was their wahine." They and the chief's other retainers followed 'Aikanaka to O'ahu, where Moehonua was born. 'Aikanaka gave the child to Kaaua to rear (as a chiefly child would be given to a *kahu hānai*), and told Keaweamahi to say the child was his own.

Moehonua became one of those government "executive officers" or "ministers" described by Malo; he exemplifies the career of the stereotypic loyal *kaikaina*. In rank, Moehonua represents an intermediate term between 'Aikanaka (a loyal warrior chief under the Kamehamehas; see Kamakau 1961:302–3) and a family of servants. Although, as the judge in the case noted, "Moehonua was not considered as a chief of

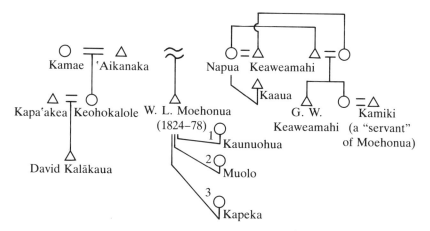

Fig. 8. Genealogy of William L. Moehonua. (From P-805, AH.)

anything like the rank of Aikanaka," he was generally considered to be an *ali'i* of some sort and was certainly of higher rank than his collateral relatives on his mother's side. The phraseology describing his relationship to the king's mother, the chiefess Keohokalole, depicts this affinal rank ordering: "She said that Moehonua was her kaikunane ['brother'] and everybody else knew it was so. Sometimes she spoke of Moehonua as a kahu, and as a makuakane ['father'] because he and Aikanaka were brought up by Keaweamahi. Moehonua was connected to Keohokalole in three ways: he was one of her retainers, was her Kaikaina, and was her makuakane" (testimony of Makue, October 10, 1878).

Wife taking is both the goal and the prerogative of high chiefs. Devoid of context "wife taking" has no predictable implications for rank relations, since the import of a union varies according to the position of the parties. For the ruling line, giving wives can be dangerous if those women are the ruler's sisters or primary wives (cf. Valeri 1972). One can therefore point to an essential tension between wife giving and wife taking: ruling chiefs seek to take wives only, but if they do so they risk rebellion from their dissatisfied juniors (Valeri 1972:41). From a dynastic point of view, wife giving is symbolically associated with eventual overthrow and defeat. This association can be seen in the legend of Kawelo (Fornander 1916–19, 5:2–71, 694–721). Like many other such histories, the Kawelo story narrates the reversal of hierarchical relations between superiors and subordinates. Two versions are given in the

Fornander collection, and the basic elements of the narrative are the same in both. Born on Kaua'i, Kawelo goes to O'ahu, where he marries matrilocally and is taught the arts of war by his father-in-law. The Kaua'i chief 'Aikanaka (not the same as the chief in the Moehonua history), described as *haku* 'lord' to Kawelo, drives Kawelo's parents from their land and Kawelo makes war on him. 'Aikanaka is defeated but rises again and his followers stone Kawelo to apparent death. Kawelo comes to life as he is about to be sacrificed, however, and defeats 'Aikanaka's forces a second time.

The Kawelo legend is similar to the 'Umi story in many respects. Both variants incorporate several stereotypic motifs of Hawaiian chiefly histories, notably usurpation by a younger brother. Taken together, the two versions depict the essential ambiguity—or the structural variability—of affinal relationships. In the first version, the defeated 'Aikanaka lures away one of Kawelo's followers (described as an 'adopted son' *keiki ho'okama*) by giving him his daughter. By exercising this ruling chief's prerogative, 'Aikanaka attempts to reassert his *haku* relationship over Kawelo's line. This act of wife giving creates indebtedness: "Kaeleha was ashamed on account of his father-in-law for not having anything with which to repay his great kindness," and he helps 'Aikanaka rebel against Kawelo (Fornander 1916–19, 5:64). In the second variant of the legend, Kawelo covets the wives of 'Aikanaka, his elder brother and lord (*kaikua'ana haku*), and seduces them by dancing. Kawelo marries matrilocally on O'ahu and defeats 'Aikanaka. But 'Aikanaka steals Kawelo's wife; in the mythic structure this corresponds to the act of giving a wife to a subordinate in the first version. 'Aikanaka's men apparently stone Kawelo to death, but a "sister" (described as a FaYoBrDa) and her husband revive him, and Kawelo reestablishes his supremacy.

As another tale of a paradigmatic usurper, the Kawelo legend depicts inherent strains in the Hawaiian chieftainship. But the story also conveys a message about the implications of marriage and the structural value of women. A primary theme is that wife taking is associated with conquest, success, power—and rebellion. In both versions Kawelo succeeds through the patronage of his wife's father. In the second version, he also takes wives from 'Aikanaka, his rightful superior. 'Aikanaka temporarily reasserts himself by wife giving in the first version and by wife taking in the second. In context, the two strategies are not contradictory. In the first variant, 'Aikanaka behaves like a lord and recruits a son-in-law as his supporter. In the second he takes a wife from the new ruler, Kawelo, who "dies" when he loses his wife. Kawelo revives through the support and care of a "sister" (*kaikuahine hanauna,* female collateral) and brother-in-law. She is called a caretaker (*mālama*). The denouement effectively reestablishes the rightful relationship between the ruler, Kawelo, and his own *kaikaina,* who should serve him loyally. There is also the suggestion that giving a lower-ranking "sister" to a subordinate is a way to ensure loyal *kaikaina.*

Ceding a sister to a junior relative carries the potential for subverting the senior line's authority in the next generation, but the danger is most acute for principal (i.e., politically consequent) unions. Although chiefesses may have been freer to have liaisons after the birth of heirs, ruling chiefs appear to have exercised control even over the secondary unions of high tabu chiefesses. There are indications that after the birth of an heir, a ruling chief was expected to cede his wives to junior collaterals (see Valeri 1972). Kawelo taunts 'Aikanaka's warriors with the words, "Why not take my sister as your wife." The opponents answer, "It is not for you to present the warrior with a wife," alluding to Kawelo's lowly birth: wife giving to a subordinate is not his prerogative.

After the birth of his highest-ranking children Kamehameha "gave" Keōpūolani to Ulumaheihei Hoapili, a junior relative and loyal counselor related to the Maui chiefs (see Kelly 1978:130). This was a "great honor" intended "to guard the ruling tabu family of Hawaii" (Kamakau 1961:352; see also Stewart 1970:125). After Keōpūolani's death Hoapili (the name means "intimate friend") married Kaheiheimalie, one of Kamehameha's widows (Kamakau 1961:387). Another of Hoapili's wives was "the tabu chiefess" Kekau'onohi, Kamehameha's granddaughter and widow of Liholiho (Kamakau 1961:208, 277). It was to Hoapili that Kamehameha entrusted his bones, lest they be discovered and "made into arrows to shoot rats with" (Kamakau 1961:215). Structurally, this wife giving to a junior relative can be seen as the fulfillment of the ruling chief's reciprocity to the junior line. But it is also true that Hoapili, as an affinal *kaikaina* identified with the Maui chiefs, was not a likely threat in any case and was a particularly safe choice to inherit the ruler's wives—another example, perhaps, of Kamehameha's "affinal strategy." The reproductive potential of chiefly women in secondary unions remains ambiguous or, more accurately, contextually variable; a child of a high chiefess by a lower-ranking male is potentially either the heir to the chiefdom, a loyal retainer, or a rebel.

Structural analysis of Hawaiian chiefly marriage supports my contention that, symbolically and politically, Hawaiian women are points of access to power and are associated with achieving and demonstrating *mana.* It is perhaps equally true that men are critical to the aspirations of women—Akahi's liaison with Līloa led to a chiefly child and an *ahupua'a* for herself—but women's strivings are not the focus of the myth-historical literature. The problem with phrasing Hawaiian chiefly relationships in terms of wife giving and wife taking is that, to be accurate, any exchange model of a Polynesian society must take into account not only "wives," but also service and adopted children. Men as well as women were the terms in this complex reciprocity. Hypergamy is the ideal for both men and women; both sought lords to serve or, like John Papa 'Ī'ī, were sent as children to be trained as chiefly retainers. And high-ranking children were given out in "feeding" adoption (*hānai*) to lesser chiefs; it was considered a great privilege thus to become a *kahu hānai,* and held promise of future security.

Reciprocity among the chiefs was not fulfilled solely by marriage; adoption must also be seen as a return on the exchange. The children of one ruling chief were commonly sent to serve the chief of a different district or island even though the other chief was a potential enemy. Kamehameha's firstborn son, Pauli Ka'oleiokū, was a retainer with his father's adversary, the Ka'ū chief Keōua Kū'ahu'ula. When Keōua surrendered himself to Kamehameha, with certain knowledge that he would be killed and sacrificed to the god, many of his chiefs and personal retainers accompanied him to become his death companions (*moepu'u*). Ka'oleiokū rode in a separate canoe and was spared by his father, however (Kamakau 1961:156–57). The 'Umi legend makes it clear that the return of a child was a weighty obligation, not to be taken lightly. When 'Umi refused to allow his daughters by an O'ahu chiefess to be adopted by their maternal grandmother, a plague of deaths by sorcery followed: "It was said that one of the causes of the trouble was 'Umi-a-Liloa's false promises. He was asked for his children, from the eldest down . . . but after a child was born he refused to give it up, saying that they must wait." The deaths were attributed to his wife's "godly ancestresses" and ceased only when a daughter was returned to O'ahu (Kamakau 1961:20).

Women and *Mana*

Since they are the key to rank differentiation, women are in a sense a pivot point between chiefs and commoners—the means by which the social rank of one's descendants can either rise or fall. Women's structural role as points of access to rank and power has genealogical, pragmatic, and symbolic dimensions. The latter become clear particularly in sources that afford some insight into Hawaiian thought, referring here not so much to conscious ideology as to connotations and implied symbolic associations. In the Hawaiian myth-historical literature women are associated with the land, with the highest tabus, with efficacy, and with the possibilities of action.

While Hawaiian chiefs as a class are symbolically foreign vis-à-vis commoners—a categorical distinction made concrete on a daily basis by enforcement of the tabus—the category of chiefs is internally differentiated along similar lines; that is, some chiefs are portrayed as more foreign than others. In the late precontact and early postcontact period the opposition had particular religious and geographical correlates: the island of Hawai'i and the sacrificial rites of Kū appear as foreign in contrast to the native chiefly lines of O'ahu and Kaua'i and more benevolent gods such as Lono (see Sahlins 1981). Certain ruling chiefs are identified with Lono and bear his name, and these are descended from women of indigenous or early lines (Sahlins 1981:12). Kamehameha was a usurper from a line of usurpers tracing back to 'Umi. Their god was Kūkā'ilimoku, the "island snatching" war god whose sacrificial cult is said to have been brought from Kahiki by the priest Pa'ao (Sahlins 1981:9–11). The high-ranking women whom Kamehameha appropriated to perpetuate his dynasty—Kalola's daughters and granddaughters—were descended from O'ahu and Maui chiefs. The *pi'o* chiefess Kalaniakua, sister of Keku'iapoiwa Liliha and aunt of Keōpūolani, was of such high rank that "she was even allowed to climb about the tabu heiaus of the tabu gods." She despised Kamehameha because of his lowly origins and committed suicide in disgust at his association with Keōpūolani (Kamakau 1961:260). Keku'iapoiwa Liliha too "was a proud woman and despised the chiefs of Hawaii, saying of them, 'They are from Keawe! They are from Keawe! they drip (*aweawe*) poi!' but the chiefs of Oahu and Maui from whom she came she held in respect" (Kamakau 1961:260).

The Hawaiian scholar Lilikalā Kame'eleihiwa (Dorton 1986) has felicitously identified the foreign and the indigenous as "the two paths to *mana*" in Hawaiian chiefly politics: the way of the god Kū signifies military conquest and violence; the way of the agricultural god Lono carries the indigenous right in the land and is associated with the strategy of marrying up. The successful conquering chief would combine these "two paths to *mana.*" Thus Kamehameha took wives related to the Maui and Oʻahu chiefly lines, and wanted his heir to be born at the temple of Kūkaniloko in central Oʻahu (Keōpūolani's illness prevented it, however). Sahlins (1981:11) describes the significance of Kūkaniloko, a famous birthing site and *heiau* where the native-born chief deposed by Paʻao was installed: "The area, the temple, and the installation rites signify an earlier, more indigenous type of ruling chief: succeeding by inherent right and tabu status rather than by usurpation."

The symbolic association of women with the land is arguably pan-Polynesian. In Hawaii women-as-indigenous figure both in cosmogonic theory and in scenarios of political usurpation (Sahlins 1981:17). The Papa and Wākea story is a transformation of a Polynesian myth accounting for the separation of earth and heaven (Valeri 1985:169–70); Papa is commonly identified as "earth mother" and Wākea as "sky father" (Sahlins 1981:14–15). In Hawaiian the word *papa* means a 'flat surface' or a 'foundation'; a secondary meaning is 'native born.' Correlating with certain structural similarities between Hawaiian and Inca society, Andean gender ideologies also associated men with conquest and femaleness with fertility and the native born (Silverblatt 1987:71–75). In Hawaii women embody the second of the "two paths to *mana.*" Through their association with high tabu and with the inherent right in the land, as opposed to the right of conquest, they signify access to rank and political authority. This symbology does not only pertain among the chiefs; a similar complex of meanings surrounds women among the commoners, for whom access to land is the analogue to chiefly status ambitions (see chap. 5).

It can be argued, however, that the symbolic value of women as outlined here reflects a male, and more precisely, a usurping male chief's point of view. Do women signify efficacy and access to power only because the available ethnohistorical materials date from a time when the politics of conquest were heating up? Most of the extant traditions recount the histories of the Hawaiʻi chiefs because they were the eventual victors; for defeated chiefs the effect is something akin to the fate of Richard III and the Plantagenets under the Tudors. For the Kauaʻi and Oʻahu lines the fate has been obscurity, since most of these chiefs are said to have been killed by Kamehameha's Maui allies. Oral histories are concerned with the salient structural issues of the time. But these symbolic associations of women resonate with a wider, and older, Polynesian symbology. The association of women with land seems fundamental, equally so among Hawaiian commoners. Rebellions were not solely a phenomenon of late precontact Hawaii, but are to some extent inherent in the structure of all chiefdoms. Where inborn rank differences between individuals at the top of society can be miniscule and there is no monopoly of force, paramount authority is shaky and often short-lived. Sahlins (1972:144) has argued convincingly that political crises "were produced in the normal course of Hawaiian society, and more than endogenic, they were recurrent. . . . They mark . . . the maturity of the Polynesian system."

Given certain propositions about the way rank was determined in early Hawaii, the identification of women with a certain political strategy—a particular "path to *mana*"—is not only logical but inevitable. Does this signification represent only a male ideology? To presume so would be to assert that women have no stake, no interest, in political and land succession. Clearly, that is not the case in Hawaii. But there is complementarity of gender roles even in Hawaiian chiefly politics. Politically significant marriages seem by definition to be those in which women outrank their husbands. Women carry the highest tabus, but it is men who are most often the protagonists in the chiefly histories and who are preoccupied with military conquest. Both men and women aspired to higher status, but they pursued their ambitions through different modes—men through warfare, women by seeing that their daughters and granddaughters married well. The saga of Kamehameha aptly illustrates that these goals were sometimes in conflict, but that women did not always lose. Both genders had political interests, sometimes in agreement, at other times opposed.

Chapter 5

The Local Group

With this right of the common people to the land is connected an inherent love of the land of one's birth. . . . men do not [willingly] wander from place to place but remain on the land of their ancestors. The Kona man does not wander to Ewa or Koolau, nor does the Ewa man change to Waialua. . . . However good the land on which he later lives he will wish to return to the land of his birth. . . . on the whole the common people remained on the land inherited from their ancestors.

—Kamakau (1961:376)

Structurally, the commoner local group is neither a microcosm nor an impoverished variant of the chiefs' tangled and fluctuating kindred, but is in form a dialectical response to the nature of Hawaiian chiefly control. Commoner social organization is both cognate and complementary to the chiefly. The interests and goals of chiefs and commoners are disparate, but analogous; the cultural alternatives for action are similar in form at both the top and bottom of society. The role of commoner women at the local level is structurally and symbolically analogous to women's significance in chiefly politics. Whatever the specific institutional context, Hawaiian women figure crucially in jural strategies, and in structurally predictable ways.

In interpersonal relations with men, commoner women living in their separate spheres appear to have enjoyed as much autonomy as their chiefly counterparts—and possibly even more. Commoner men did not have at their disposal the ritual sanctions that could be exercised by *ali'i* men over women. Enforcement of the ritual tabus was the prerogative of male chiefs in the priestly ranks (*kāhuna*), who held life-and-death authority over all commoners, male and female. Family histories related in land and court records give us no indication of male dominance or authoritarianism within the kin or residential group. Indeed, gender relations appear to have been strikingly egalitarian. Among the commoners there is no analogue to the virtual house arrest reported for certain high tabu chiefesses, their sexuality guarded in order to protect a political dynasty.

Admittedly, the life of ordinary Hawaiians is the least known aspect of the early society because European visitors interacted primarily with male chiefs. We have numerous accounts of life in the households of the chiefs surrounding Liholiho; would that we had one detailed account of a day in a commoner household. In addition to ethnohistorical works, my analysis draws on the testimony of Hawaiians in nineteenth-century courts cases as well as genealogies and household groups reconstructed from land records. At issue here is the basis of social integration within the *ahupua'a*. Were the *maka'āinana* internally ordered by rank and kinship, or was integration imposed by an alien hierarchy of chiefs and *konohiki?* Fundamentally, what held together local-level society?

The *'Ohana* Theory

In chapter 4 I discussed the lack of fit between the conical clan model and Hawaiian chiefly relationships and suggested that anthropologists (perhaps influenced by African descent models) previously tended to oversystematize Polynesian social organization. Perhaps as a corollary of this yen to formalize according to familiar models, older ethnography understated women's personal authority and structural significance in Polynesian societies, among both chiefs and commoners. It seems more or less predictable that the more a theory draws on ethnographic examples of societies with patrilineal descent groups, the less appropriate the reconstruction will be for Polynesian societies such as Hawaii, with bilateral reckoning of kinship and rank.

A central question in reconstructing the Hawaiian local group is whether land divisions such as the *ahupua'a* and the *'ili* were the province of particular descent groups that developed historically in situ. Was the integrity of the commoner Hawaiian community an extension of kin group solidarity—a development from the ground up, so to speak—or a creation of political authority, imposed from above? By the logic of the ramage model, the people on the land should be internally rank ordered by the same principles that applied among the chiefs. Theoretically, the conical clan structure pervades an entire chiefdom. People living in the valleys would then comprise localized descent groups and the local group of commoners could be identified with a clan segment. I argued that there were no ramages among the Hawaiian chiefs. I will now carry the point further: neither were there corporate descent groups of any kind among the commoners, as far as can be ascertained from Māhele land records and other ethnohistorical evidence.

The most famous theory of the Hawaiian local group—the *'ohana* model originally outlined by Handy and Pukui (1972) in the late 1950s—was heavily influenced by the contemporary anthropological understanding of Polynesian chiefdoms. But the *'ohana* as described by Handy and Pukui represents a level of solidarity and integration that the Hawaiian local group never achieved. In my view the term *'ohana* has suffered some oversystematization in the hands of academics. Hawaiians themselves have been influenced by this scholarship, and many now believe that *'ohana* describes an indigenous, ancient social grouping. I believe that Hawaiians had *'ohana* in the sense of an egocentric network of family or relatives, but not *'ohana* in the sense of a bounded, rank-ordered, ramified descent group. Once again, Hawaiian social organization does not fit neatly into established anthropological categories.

In their reconstruction Handy and Pukui (1972:2) reason that Hawaiian land divisions had a genealogical foundation. They describe the *ahupua'a* as composed of several *'ohana*, which they describe as localized cognatic descent groups:

> The fundamental unit . . . was the dispersed community of *'ohana*, or relatives by blood, marriage, and adoption, living some inland, some near the sea but concentrated geographically in and tied by ancestry, birth and sentiment to a particular locality which was termed the *'aina*.

The strength of patrilineal affiliation in the *'ohana* is unclear in the Handy and Pukui model. Although in their description the *'ohana* is cognatic, the "functioning head" or *haku* of the entire group—that is, of all the households comprising the *'ohana*—is said to be "the elder male of the senior branch" (1972:6). The ramage logic is also apparent in their speculation that the *'ili* was "probably originally the province of a single *'ohana*." From this natal locality, they surmise, the family "would ramify throughout the *ahupua'a*, and ultimately into neighboring *moku*; though there would remain a concentration of closest-related *'ohana* in the original *'ili*" (1972:5).

The most striking discrepancy between the *'ohana* theory and local-level society as revealed in ethnohistorical materials is the issue of genealogy. Handy and Pukui report that every *'ohana* had a family genealogist who knew the names and deeds of the ancestors; to persons of rank, this was "the most precious of all heritages" (1972:196). But they also imply that the transmission of genealogies was a practice of those who had some "claim to distinction." According to Kamakau (1961:242), in ancient times there were genealogical experts who kept the histories even of the commoners, but after 'Umi's time "genealogies became tabu to commoners and the children of commoners."

In Māhele records and post-Māhele court cases, where it would have been materially advantageous to know one's genealogy, Hawaiian commoners usually could trace back no further than the grandparental generation (cf. Sahlins 1985:25). There is no evidence that the people living in an *ahupua'a* stipulated or reckoned overall common kinship beyond the normative ideology of all Hawaiians' shared ancestry. Among commoners there is a gradual attrition of specifiable relationships the further one moves from immediate bilateral kin. Genealogical details fade into distant degrees of collaterality as the reciter moves upward and outward. Chiefly and commoner genealogies are complementary in shape; in contrast to the soaring, intertwined lineages of chiefly pedigree, commoner genealogies are shallow but broad, specifying primarily sibling and affinal relationships. I will return to the political implications of the commoners' "structural amnesia" at the end of this chapter.

A major problem with Handy and Pukui's *The Polynesian Family System* is that it mixes informant data from Pukui's youth in Ka'ū with reconstruction of an earlier Hawaiian society—time referent unclear. The work is a superb source of insights into Hawaiian culture; the difficulty is separating Pukui's firsthand reportage from speculation about what the society was like in former times. In the latter task she was certainly influenced by her anthropological training and her association with Handy. As anthropologists have often surmised in studies of acculturated societies, Handy and Pukui conclude that the twentieth-century Hawaiian local group reflects a devolution from a more orderly past state. They speculate that the granting of individual *kuleana* in the Māhele contributed to the disappearance of the *'ohana*. Had awards been made as *'ili* to *'ohana*, they suggest, local-level social organization might have preserved its indigenous solidarity (1972:17).

It is true that most Māhele claims appear to have been filed on behalf of an entire household or extended family. But there is no evidence that the residents of the *'ili* comprised a single extended family or descent group at any time in the postcontact period; indeed, the land records conclusively contradict this theory. Lesser chiefs, *konohiki,* and commoners were placed on the land in a political hierarchy of land givers and land takers (Sahlins 1985:24–25). It can be argued that the political basis of land tenure was a late development in Hawaiian society, an artifact of conquest land redistribution, and that centuries before European contact, when the population was smaller and presumably less stratified, land divisions were indeed identified with descent groups. Kirch (1984:258), for example, calls late precontact Hawaii a "territorial system" in contrast to an "ancestral Polynesian system" where landholding was associated with corporate descent groups.

I am not comfortable imputing from eighteenth- and nineteenth-century ethnohistorical materials a model of Hawaiian society circa A.D. 500 or even A.D. 1000, and I will leave the debate over proto-Polynesian social forms to the archaeologists and historical linguists. The salient point is that anthropologists, like indigenous nationalists, at times tend to idealize ancient social forms and to impute to them a fixity and structural predictability that they may never have had. Often, such reconstructions implicitly assume categorical male authority. The importance of women in the Hawaiian local group, however, correlates with the relative lack of emphasis on patrilineality and male dominance. If, as I argue, women embody the alternatives of praxis and the possibilities of agency in the Hawaiian system, then unitary models are bound to write women out of the picture.

A Segmentary Economy

It is a truism in anthropology that political forms are related to a society's mode of production. From Sahlins's (1958) early work on social stratification to studies by Kirch and other archaeologists, students of Polynesian chiefdoms have been much concerned with the link between economic transformation and changes in political integration. Inverting the perspective, I will here examine the organization of production among the people on the land in pre-Māhele times.

The Handy and Pukui model of the local-level Hawaiian economy is similar to Barth's (1956) famous description of ecological specialization in Swat, North Pakistan. Handy and Pukui (1972:6) assert that segments of the *'ohana* living upland and seaward in an *ahupua'a* land section were economically specialized and exchanged complementary products through gift giving. No one familiar with Polynesian societies can doubt that such reciprocal gift giving took place in early Hawaii; my own work on exchange in a modern Hawaiian community (Linnekin 1985) notes the prevalence of exchange-in-kind and confirms the general principle that different things travel in different directions and at different times. One gives fish, when one has them, to someone who does not have fish. The donor can be confident that the gift will be reciprocated at a later date, and with a different sort of item, under the ethic that Sahlins (1965:147) called "generalized reciprocity."

Judging from Māhele land records, however, the Hawaiian economy was organized politically, not by symbiotic internal trade—which is not to say that such trade was lacking. In most *ahupua'a* claims tend to replicate each other. Complementary exchanges such as described by Handy and Pukui assuredly took place, but not because of ecologically circumscribed use rights. In most *ahupua'a* household production was generalized, each family having access to a range of resources. The most relevant model for the household economy appears to be the *lele* rather than *mauka/makai* specialization, for the *lele* were located in different productive zones and thus guaranteed that every household had access to the uplands, to taro lands, and to the sea, making each household theoretically capable of self-sufficiency.

The local economy was segmentary in the sense that households in the *ahupua'a* carried on largely the same set of productive activities, though there were certainly regional variations. My sample includes a preponderance of windward taro-growing districts, while the familial specialization reported by Pukui for Ka'ū may have been more prevalent in leeward areas. In the 1970s elderly informants described to me much the same sort of symbiotic exchange for Kaupō, on the dry side of Maui. A *kama'āina* of Kaupō related that in her childhood, her upland-dwelling family exchanged pig and dryland taro for fish with the people who lived at the seashore. Further, she claimed to know nothing of fishing skills and her sister avowedly disliked fish. Specialization between fishing folk and dryland cultivators living upland would help to explain the relative dearth of Māhele claims from certain leeward areas such as South Kona. Claims for land may simply have been less relevant for fishing people.

It was also in leeward fishing areas that settlements tended to cluster at the shore (Cook and King 1784, 7:118, 129; Ellis 1782:178; Lapérouse 1799, 1:340–41; Loomis ms.:7–8). In Kona, King (Cook and King 1784, 7:105) noted that they saw "no villages at a greater distance than four or five miles from the sea." In wetland taro-growing valleys houses were dispersed throughout the *ahupua'a* (see Ellis 1969:194–95; Menzies 1920:51). Menzies (1920:177; see also Whitman 1979:59) witnessed internal trade at Honomalino, South Kona, in 1794:

> The country round us at this place was so rugged and dreary and barren that the natives are obliged to depend a good deal upon the sea for their sustenance. When the fishing canoes came into the bay in the evening . . . the whole village and people even from other villages flocked about them and a brisk market was kept up till they disposed of all their fish for small nails and bits of iron. . . . Of these nails the fishermen make their fish hooks, and no doubt are obliged in their turn to purchase potatoes, yams, cloth, etc., from the planters.

Despite these early descriptions of coastal villages in leeward areas, the Hawaiian settlement pattern was essentially dispersed. There were no market towns or administrative centers before European contact. The coastal settlements reflect particular ecological contingencies rather than economic or bureaucratic centralization.

Although the *ahupua'a* was by and large a self-sustaining economic unit, Hawaiians also carried on regional and interisland trade in certain necessities and manufactures. Salt, for example, was processed on the dry sides of the islands. Whitman (1979:64) attests that Maui salt was "of a quality superior to any made on the other Islands. It is put up in bundles of leaves and sent to the other Islands where it is highly esteemed and bartered for other commodities." Another major article of regional trade was *olonā* fiber, which made durable, salt-resistant fishnets and lines. *Olonā* grows grows in cool boggy areas, and according to Kamakau the lands producing it prospered through trade: "*Olona* was an article of barter for 'food' and 'fish,' valuables, and necessities. . . . Maui and Molokai people were noted in the old times for growing and scraping *olona* . . . and that was the source of wealth of those lands."

Different islands were noted for excellence in products manufactured by both women and men, such as mats and tapa, canoes and paddles: "Owhyhee and Mowee furnish the best canoes, Morokie the most beautiful pows [*pā'ū*]. The *tarpers* of Mowee are generally esteemed the handsomest and those of Owhyhee the strongest" (Whitman 1979:60). Campbell (1967:145) writes that in 1809 the Hawaiians of O'ahu traded tapa with Kaua'i for canoes, paddles, and spears. Interestingly, this was during the occupation of O'ahu, when Kamehameha was actively preparing to invade Kaua'i; that island did not submit to the rule of the Kamehamehas until 1810 and retained political autonomy until 1821. Kaua'i mats were considered finer than those made on other islands: "one Attooi mat of the finest quality is worth three of the best that are made on any other of the Islands" (Whitman 1979:60). The material exchanges, evidently conducted by ordinary Hawaiians, continued despite the political hostility; an analogy can be drawn here to the ongoing barter between Hawaiians and the English in the tense aftermath of Cook's death. Another notable aspect of this exchange is that female goods (mats and tapas) were being exchanged for male goods (things made of wood). This separation by gender of mats and cloth from wood manufactures is, incidentally, precisely the distinction between the Samoan gift categories *'ie toga* 'female wealth' and *'oloa*, traditionally food, canoes, and tools (Shore 1982:203–8). Unfortunately, we have no data as to how Hawaiian internal trade was organized. As discussed in previous chapters, however, Hawaiian women had rights over their own manufactures and their own personal possessions, and it is likely that they benefited from the specialized trade as much as the men.

By describing the Hawaiian economy as segmentary or generalized rather than symbiotic I mean that the Hawaiian local group was, with the exception of a few traded articles, economically self-sufficient. Economic institutions did not significantly articulate or integrate commoner society. Ecological determinants did not dictate an economic center in Hawaii, nor was ecology a disqualifying factor in political fortunes; dry and rather barren Kona and Kohala supported the dynasty that eventually prevailed in conquering the islands. The implication of this portrayal, in conjunction with the preceding discussion of the *'ohana*, is that the society of the *maka'āinana* was composed of essentially autonomous household groups. No autochthonous institutions—neither localized descent groups, nor symbiotic exchange networks, nor an internal rank hierarchy—united the commoners. The political or "territorial" (Kirch 1984:258) organization of the Hawaiian economy, with the *ahupua'a* as the fundamental unit, is further supported by the structure of Māhele claims. Although commoners frequently claimed dispersed resources within the *ahupua'a,* very few claims—only about 100 out of 4,400—include parcels in two or more *ahupua'a,* and almost all of these are by chiefs.

"Moe Aku, Moe Mai"

Commoner marriage is analogous to the chiefly in that it opened paths, and women figured importantly as protagonists and as points of access to possibilities. These paths necessarily differ in their specifics depending on one's position in the Hawaiian social hierarchy. Marriage among the commoners could not have the dynastic ramifications of chiefly alliances. Fine rank distinctions did not pertain, and the status rivalries discussed in chapter 4 are not of much relevance. Commoners may have aspired for their children to marry up (see Sahlins 1985:25–26) or to "seek a lord" to serve among the chiefs. But despite the mythic preoccupation with chiefly matings in the bush, I do not believe that sexual attachments between chiefs and commoners were of great significance in the everyday lives of the *maka'āinana.* Marriage on the local level had to do with other pragmatics such as securing residence and use rights, and with structuring relationships of the commoners to each other.

Early ethnohistorical sources are in near-universal agreement that Hawaiian marriage was unmarked, casual, and ephemeral, that attachments were easily entered into and easily broken (Boit ms.:28; Campbell 1967:136; Ellis 1969:434–35; Mathison 1825:474–75; Thurston 1921:89). Hawaiians were initiated early into sex (Handy and Pukui 1972:95, 110), and they remained sexually active throughout their lives. Indeed, one could debate whether the Hawaiians had formal marriage at all, as differentiated from liaisons and cohabitation (see Sahlins 1985). In the words of a Hawaiian testifying in court in 1854, "In the old days, before the custom of marriage became general, it was moe aku, moe mai ['sleep there, sleep here']" (P-805, AH). The fragility of the Hawaiian conjugal tie does not rule out a structuring capability, but it does imply a multiplicity of affinal links rather than a long-term bond between corporate groups.

To Western moral sensibilities in the early postcontact period, the freedom of attachments among Hawaiians was shocking. The American missionaries had a word for Hawaiian marriage: they called it adultery (*"moe kolohe"*) and labored—largely in vain—to introduce a binding conjugal tie. Adultery headed the list of crimes reported for 1839, with 246 convictions. "Lewdness" was the next most frequent offense with 81 cases, followed by theft and falsewitness at 48 each (Anonymous 1839:234). In a list of crimes tried before the lower court of Honolulu in 1846, the most numerous offense is "adultery fornication etc.," with 126 male and 127 female offenders. The government newspaper reported this as "the predominant vice of the natives . . . their standard of morality is still exceedingly low, though crimes are rare" (*Polynesian* January 9, 1847).

Early observers report that the *maka'āinana* usually lived with one spouse at a time, but polygamy was certainly acceptable and instances of the *punalua* 'co-spouse' custom (see Handy and Pukui 1972:56–60) can be found thirty years after missionization in the Māhele records. In a few claims witnesses stated that they received land from or resided next to their *punalua*. Pukui's recollections of early twentieth-century Ka'ū (Handy and Pukui 1972:109) make it clear that nearly a century after the arrival of Christian missionaries there was still no stigma attached to polygamy in this rural district. Instances of sororal polygyny, fraternal polyandry, the sororate, and the levirate occur in nineteenth-century family histories; analogous cases can be found in some modern Hawaiian families where sets of sisters have married sets of brothers. Pukui explains the cultural logic behind sororal polygyny and the sororate:

> Should a man take his wife's younger sister or cousin for a mate with his wife's approval, no one worried about it, because, "*O lakou no ia.*" (They all belong to each other). . . . A wife might say to her husband, "I love my cousin so much that I do not want her to go away, so you take her for your wife." . . . The children of one were the children of the other. (Handy and Pukui 1972:109)

Nowhere in the nineteenth-century archival materials do Hawaiians describe any major ritual or exchange on the occasion of marriage. There are no distinct terms for the statuses "husband" and "wife"; the words used are *kane* and *wahine,* 'man' and 'woman.' In land records and court testimony the Hawaiians use the terms *moe* 'sleep, lie' or *noho* 'stay with, stop at' to describe sexual attachments in personal and family histories (on *noho pū* cf. Handy and Pukui 1972:108). Ellis (1969:434–35) reports: "We are not aware that the parents of the woman receive any thing from the husband or give any dowry with the wife. Their ceremonies . . . are very few, and chiefly consist in the bridegroom's casting a piece of tapa . . . over the bride" (cf. Mathison 1825:474–75). But Kamakau (1964:25–26) distinguishes between cohabitation, the most frequent type of attachment, and "the binding form of Hawaiian marriage," called *ho'āo pa'a* (1961:347; cf. Handy and Pukui 1972:52). In cohabitation, "men took many wives and women many husbands." The *ho'āo pa'a* tie, in contrast, "could not be dissolved." Kamakau describes a betrothal ceremony and a series of reciprocal exchanges between the families that marked the union as a lasting one:

> the relatives of the man gave them rich gifts, and land, if they had it, and the woman's relatives also gave them gifts and land, if they owned land . . . the children born to them sealed the relationship between the two families. (Kamakau 1964:26)

The latter phrase is particularly significant for the meaning and social context of this binding arrangement. Kamakau's description of *ho'āo pa'a* conflicts with the early accounts of Hawaiian marriage. A convert to Christianity, Kamakau clearly disapproved of the usual loose type of marriage and may have sought to deemphasize it as a backward and discarded custom: "The taking of many women as wives was a cause of trouble in old days. Women too took many husbands. This broke up the family and brought about quarreling and jealousy. Some women went off with whatever husband they pleased" (1961:234–35). But Kamakau also states that *ho'āo pa'a* was the custom "of the chiefs and the first-born children of prominent people and family pets" (1964:26). In other words, binding unions had something to do with a family's destiny and inheritance. Chiefly unions of major political consequence—that is, involving high-ranking women with critical kin connections—were indeed more lasting than casual liaisons, even if male chiefs had to exercise a degree of coercion to keep certain *ali'i* women from initiating other relationships. Among the commmoners, "first-born children of prominent people and family pets" were those most likely to become *haku 'āina* in the family, as senior siblings or chosen favorites (*punahele*).

An apparent digression into inheritance issues is unavoidable here, for the meaning of marriage among the common people is inseparable from their relationship to the land. Sexual freedom was firstly a life cycle phenomenon in Hawaii—the behavior appropriate to young adulthood and social immaturity. But the nature of Hawaiian sexual attachments also varied with the different destinies of senior and junior siblings. The land transmission statistics suggest that one sibling became the landlord or *haku 'āina* in the family. This was most frequently the eldest son (cf. Handy and Pukui 1972:47), but another sibling—male or female—might well be chosen to fill the role if possessed of superior abilities.

Not only were all commoners subordinate to chiefs and *konohiki*, but the nineteenth-century materials reveal that many—perhaps most—commoners and commoner families lived as dependents under other *maka'āinana*. The family inheritance—the right to occupy and use certain plots of land under the chief—was impartible in the sense that one sibling was acknowledged to have the care of the place and authority over the younger siblings; the land was not divided into smaller and smaller plots over time to accommodate all members of the family. Junior siblings were not forced to leave the household or the *ahupua'a*, but clearly many did, for variable periods of time. Commoners too could seek a lord elsewhere. Those who did might attach themselves to a household, locally or in another *ahupua'a* as *ōhua* 'dependents' (Handy and Pukui 1972:5) by asking the household head for a taro patch or two to work and permission to reside there. In the land records the term *hoa'āina* 'tenant' is sometimes used to describe someone living under a *kuleana* holder. *Lōpā* 'poor tenant farmer' is a similar but more denigrating term. Thus some *kuleana* supported large residential groups occupying several dwellings.

What of *moe aku, moe mai?* For the young, for peripatetic junior collaterals (cf. Ortner 1981), and for the mass of Hawaiian commoners during most of their lives, cohabitation was the norm. Whether or not *ho'āo pa'a* was a recognized social practice in pre-Christian times, the notion encapsulates a certain truth: that some conjugal relationships among the commoners were expected to create a bond between families. These attachments were marked by feasts and exchanges, while casual liaisons were not. Sororal polygyny, fraternal polyandry, the sororate, and the levirate illustrate repeated affinal ties between families; clearly not all sexual relationships among the commoners were short-lived cohabitation arrangements. But it was the birth of children, more importantly than marriage, that sedimented Hawaiian affinal relations. In contrast to the unmarked marriage custom, birth was the important ceremonial occasion, the event that, as Kamakau writes, "sealed" the relationship between the families (see also Handy and Pukui 1972:69–70, 80–86; Kekoa 1865). The birth of children also secured the family's continuity and succession on the land. In Hawaiian thought grandchildren (*mo'opuna*) replace their grandparents (*kūpuna*). Grandparents have the right to ask for their *mo'opuna* in adoption, and it is they who rear the children born to young adults who have not yet settled down. Proverbs and normative statements celebrate the solidarity, mutual care, and affection in these relationships (see Handy and Pukui 1972:179–80).

Where chiefly marriage structured relations between island chiefdoms and senior/junior lines, the more binding unions among commoners articulated household groups within and between *ahupua'a,* creating reciprocal expectations and possibilities. Sahlins (1985:23) notes that a man's wife is termed his *kuleana,* his claim or right in her family (cf. Handy and Pukui 1972:70). In his description of *ho'āo pa'a* Kamakau (1964:26) revealingly refers to the gifts exchanged between the families as *lou* 'hooks.' *Lou* means generically any kind of hook (Pukui and Elbert 1971:196), but refers particularly to breadfruit books—long sticks with a cross or "V" of sticks lashed at the end, and used to pluck the fruit from the trees.

Mobility

In order to comprehend fully the political and economic transformation of Hawaii in the nineteenth century, we must examine the movements of ordinary Hawaiians. The Hawaiian sources as well as historical examples of other colonized, "peripheralized" societies tell us that rural society was disrupted and that gender roles in the family are likely to have been altered by economic changes. Postmarital residence and mobility patterns have critical import for women's kinship role and authority in the household. Through the lens of ethnohistory the local commoner community seems static and opaque. Reconstructing the dynamics of commoner household arrangements is perhaps the most difficult task of all. Nonetheless, there are various indicators and measures that can be assembled from the ethnohistorical record, and I will herewith hazard some informed guesses about the commoners' residential stability through the early postcontact period.

The statement by Kamakau quoted at the beginning of the chapter suggests that the commoners were a stable population: that for the most part ordinary Hawaiians lived out their lives in the *ahupua'a* where they were born. Hawaiian ideological associations portraying the chiefs as "stranger kings" and the commoners as people of the land also support this conclusion. Yet the political basis of land tenure and the chief's right of eviction stand in apparent contradiction to the commoners' permanence. The residents of the *ahupua'a* depended on the severance of their chief and *konohiki* for rights in land. As a witness in a land case testifed in 1876, "The chiefs used to give lands to their people, and take them away when they liked" (L-1958). Foreigners concluded that in traditional times the islands were full of dispossessed people at the mercy of the chiefs for land. Observers' comments on the Hawaiians' "migratory and locomotive character" (L. Lyons, 1848 Report of Waimea Station, HMCS) also point to high mobility.

We have, then, two conflicting indications of the commoners' stability on the land. These portrayals point to radically different understandings of the Hawaiian local group, for mobility is not only a function of political relations, but also reflects the nature of marriage and land tenure. Which characterization is correct? Was the ideal for all siblings in a family to remain in their natal *ahupua'a?* Pukui (Handy and Pukui 1972:110) reported that "the people of Ka-'u married mostly within their own district and discouraged marriages to those of the outside district or islands." One would then expect to find a high frequency of local endogamy—marriage within the *ahupua'a.* But if, as the land inheritance statistics suggest, one senior sibling became the landlord or *haku 'āina* in the family, would not younger siblings have tended to marry out? Obviously, these questions cannot be answered with certainty since commoner Hawaiian society is no longer intact. As noted earlier, it is also difficult to find explicit normative statements about marriage and residence preferences in the Hawaiian materials; this absence of stated prescriptions is one aspect of what Sahlins (1985:26) calls the "performative" quality of Hawaiian social structure.

Statements by nineteenth-century Westerners, however, are not a reliable indicator of the commoners' mobility in earlier times. Many foreign writers were convinced that the chiefs were tyrants or chose to portray them that way to support a particular political agenda. Westerners could not conceive of secure tenure without the guarantees of exclusive, private ownership. This evaluation by the missionary J. S. Emerson is representative of their assessment:

> I do not think that the people generally have had till recently an idea that they had a right in the soil, or, at least, such a right as they could not be made

to yield at any time by the command of a high chief. . . . The removals of the people from one island to another made them feel like tenants at will. (Wyllie 1846:44–45)

The nineteenth-century Westerners also project onto precontact Hawaii a picture of rootlessness derived from disrupted times. After European contact and increasingly after Kamehameha's conquest, political and economic upheavals resulted in increased mobility among the commoners. Granted, it was the *konohiki's* long-established right—and, moreover, a duty—to distribute and reallocate land among the commoners. But as I argued earlier, there were moral and effective political limits to the frequency of eviction. Both early observers' reports and Hawaiian accounts indicate that the threat of dispossession impacted lesser chiefs and *konohiki* more immediately than the commoners. In comparison to the chiefs the commoners were indeed people on and of the land, both in ideology and in their residential continuity. Yet Hawaiians were also a traveling people. Not all members of a household resided in the *ahupua'a* from birth to death. Even before the arrival of Europeans adoption, marriage, and seeking a lord would have absented many Hawaiians from their natal lands for variable periods of time.

One must first of all distinguish—as the Hawaiians did—between frequent visiting, or high short-term individual mobility, and true wandering by dispossessed persons who "belonged" to no particular place. It is one thing to say that Hawaiians had a peripatetic character and carried on reciprocal visiting with relatives in other places; it is quite another to claim that absent family members lost their identification with their natal land, symbolized in their right of burial there, and their right to return. The latter is clearly not the case. True land alientation—the loss of residence and use rights in the land of one's origin—is a nineteenth-century phenomenon in Hawaii. Some evictions occurred in earlier times as a result of conquest land redistribution, but there was no advantage for a conquering chief to throw off the *maka'āinana*. After all, the people on the land fed the chiefs and supported their retinues. Kamakau (1961:376–77) noted that "land irregularities" intensified during the late-eighteenth-century wars of conquest. But even when Kamehameha brought an occupying army to O'ahu in 1804, his soldiers and retainers were for the most part settled in over the indigenous population, who remained in place (Kirch and Sahlins, ms.). The result of this new wave of settlement was not wholesale dispossession, but intensified local production.

What I am calling "mobility" is largely a process of household development—a cycle whereby familial groups expand and contract over time. Even through the period of the Māhele mobility among the commoners is rarely a matter of entire household groups moving from one land to another. Short-term, periodic absences of household members did not by any means result in loss of use rights in the *ahupua'a*. There was no economic necessity compelling all family members to be continuously present. The staple crops of Hawaii need little maintenance after planting, as long as production is geared primarily to subsistence needs. Taro does not need to be harvested all at once. The mature corms can be left in the patch for a few months without suffering. Even today Hawaiian taro farmers customarily pull only what is needed for the day's use or the immediate market order. If neglected, wetland taro will become choked with weeds. The corms will be smaller and the yield of the patch correspondingly less. But given the high productivity of taro, maximizing yields was not necessarily an overriding concern for the early Hawaiians; chiefly demands would be the most significant variable in determining production goals. An observation by the missionary Ellis (1969:344–45) suggests that frequent visiting, or high short-term mobility, may even have functioned as a means of reciprocal interhousehold exchange:

> It is not unusual for a family, when they have planted their field with sweet potatoes, etc., to pay a visit for four or five months to some friend in a distant part of the island. When the crop is ripe, they travel home again, and, in return, are most likely visited by a friend, who will not think of leaving them so long as any of their provisions remain unconsumed.

Māhele testimony offers some indication of the relative time depth of local populations at midcentury, in the form of claimants' statements about when they received their *kuleana*. It seems axiomatic that, in general, landholders in rural out-districts—the *kua'āina* 'back land'— would trace their tenure back further than residents of districts near the ports. While other ethnohistorical sources certainly support this inference, table 3 shows that the evidence from the land records is not so simple: nineteenth-century political events and contingencies—some local, some national in scope—had a major impact on the commoners' reported length of tenure. In this sense, there may be no such thing as a "typical" rural or urban *ahupua'a*.

As noted in the first chapter, most Māhele claimants traced their *kuleana* to political superiors. In part this reflects intensified land redistribution after the conquest. As Oʻahu became the political center of the islands, the lands near Honolulu were repeatedly partitioned among the relatives and supporters of the Kamehamehas. Particularly desirable were the verdant valleys located back of the town, such as Mānoa, Nuʻuanu, and Kalihi, which were close to the market center but also provided a cool refuge from the heat of Honolulu's plain. These *ahupuaʻa* were not awarded in their entirety to individual chiefs; instead, the *'ili* within them were redistributed to numerous lesser chiefs and foreigners who had served Kamehameha. The format of the testimony itself may also have encouraged Hawaiians to report a political source, as opposed to familial inheritance. Since the *konohiki* was present and essentially had the authority to veto a claim, commoners may have felt that their claim would have greater legitimacy if they cited a chief or former *konohiki*.

Waves of settlement are clearly discernible in the data on length of tenure, and the residents of an *ahupuaʻa* can be categorized or stratified according to when they received their land (Kirch and Sahlins ms.). In testimony the Hawaiians themselves identify land-giving eras as the "times of" particular chiefs and *konohiki*. The earliest period in table 3 represents *kamaʻāina*, old-time residents who traced their tenure "from olden times" or, more often, from the time of Kamehameha I. Although long established by the time of the Māhele, many of those who traced their occupation to the time of Kamehameha I were not indigenous residents, but settlers placed there after the conquest. On Oʻahu, the wave of settlement resulting from the occupation of 1804–12 is particularly evident in the numbers of claims tracing to Kamehameha's time. From Kamehameha's death until the Māhele, epidemics, emigration,

TABLE 3.   Tenure Reported in Māhele Claims in Four *Ahupuaʻa*

Time Land Received	Mānoa, Oʻahu		Punaluʻu, Oʻahu		Paʻalaʻa, Oʻahu		Waiheʻe, Maui	
	N	%	N	%	N	%	N	%
Before 1820	14	18	22	73	19	34	24	21
1820–29	25	31	0	0	12	21	41	35
1830–39	29	36	2	7	16	29	26	22
1840–48	12	15	6	20	9	16	26	22
Total	80		30		56		117	

and escalating tax demands disrupted the local population. The mid-1830s, the time of the premier Kīna'u and the "troubles of Kaomi," saw another period of intensified local land redistribution as a result of power struggles among the chiefs.[1]

The contrasts between land sections in table 3 reflect their differential economic and political significance to the monarchy. Mānoa Valley, actually the upland (*mauka*) portion of the *ahupua'a* of Waikīkī, was well-watered, productive, and close to the port of Honolulu. The relatively shallow time depth of the Mānoa landholders reflects the *ahupua'a*'s importance as a political prize, as well as the immigration of ordinary Hawaiians to the Honolulu area. Not only were Mānoa's 'ili distributed among numerous chiefly landlords, but every land section saw a superstratification of *konohiki* levels, from the chiefly owner or owners to the local land manager to the *luna,* a resident subagent or overseer who supervised the labor of the commoners. Punalu'u, a *kua'āina* 'back land' place located far from Honolulu on O'ahu's windward side, provides a neat contrast to Mānoa: 73 percent of the landholders traced their residence to the time of Kamehamaha I or earlier, as opposed to 17.5 percent of the Mānoa claimants. Unlike Mānoa, Punalu'u had a relatively simple *konohiki* structure, with a single chiefly owner and local land manager. Punalu'u was not particularly populous or strategically important, and Māhele claims indicate a long-established and relatively stable commoner population.

A land's political significance did not necessarily diminish with distance from Honolulu, however. Fertility and productivity were also factors. Pa'ala'a, in Waialua district on O'ahu's north shore, saw a major immigration of Kamehameha's followers during the occupation. In the 1830s and 1840s Waialua served as a poi bowl and supermarket for the government in Honolulu. Letters of request arrived almost daily for Gideon La'anui, the district chief, itemizing foodstuffs and supplies to be sent to the chiefs in Honolulu (Kirch and Sahlins ms.). The missionary Emerson described Waialua as having "seven lords, one above the other, and all of them are over the people, and claim services from them occasionally" (Wyllie 1846:44–45). That Pa'ala'a had more claimants receiving land after 1830 than other rural districts is consistent with this more complex—and more oppressive—political structure. Yet as revealed by the figures for Waihe'e, a productive taro-growing valley on West Maui, few areas could be called "pristine" by the time of the Māhele. Claims in Waihe'e are more or less evenly distributed over time, with a bulge during

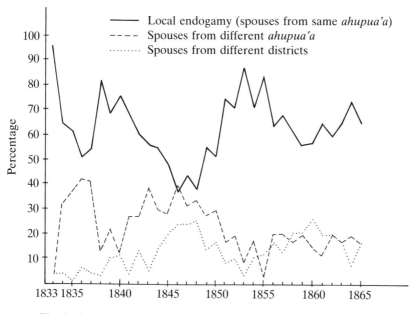

Fig. 9. Local endogamy and exogamy, Waimea, Hawai'i, 1833–65

the 1820s that may be related to the movements of the chiefs; Liholiho's mothers favored Lāhaina as a residence, and West Maui districts such as Waihe'e would have been required to intensify production to support them. Even in rural and outer-island areas the land transmission statistics appear highly sensitive to historical events—testimony to the effectiveness of chiefly control over the local level.

Local Endogamy

Missionary marriage books provide further evidence of the stability of *maka'āinana*. Quantitative material is uncommon in ethnohistorical materials, but nineteenth-century missionaries in Hawaii kept tallies of events requiring their pastoral duties, such as births and marriages. In recording marriages that they performed some pastors also noted the geographic origins of the spouses. The few detailed lists that have survived offer some indication of the extent to which commoners married within their home *ahupua'a*. Figures 9 and 10 graph local endogamy and

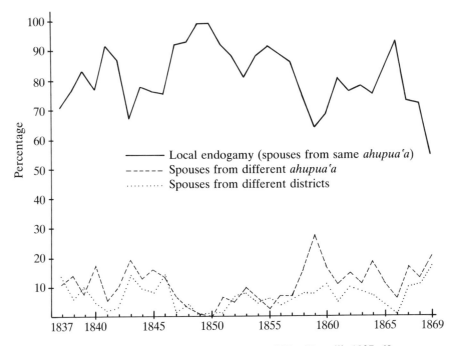

Fig. 10. Local endogamy and exogamy, Hilo, Hawai'i, 1837–69

exogamy over time in two Hawai'i island districts: Waimea from 1835 to 1865, compiled from the marriage book of Lorenzo Lyons, and Hilo from 1837 to 1869, drawn from the marriage records of Titus Coan (both originals in AH). By "local endogamy" I mean cases were the place of origin is identical for both husband and wife. Another line plots instances where one spouse came from a different *ahupua'a* in the same district, and the third line represents the proportion of marriages in which the man or woman originated in a different district. Tables 4 and 5 present the frequencies on which the graphs are based.

The most significant overall characteristic of these graphs is that in almost every year, the number of marriages varies inversely with the distance between the spouses' original homes. The incidence of local endogamy is generally quite high, both before and after the Māhele. The figures can hardly be taken as representative of the pre-European period, and yet the suggestion of high local endogamy is compelling, since one would expect that the economic and social upheavals of the nineteenth century must have led to increased out-marriage. According to the missionary Emerson, the chiefs encouraged local endogamy in order to prevent the attrition of their followers: "It has been repeatedly stated to me, that some of the head men forbid women to marry men of another land, unless the man will come and live with the woman. But that this is the fact in many cases I can not certify" (Station Report of 1836–37, HMCS; cf. Handy and Pukui 1972:110).

TABLE 4. **Marriages by Origin of Spouses, Waimea, Hawaiʻi, 1833–65**

Year	Same Ahupuaʻa		Different Ahupuaʻa		Different District		Total
	N	%	N	%	N	%	N
1833	28	96	0	0	1	4	29
1834	52	65	25	31	3	4	80
1835	58	62	34	37	1	1	93
1836	84	51	70	42	12	7	166
1837	70	54	53	41	7	5	130
1838	76	83	11	12	5	5	92
1839	20	69	6	21	3	10	29
1840	60	76	10	13	9	11	79
1841	31	69	12	27	2	4	45
1842	38	69	17	27	8	13	63
1843	50	56	35	39	5	5	90
1844	28	55	15	29	8	16	51
1845	24	49	14	29	11	22	49
1846	23	36	25	40	15	24	63
1847	31	44	22	32	17	24	70
1848	23	38	21	34	17	28	61
1849	48	56	24	28	14	16	86
1850	32	51	19	30	12	19	63
1851	42	75	9	16	5	9	56
1852	60	70	17	20	9	10	86
1853	78	88	8	9	3	3	89
1854	44	71	11	18	7	11	62
1855	45	86	1	2	6	12	52
1856	34	63	11	20	9	17	54
1857	34	68	10	20	6	12	50
1858	26	62	7	17	9	21	42
1859	40	56	14	19	18	25	72
1860	30	57	14	27	8	15	52
1861	27	66	8	20	6	14	41
1862	18	60	6	20	6	20	30
1863	23	66	6	17	6	17	35
1864	23	74	6	19	2	7	31
1865	23	66	6	17	6	17	35

Source: Compiled from Marriage Book of Lorenzo Lyons (AH).

Granted, Emerson's comment dates from an era when chiefly demands were increasing as the local population was shrinking. But as I argued in chapter 4, there is ample myth-historical evidence that chiefly authority relied on the people's loyalty and labor. Chiefs needed not only to recruit warriors, but also to maintain an underlying populace of producers. I do not believe that the chiefs' interest in preventing emigration was solely a postcontact phenomenon. Despite their attachment to

TABLE 5. Marriages by Origin of Spouses, Hilo, Hawai'i, 1837–69

Year	Same Ahupua'a		Different Ahupua'a		Different District		Total
	N	%	N	%	N	%	N
1837	50	72	8	11	12	17	70
1838	112	76	21	14	14	10	147
1839	135	83	11	7	16	10	162
1840	134	77	31	18	9	5	174
1841	104	92	6	5	3	3	113
1842	77	87	9	10	3	3	89
1843	58	67	17	19	12	14	87
1844	75	78	12	12	9	10	96
1845	116	75	25	16	13	9	154
1846	87	74	15	13	16	13	118
1847	66	92	5	7	1	1	72
1848	71	93	2	3	3	4	76
1849	192	99	1	0.5	1	0.5	194
1850	151	99	0	0	1	1	152
1851	125	92	9	7	2	1	136
1852	66	88	4	5	5	7	75
1853	89	81	11	10	10	9	110
1854	83	88	6	7	5	5	94
1855	73	91	2	3	5	6	80
1856	74	89	6	7	3	4	83
1857	58	87	5	7	4	6	67
1858	45	74	10	16	6	10	61
1859	32	64	14	28	4	8	50
1860	25	69	6	17	5	14	36
1861	30	81	4	11	3	8	37
1862	31	76	6	14	4	10	41
1863	21	78	3	11	3	11	27
1864	32	74	8	19	3	7	43
1865	42	84	6	12	2	4	50
1866	32	94	2	6	0	0	34
1867	22	73	5	17	3	10	30
1868	34	72	6	13	7	15	47
1869	16	55	6	21	7	24	29

Source: Marriage Records of Titus Coan (AH).

the land of their birth, commoners too could seek a lord elsewhere, and even in pre-European times there would still have been a significant secondary pattern of out-marriage.

Admittedly, these figures represent a very limited sample of unions occurring in the *ahupua'a*. First, only Christian marriages are represented. At least some of the reported marriages may therefore have been analogous to the "binding" unions described above, and some of the parties may have been prospective household heads who intended to remain on the family land. Judging from contemporary missionaries' complaints, however, many other Hawaiians were living in cohabitation arrangements; nor do the lists tell us anything about temporary liaisons. Furthermore, the lists report only marriages among those who remained in the *ahupua'a*. They give no indication of marriage patterns among those who emigrated, and it is well documented that Hawaiians were constantly leaving rural and outer-island areas for Honolulu and other port towns during this period. Despite these qualifications, I believe that the missionaries' marriage records do tell us something about the commoners' overall stability in the *ahupua'a*. As described by Lyons in his letters and journals (Doyle 1953), Waimea was an impoverished and isolated area little touched by the market economy. The port of Hilo was officially opened to foreign commerce in 1850. Coan's figures could therefore be expected to show some effects of in-migration from the countryside, but his data are nonetheless comparable to the Waimea graph.

Especially striking is the fact that, despite differences in absolute percentiles, the frequency polygons for the two areas are remarkably similar in shape from 1837 through the 1860s. The fluctuations over time appear to reflect historical exigencies affecting at least the island of Hawai'i. Moreover, the diachronic variations correlate well with certain major economic events. Increased out-marriage from Waimea during the 1840s—a trend evident but less pronounced in the Hilo data—can be attributed to intensified tax demands on an already impoverished populace. As poignantly documented by Lorenzo Lyons, Hawaiians in this remote district were still using stone adzes in 1847 (Doyle 1953:145). Waimea's plight during this period was far from unique in rural Hawaii. The whaling trade's demand for provisions stimulated agricultural production during the 1840s and 1850s (see Morgan 1948:150–54), but this differentially affected areas near foreign ports. People living in remote and outer-island areas could remain as overburdened cultivators under the chiefs or migrate to the towns. In both graphs there is a marked upturn in local endogamy beginning in 1846, and lasting through the period of the Māhele. The possibility of obtaining land titles was evidently an incentive for people to stay in their natal *ahupua'a* at least for the short term.

Another event encouraging rural Hawaiians to stay on the land at this time was the California gold rush, which enormously boosted the Hawaiian provisions market and sparked a potato boom on the island of Hawai'i (Doyle 1953:153). The completion of the land division appears to have again encouraged mobility among Hawaiians. But though the Māhele effectively disenfranchised many of the people, numbers continued to live on the land as tenants under relatives and friends or as "squatters" (in the view of their foreign landlords) on former *konohiki* lands. With some local variations, the exodus from rural lands appears to have been steady but gradual through the latter half of the century. Out-marriage increases until 1859, after which there is another upturn in local endogamy. This correlates with the collapse of the whaling trade that began in 1859, after which prices for provisions crashed (Morgan 1948:153). Marriages within the *ahupua'a* increase between 1859 and the mid-1860s, correlating with depression and disarray in the external market. During this period commoner Hawaiians may have been less drawn to leave the land for Honolulu and the other ports (see chap. 6).

The missionaries' marriage books tell us, minimally, that local endogamy was high among commoners who remained in the *ahupua'a*, even through the nineteenth century. To this extent Handy and Pukui (1972:110) were correct in saying that Hawaiians usually married within their home *ahupua'a*. But given the limitations of the nineteenth-century marriage data, it is risky to attach a statistical estimate to "usually." We have no way of quantifying casual liaisons, short-term cohabitation arrangements, and the seekings of junior siblings. We *can* examine the countervailing forces encouraging commoner men and women to stay or leave and the pragmatic alternatives open to people in certain structural positions. There was both a normative preference and some external pressure for Hawaiians—both male and female—to settle eventually in their natal *ahupua'a*. Before the monarchy and the market created urban centers, the inducements to leave the land were presumably fewer and it may have been more difficult for the people to evade the authority of local chiefs.

The *Ma*

Changes in commoner women's authority over land in the nineteenth century must be understood in the context of their roles as mothers and sisters in the extended family. The fundamental unit of local-level Hawaiian society was a bilateral household group which I call the *ma*.[2] As defined in the nineteenth-century Andrews dictionary (1865:356), *ma* is a particle,

> which mostly follows proper names of persons, and signifies *an attendant upon,* or *persons belonging to,* or *accompanying; as ke alii ma,* the chief and his train; . . . Hoapili *ma,* Hoapili and *those known to be about him.* It includes persons in all capacities, from an equal with the one named to all connected with him, even to his servants.

According to Handy and Pukui *ma* means "and family" but the earlier Andrews definition more accurately captures the broad inclusiveness of the term in Hawaiian usage. Hawaiians today use the word "them" instead of *ma* to indicate people associated with an individual, as in, "Let's go visit Annie them." My sense is that "them" used this way has a short-term referent and means associates at a particular time, not necessarily a long-standing or permanent group. "Them" clearly does not refer only to relatives. The nineteenth-century evidence supports Handy and Pukui's (1972:5) statements that "the household included members of the family proper of all ages plus attached but unrelated dependents and helpers." They write that true family (*'ohana*) were differentiated from unrelated add-ons, who were called *ōhua,* signifying "passengers on a canoe or ship exclusive of owner and crew." The nineteenth-century family histories attest that *ōhua* who remained permanently attached to the household would over time be assimilated as fictive or stipulated kin, a process facilitated by the commoners' shallow genealogies. Kinship categories did not define the composition of the *ma;* rather, putative kinship could follow from coresidence.

In sum, Hawaiians recognized numerous options for coresidence. Essentially any form of relationship—kin, affinal, or friendship— constituted a potential accessway or path into a household. The residential group was not shaped by prescriptive rules, other than an apparent preference for the elder brother to assume an authority role; I have not found in any ethnohistorical source a stated norm of postmarital residence. Neither does a clear statistical norm emerge from reconstructions of nineteenth-century household groups. However, the evidence definitely does not support Handy and Pukui's (1972:44, 107) statement that "the boy or man went . . . to live with the girl's folks: never the girl to her husband's." Residential choices responded to pragmatic and situational dictates, varying with position in the sibling set and aspirations. The pattern of these choices appears to be nearly bilateral among the commoners. An agnatic line of land succession might be present in the household, but the landholder's *ma* also included attached affines—both male and female and adopted children, as well as related and unrelated dependents.

As discussed earlier, uxorilocality was always possible in the indigenous system and was particularly a recourse of younger brothers who found it difficult to live peaceably "under" their seniors. The pre-1848 inheritance statistics (see table 12) indicate a 10.4 percent incidence of land transmission from the wife or wife's relatives. This is not an accurate statement of the frequency of uxorilocality, however, since the numbers reflect only the statements of those who claimed *kuleana*. Most affines who married into a family would assume a subordinate position vis-à-vis the landholder. Therefore, the statistics must understate— perhaps dramatically—the incidence of uxorilocality in the Hawaiian residential group.

Given the Hawaiian penchant for visiting relatives and the ease of sexual liaisons, the composition of the *ma* may have varied from day to day, its potential membership far exceeding the number of residents at a given time. Lt. King (Cook and King 1784, 3:118) estimated five residents per household, a number that seems too low in the context of other early reports. In the 1820s travelers noted families ranging from ten to twelve (Loomis 1824–26:8; Macrae 1922:8, 16). According to Macrae, three- and four-generation households were common. The missionaries were often shocked by the number of people occupying a single thatched house. Lyons (Doyle 1953:62) and Ellis (1969:68) wrote that many houses contained two or three families—presumably they meant nuclear families. In his 1848 station report (HMCS) Emerson described a dwelling inhabited by "fourteen souls of men." Ellis, in his tour around the island of Hawai'i, visited several commoner habitations. In one "solitary hamlet" of four or five houses, "three or four families were residing" (1969:214). One of their hosts lived in the same house with his two sisters (1969:218).

The examples in figure 11 illustrate some of the empirical variations

a) Waimalu, Oʻahu (from P-2190)

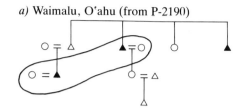

b) Waiau, Oʻahu (from Land Court Applications 114 and 334)

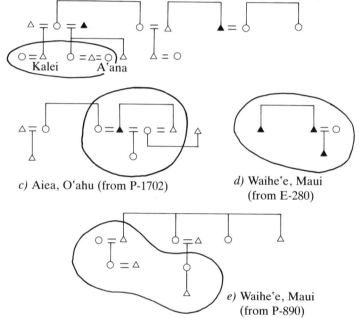

Kalei   Aʻana

c) Aiea, Oʻahu (from P-1702)

d) Waiheʻe, Maui
(from E-280)

e) Waiheʻe, Maui
(from P-890)

Fig. 11. Variations in nineteenth-century household composition

found in nineteenth-century residential groups, as reconstructed from Māhele testimony and post-Māhele court cases. It is important to note that the outlined figures do not fully exhaust the membership of these households, since they delimit only the individuals who were specifically said to be coresident. Nor can static diagrams capture the process of household development: the short- and long-term fluctuations in the size and composition of the *ma*. The time frame ranges from the 1840s through the 1880s; greater precision is difficult because witnesses in these sources are vague about Western dates, but it can be said that most of these family groups were in existence at the time of the Māhele. The first two examples (figs. 11*a* and 11*b*) are from Oʻahu's Ewa district, located to the west of Honolulu. Fig. 11*a* diagrams an extended family as it existed just prior to the smallpox epidemic of 1853. The two brothers and their older brother's son claimed land in the same *'ili*. Kahiki lived with his father's younger brother Kuheuheu, but it is not possible to say which other family members were present. When Kahiki and Kualu died of the smallpox in 1853, Kuheuheu inherited their land. The second example (fig. 11*b*), from Waiau *ahupua'a*, is an expanded family based on a pair of uterine half-siblings. This case attests that, even though commoner genealogies are shallow, similar sorts of conjugal and affinal relations are found among the *maka'āinana* as among the chiefs. The testimony of a dependent, relationship unknown, illustrates the short-term mobility and siblinglike role expectations of household members:

> Kalei used to take care of us. He supplied us with food and all the necessities of life. Anything that Kalei had, we all ate. Kanakanui and his wife would stay there sometimes, sometimes not. After Kanakanui died Aana lived there until she sold the land. While she was there, Kalei would supply her with food. (Land Court Application 114)

In another case involving an Ewa landholder (fig. 11*c*) the household included adult brothers, affines, a friend (*aikane*), and the *aikane*'s adopted child, who married the two brothers in succession. An unrelated member of Kami'i *ma* testified that he had formerly lived with the landholder's younger brother in Waikīkī: "I knew Kamomokualii. He was my aikane. He lived at Waikiki. We all then lived there. Kameahaiku was a child I brought up, and gave her to Kamomokualii" (P-1702, 1873, AH). The witness explained that Kameahaiku first lived with Kami'i "because she was the wife of his brother." In other nineteenth-century cases Hawaiians similarly attribute instances of the levirate and sororate to the affection that develops with coresidence. Such statements further support the interpretation that, despite a degree of exogamy and *'imi haku*, the core of the *ma* was a set of adult siblings.

I stated earlier that commoner marriage created and defined relationships among local landholders, who did not trace overarching common descent. Figure 11 gives examples of the composition of residential groups, and figure 12 illustrates various ways in which commoner households in the *ahupua'a* were related to one another. The examples offer a set of empirical variations on interhousehold ties at the local level. Many of the links are affinal: male landholders are related as brothers-in-law or as father-in-law/son-in-law. But one also finds sibling relationships

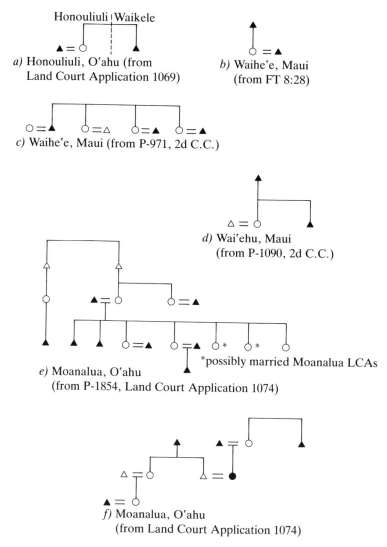

Fig. 12. Variability in local-level relationships

among landholders, and this has bearing on the issue of local endogamy. A sibling who did not become the *haku* in the family did not always have to accept a subordinate position in a household, but could ask the *konohiki* for land in his own right; I use the male pronoun here because *konohiki* were much more likely to give land to men than to women. Particularly by the time of the Māhele, with the Hawaiian population

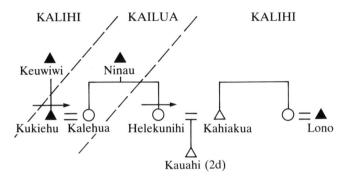

Fig. 13. Marriages between Kalihi and Kailua

reduced to a quarter or less of its precontact size, there was ample land available in most rural districts and local chiefs must have been eager to keep people. The brother/brother ties between landholders again suggest that most commoner Hawaiians preferred to settle in their natal *ahupua'a,* but it is open to debate whether and at what period that "majority" was closer to 60, 70, or 90 percent. And of those who left, how many eventually returned?

The Hawaiian custom of *noho pū* 'living together' points to a pattern of dispersed alliance. In other words, a family would have numerous in-law relationshps—and therefore "*kuleana,*" potential claims on people—both within the *ahupua'a* and elsewhere. The nineteenth-century materials document many instances of intermarriage between *ahupua'a,* and repeated unions between certain lands and residential groups are common. Pragmatically, these can be explained by the Hawaiian penchant for visiting relatives in other lands. Structurally, the recurring marriages have the effect of creating exchange relationships between certain *ahupua'a* and residential groups. The long-established affinal tie becomes a recognized alternative, a known path open to family members who leave their natal *ma.* As illustration, figures 13 and 14 document a composite family history reconstructed from several sources, showing migration between *ahupua'a* and affinal links between landholders (Naai and Kealani vs. Nalimu and Kainapau, 1880; P-364, P-1328, P-1883, P-2038, AH).

Figure 13 diagrams marriages between Kalihi and Kailua, *ahupua'a* lying on the leeward and windward sides of O'ahu. In the Māhele Keuwiwi was awarded land in Kalihi, but his son Kukiehu married into a Kailua family and received land there. His wife's sister, the younger daughter of the Kailua landholder Ninau, in turn married into Kalihi;

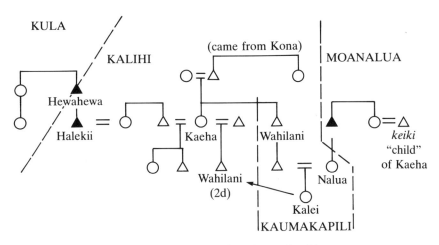

Fig. 14. Kaeha *ma,* showing places of residence

her son Kauahi, born around 1851, was the namesake of a Kalihi awardee whose relationship to the *ma* cannot be determined. Figure 14 shows a more complex set of movements between *ahupua'a.* Hewahewa, a lesser chief and *konohiki* who participated in the 1848 Māhele with the king, received land in Kalihi, as did his son Haleki'i. But according to court testimony (E-165, 1871), his sister, sister's daughter, and several other dependents lived under him in Kula, in the uplands of Maui. One of these *ōhua,* explaining his attachment to the *ma,* testified: "I consider myself a distant relative" of Hewahewa's sister.

Hewahewa's several dispersed landholdings are attributable to his status as a Kamehameha supporter, but the evidence suggests that alternating residence was a long-term reality for many Hawaiians—a point I will return to below. Kaeha *ma* is said to have come from Kona, Hawai'i, to Kaumakapili, Honolulu, where Kaeha's brother Wahilani resided. Kaeha married Kekohai and lived in Kalihi. Her son, the namesake of his mother's brother, married his classificatory daughter Kalei, whose mother had come from Moanalua, the *ahupua'a* immediately to the west of Kalihi. A child (*keiki*) of Kaeha's is said to have married into Moanalua earlier.

It is tempting to see a pattern of restricted exchange in the movements of these individuals (fig. 15). That the evidence is partial perhaps increases the temptation: if we but had the whole picture, a classic case of balanced reciprocity might emerge, with residential groups in different lands exchanging people over time through marriage and adoption.

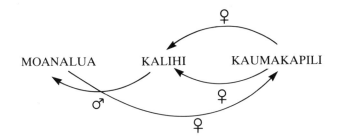

Fig. 15. Marriages between Kalihi, Kaumakapili, and Moanalua

To an extent, this sort of exchange did take place—even, I have argued, among twentieth-century Hawaiians (Linnekin 1985). I am convinced that an egalitarian ethic—the notion that a gift must be repaid eventually with one of equal value—was observed among the commoners, who were not internally differentiated by rank. When a child left the natal *ahupua'a* for the long term through marriage or adoption, the *ma* could expect a return at some future time through in-marriage, adoption, or service. (This ethic can account for the prevalence of grandparental adoption, particularly of a daughter's child, among modern Hawaiians.) Nevertheless, even if we had complete nineteenth-century family histories and genealogies, there is no indication that relationships among the commoners could be explained in terms of a structural master plan. Hawaiian marriage remains a "complex system," in Lévi-Strauss's (1969) terms, where alliances are dispersed, where choices respond primarily to pragmatic considerations, where *noho pū* creates and structures more than it is structured a priori.

There is another problem of fit between the nature of Hawaiian society and anthropology's established rubrics. We tend to describe exogamy, endogamy, and the local group in static terms, as if they described enduring arrangements. In societies where marriage is sealed by major material exchanges and divorce is correspondingly difficult, it is appropriate to assume that postmarital residence and group affiliation have a degree of permanence. But what of a society where people engaged freely in liaisons and might live in several different locales in the course of a lifetime? Granted, some unions among the commoners were more permanent than others. Hawaiians might leave their natal *ahupua'a* permanently and come to identify with a different place. A story published in a nineteenth-century newspaper (Anonymous 1868) tells of a woman who married an elder brother, a landholder, and in time "became a native and an ancestress" in his *ahupua'a*. But in many documented cases Hawaiians alternated residence between their own and affinal residential groups:

> I was married into this family before I went away about two years. . . . I came from Hilo. (L-1860)

> He did not reside constantly. He visited Hawaii and Kauai and was in the habit of going to Moanalua where his wife lived with her brother. (P-1870)

The fragility of Hawaiian marriage complements the integrity of the *ma,* with a sibling set at its core. The *ma* gives away its brothers and sisters, but often only temporarily. High short-term mobility tends to mask the essential stability of the fundamental unit associated with land. Over the long term a set of cross-sex siblings was the nucleus for attached dependents. Given the ephemeral nature of most conjugal relationships, affines were structurally extraneous members of the household. Consanguines could always return to their natal *ma,* to the land where they "belonged." Whether and at what phase in life they chose to do so varied with situation, depending on their age, gender, relative position in the sibling set, the constraints of status, and the individual's unique biography.

Commoner social organization represents a statistical rather than a prescriptive system. There was no single normative destiny for all siblings, nor even for all men and all women. But we can identify the options available to people in particular structural positions and reckon the likelihood that men and women, seniors and juniors, would pursue certain paths. The local group was the outcome of men and women availing themselves of culturally defined alternatives. The most contentious point in a reconstruction is estimating statistically how many siblings stayed in the *ma,* how many married within the *ahupua'a,* how many married out but eventually returned, and how many left permanently to reside elsewhere. The statistics, which necessarily represent snapshots in time, are merely an aid to understanding these dynamics.

Brothers and Sisters

The preceding discussion underscores the bilaterality of the Hawaiian residential group and points to the structural importance of sibling relationships on the local level. The *ma* is similar to the domestic group in any bilateral society in that group affiliation is optative. Theoretically, siblings' residential choices could approach 50/50, with half staying in the natal household and half leaving. In reconstructed household groups it is common to find at least one cross-sex sibling pair, an adult brother and sister, remaining in the *ma* for the long term. Hawaiian and, more broadly, Polynesian cultural logic suggests that the elder sister would be most likely to stay, but this is difficult to corroborate quantitatively from the ethnohistorical evidence. It is the descendants of the sibling set who have the right to use and occupy the family's land, and senior brother and sister are custodians of this inheritance. The fundamental bilaterality of the Hawaiian concept of family accounts for the prevalence of inheritance from ancestors (*kūpuna*) and parents (*mau mākua*) in Māhele testimony. The referent in familial land giving is ultimately the sibling set in the senior generation.

While the brother/sister tie is particularly central in societies that reckon kinship bilaterally, since Burridge's (1959) seminal paper anthropologists have treated siblingship as a structural principle with much wider relevance (Kelly 1977; Marshall 1979; Smith 1983). Except for the presence of matrilineages, the Palauan case (Smith 1983) is strikingly similar to Hawaii. Social structure can be treated as "a model of defined parts" (Schneider 1965:78) in which siblingship and descent are complementary principles that vary in relative significance and domains of operation. Siblingship can refer to the mode of relations pertaining among parallel siblings, but most writers focus on cross-sex siblingship, that is, on normative, structural, and/or sentimental aspects of the brother/sister tie. As I use it here, siblingship refers to a symmetry in relationships, a mutuality and equivalence of which the brother/sister bond is the archetype in Hawaiian social organization. My argument is that relationships on the local level, both within the *ma* and between household groups, are normatively expected to fulfill the ethic of siblingship.

Yet the *ma* harbors an internal contradiction. Members of the *ma* participate in symmetrical exchanges, but the land relation is intrinsically hierarchical. Siblinglike relationships and obligations within the *ma* enjoin solidarity and mutual care, but some members of the *ma* are explicitly subordinate to others and are expected to serve. The contradiction between siblingship and hierarchy can account for the wanderings of many Hawaiians from one household to another. The apparent fluidity of the Hawaiian residential group is related to an underlying conflict in normative expectations that renders certain residential arrangements (such as the coresidence of older and younger brother) structurally untenable over the long term. Frequent and periodic absence is one means of defusing tension; uxorilocality is another.

A normative and sentimental contrast between same-sex and cross-sex relationships pervades Hawaiian social organization. The ideals of aloha and mutual care are realized most fully in cross-sex relationships such as brother/sister and mother/son, which are in general more solidary than same-sex ties such as brother/brother and father/son. Same-sex relationships are intrinsically hierarchical and asymmetrical (cf. Burridge 1969:xxii) and may be weighted with tension over jural succession. Same-sex siblings are always terminologically ranked vis-à-vis one another as older (*kaikua'ana*) and younger (*kaikaina*). In contrast, cross-sex siblings use the reciprocal terms *kaikunane* 'brother,' female speaker, and *kaikuahine* 'sister,' male speaker, which do not imply relative rank (cf. Marshall 1979:11 for other Oceanic cultures). Within the same generation, full siblings are not distinguished from half-siblings and cousins, although terms such as *he hanauna* (see Andrews 1865:149; Handy and Pukui 1972:68) and *hoahānau* (Andrews 1865:167) can be used to designate distant collateral relatives. The category *mākua* 'parents' includes all related members of the ascending generation, whether related by collaterality, adoption, or secondary marriage.

In later nineteenth-century materials Hawaiians sometimes use the qualifier *pono'ī* 'true, own' apparently to distinguish an immediate sibling or parent from a classificatory or putative relative. Handy and Pukui (1972:67–68) report that the word *luau'i* has this function, but also cite the expression *'i'o pono'ī* 'own flesh' (1972:48, 129). *Pono'ī* appears only a few times in thousands of Māhele claims, and is more common in post-Māhele cases where haole judges presided over conflicting claims to land. In this context the term was clearly used to make a Western-style distinction. Even so, the Hawaiian and Western interpretations seem to have been divergent. In one instance a Hawaiian used *pono'ī* to refer to his parent's sibling as a "true parent." Where Westerners would tend to view the nuclear family as the referent of *pono'ī*, Hawaiians may have seen the adult sibling set as the circle of *pono'ī* kin, true relatives who had rightful claim to the family's inheritance.

In any case, the infrequency of *pono'ī* in Māhele testimony suggests that the criterion of genealogical closeness was foreign and largely irrelevant to the Hawaiians before private land titles were established. One implication of the commoners' "structural amnesia" is that kinship is readily attributed to those who behave like relatives: in other words, Hawaiian kinship has a marked performative aspect. Perhaps a kin relationship cannot be specified precisely, but neither can it be ruled out. Those who attach themselves to the household are likely to be called relatives in time (cf. Handy and Pukui 1972:65). Through classificatory siblings and collaterals to those who are "related in some way," Hawaiian kinship can extend horizontally almost indefinitely.

Lévi-Strauss (1963:38–44), among others (see Marshall 1979 for comparative data from Oceania), has pointed out that where the husband/wife bond is weak, the brother/sister tie tends to be strong and solidary; this correlation is borne out in Hawaii. The role expectations of cross-sex siblings include loyalty, mutual care, affection, and nurturing:

> Women in those days were especially devoted to their brothers, and brothers to their sisters. It was common to see younger sisters sitting in their brothers' laps. Brothers chanted verses composed in honor of their sisters, and sisters of their brothers as a sign of devotion. (Kamakau 1961:315)

This solidarity makes possible the amiable long-term coresidence of brother and sister, and in part explains alternating residence between natal and affinal households. Normative and legendary portrayals of brother/sister relationships contrast markedly with descriptions of the fragile marital tie. Handy and Pukui (1972:54–56) report a "platonic marital relationship," a form of adoptive affinity contracted between individuals who treated each other "with great respect and affection" and "were as good to each other as brother and sister." In one chiefly history, a woman displays such uncommon devotion to her husband that the conjugal bond is assimilated to siblingship: the wife of Kihaapi'ilani "was his companion in his trials and tribulations, even in those that might mean death. He made a sister of his wife" (Kamakau 1961:25).

Within the same generation, members of the *ma* were either classificatory siblings or were assimilated to the group by means of siblinglike relationships. Terms such as *hoahānau, pili makamaka* 'close friend' or 'host' (see Handy and Pukui 1972:73–74), and *aikane* 'intimate friend' suggest equivalence and solidarity among coresidents of the same sex. Sahlins (personal communication) has called the *aikane*, a close friend of the same sex (Andrews 1865:25), an "unranked brother." The use of this term of friendship induces an ethic of siblingship rather than hierarchy, which normally characterizes the brother/brother tie.

The *punalua* 'co-spouse' tie similarly proscribed hostility between co-wives or co-husbands. Morgan's paradigm of the Punaluan family was based on a later usage of the term (Handy and Pukui 1972:60–65), of men married to sisters (*punalua* = WiSiHu) or of women married to brothers (*punalua* = HuBrWi). In premissionary times co-spouses were *punalua* to each other and "had joint responsibility for the children of the family" (Handy and Pukui 1972:56). A man's wife would also be *punalua* to his former lovers (Handy and Pukui 1972:57). The nineteenth-century Andrews (1865:498) dictionary provides further insight into the ethic of the relationship: as a verb, *punalua* means 'to make an equal of one; to come on terms of reciprocity with one.' As a noun *punalua* is glossed 'a friend on equal terms with one.' Functionally, the *ma* thus preserves internal solidarity by transforming attached affines into unranked siblings. Male *punalua* should be like brothers, without the potential hostility, and female *punalua* like sisters: "True *punalua* received each other as sisters and accorded each other the same treatment as one would a relative" (Handy and Pukui 1972:60).

Other terms for affinal relatives are reciprocal and do not imply relative rank. At the formal structural level, this supports my earlier contention that Hawaiian affinal relationships are not implicitly ranked and underscores the importance of marriage as a mechanism of alliance. For the local group, the reciprocal in-law terms imply normative egalitarianism among the people on the land, or at least between households related through marriage; and the reconstructed family groups indicate that landholders in the *ahupua'a* were more likely to be related by marriage than by consanguinity. *Pūluna* 'co-parents-in-law' was used between the parents and relatives of a married couple—a relationship that, according to Pukui, was "sealed (*ua pa'a ka pili*) only by the birth of a child" (Handy and Pukui 1972:69–70). While a man's wife's sister called him *kane* 'man' or 'husband' and a woman's brother-in-law referred to her as *wahine* 'woman' or 'wife,' brothers-in-law used the reciprocal term *kaiko'eke* 'WiBr/SiHu' for one another (as would two sisters-in-law). Within the local group the affinal tie established an exchange relationship between sibling sets, a tie that was normatively symmetrical. Adoption figured in this exchange as the fulfillment of reciprocity and accomplished equivalence between affines. Actual sister-exchange (which also implies equivalence) appears to have been rare; Hawaiians effectively maximized the number of affinal links to other *ma,* both within and without the *ahupua'a.* It is worth emphasizing here that commoner women exerted considerable and perhaps nearly complete autonomy in marriage choices. In other words, the formation of alliances among commoners was not accomplished through a male-controlled traffic in women, but through women making their own decisions and pursuing their own "political economy of love."

Adoption serves as another indicator of the mutual expectations and structuring capability of the brother/sister tie. Table 6 shows a high frequency of adoptions (11 of 14 known) occurring between cross-sex siblings: in other words, a child is adopted by the father's sister or mother's brother (for a comparative case see Smith 1983:264–65). However, these figures are markedly at odds with the prevalence of grandparental adoption among modern Hawaiians, as noted by several researchers. In my own fieldwork 65 percent of the adoptions recorded were by the maternal grandparents (Linnekin 1985:183–93). Admittedly, table 6 offers a fortuitous sampling of adoptions occurring variously between 1830 and 1860, in only three land sections. These are cases where the child was specifically described as adopted, as opposed to "living with" or "staying at," and where the adopter's relationship to the child could be determined from the land records or other legal documents. The ten unknown cases may represent adoptions by grandparents; the data are simply too fragmentary to tell.

It is also true that marriage and residence patterns in the modern Hawaiian community where I worked differ greatly from those in the nineteenth-century *ahupua'a.* The vast majority of those born in Ke'anae marry out and leave the area. There is a strong preference for a young couple to establish an independent household or, if that is not possible, for a women to go to her husband's home. These ideals likely reflect the influence of American culture and the lesser participation of modern rural Hawaiian women in the external economy. Children are thus likely

TABLE 6. Adoptions in Three *Ahupua'a*

Ahupua'a	Relationship of Adopter						Total
	FaSi	MoBr	FaBr	MoSi	FaFaSi	Unknown	
Mānoa	7	2	2			4	15
La'ie					1	5	6
Punalu'u		2				1	3
Total	7	4	2		1	10	24

to move away, but their offspring may return as *hānai* children to serve and care for the grandparents. The figures presented in table 6 are logical if local endogamy was high and postmarital residence choices were about evenly divided. Minimally, these figures indicate that adoption between brother and sister occurred to a significant extent and suggest an ethic of equivalance and *aloha* between cross-sex siblings and between *kaiko'eke*.

Through local in-marriage the brother/sister relationship is the interstitial link between households in the *ahupua'a,* creating a symmetrical exchange relationship between *kaiko'eke.* If we can assume that egalitarianism prevailed among the commoners (with the possible exception of the resident *konohiki*), then the interhousehold material exchanges described by Pukui would be facilitated by a kin or affinal relationship. I am in part extrapolating from my own observations of exchange-in-kind among modern rural Hawaiians when I suggest that gift giving and mutual aid are easier between relatives, among whom the ethic of "generalized reciprocity" prevails. But many anthropologists (perhaps most eloquently Sahlins 1965) have drawn similar conclusions about the ethic of exchange in non-Western societies. Hawaiian concepts of marriage gifts as "hooks" and of a spouse as a *kuleana* in another family offer indigenous cultural evidence that affinally related households were seen as linked in reciprocal exchange. Kirch (1979:29) has provided some archaeological corroboration for mutual aid between *kaiko'eke.* In the Anahulu River valley, on the north shore of O'ahu, a landholder's irrigation ditch was constructed to bypass that of an unrelated neighbor, so the farmer would receive his water supply from his brother-in-law.

I have suggested that Hawaiian kinship embodies an important cultural distinction, encoded in terminology and manifested in normative expectations, ethics, and behavior, between relatives who are ranked vis-à-vis one another and those who are mutually unranked. Within the same generation this is a distinction between same-sex and cross-sex siblings, but same-sex ties (particularly Fa/So, which is often the path of jural succession) are more likely to be strained than are cross-sex ties such as Mo/So or Fa/Da. The internal cohesiveness of the *ma* rests on siblingship, which I have defined as the ethic of mutuality and equivalence embodied in cross-sex relationships. Those who find it difficult to behave accordingly will leave the residential group. Thus younger brothers are likely to marry out of their natal household, and brother and sister are more likely to comprise the long-term core of the *ma,* the point of attachment for dependents. The *ma* is fundamentally a bilateral group, an assemblage of people who are categorically siblings to one another.

Conclusion

In organization and solidarity the commoner community was the complement to the chiefly. The chiefs were tenuously related to the people on the land and were always susceptible to rebellion. As a corollary to the fragility of their rule, commoner Hawaiian society was fragmented into autonomous household units linked by marriage in dyadic exchange relationships. The chieftainship could not have withstood the opposition of solidary local groups, and it consistently subverted any such development with exercise of the tabus, confiscation, and land redistribution. Political integration at the local level was imposed from above in the form of an alien leadership. This is not to say that the *maka'āinana* had no organization, for as I have detailed the people in the *ahupua'a* were interrelated in numerous ways. But the commoners were not unified in and of themselves as a political or a territorial force. Rather, they looked to chiefly authority for direction: in political matters, the commoners were destined to serve.

The chiefs were not of the people; they were not the heads of localized lineages. Although they were putatively related to the commoners the ties could no longer be specified. For administration of affairs the commoners looked to their *konohiki,* as exemplified in maintenance of the irrigation system. The *konohiki* was responsible for the allocation of water and other use rights within the *ahupua'a* and organized the cleaning and repair of the ditches. For some time after the Māhele this function was assumed by the tax collector, but with the end of the *konohiki* system effective regulation ceased. Water disputes increased in the aftermath of the Māhele, for there was no longer a central authority over land and water: the land now belonged to many individual owners, and there was no one to order the repair of the sluices after rains and floods. As a witness in a water rights case lamented, "The common people are konohikis now. . . . Everybody that has a kuleana of his own is a konohiki" (E-305).

Though the local *konohiki* might be a commoner elevated through service, the *maka'āinana* were by and large internally undifferentiated by rank. Since commoners were by definition people without genealogies and since land was subject to reallocation by the chiefs, descent groups associated with land could not develop or had been fragmented by the late precontact period. Lineal descent had limited relevance among the commoners and was largely restricted to inheritance of authority over land and customary use rights. Siblingship, rather than descent, is the dominant principle ordering the local group. The residents of the *ahupua'a* were for the most part related horizontally rather than vertically, by sibling and affinal ties. Reciprocal exchanges between households were transactions between peers. Identification with a place and the right to reside there (albeit under someone else) fell bilaterally to the descendants of a sibling set.

What of the intersection of rank and gender? The analogues between chiefly and commoner women's roles and structural efficacy are apparent. For all women, the Hawaiian materials point to gender parallelism, personal autonomy, and relative sexual egalitarianism. Chiefly women had their own retinues and loyalists and commanded the productivity of lands in their own right. As vessels of high rank and as potential mothers chiefly women were essential to the dynastic strategies of male chiefs. "To seek a lord" was to seek a chief's high-ranking daughter. As the sisters of other male chiefs, they were also critical as the means of forging alliances. This significance is aptly illustrated by Kamehamaha's marriages numerous to Maui-descended women, and is personified by the powerful Ka'ahumanu, the ultimate political sister but never herself a biological mother.

Fundamentally, the extent of men's control over women in Hawaii is questionable. Granted, the chiefs could put to death any women who flouted the tabus, but this penalty appears to have been exacted rather erratically. The ethos of Hawaiian women was clearly not passive or acquiescent. There is no clear evidence for an explicit norm of wife deference, as Gailey (1987:62) asserts for Tonga. Commoner women may have had more freedom of choice in selecting marital partners than their chiefly counterparts. Women of high *kapu* rank were certainly constrained by their consorts for political reasons, and some vigorously fought their husbands' attempts to prevent liaisons. *Ali'i* men had priests, enforcers, and guardians (*kahu*) to protect their high-ranking wives. In the analogous circumstance jealous commoner men could only rely on physical intimidation.

The ethnohistorical materials on commoner households suggest that the ideology of female pollution, while dictating separation, did not produce a consistent asymmetry in male/female authority. Again, the extent to which ritual logic carries over into interpersonal and domestic relations is problematic. Even more problematic, and analogous to the contradiction in the status of female chiefs, is the potential conflict between gender hierarchy and age hierarchy in Hawaiian families. The land transmission statistics indicate a preference for male heirs, but it is also clear that older women, particularly older sisters residing in their natal households, wielded considerable authority and could serve as household heads (see chap. 7). In Hawaii the older sister's status is not formalized or institutionalized, however, as it is in the case of the Tongan "sacred sister" (see Gailey 1987; Herda 1987; Rogers 1977).

In Hawaii women both chiefly and common represent a certain *mana* or efficacy, a path to structural alternatives. The practical "stakes" among the commoners were *kuleana* such as land and use rights rather than political power and dynastic rank, but at both levels of society women symbolized the realization of potential, the way to make a difference in one's destiny. The dual roles of sister and mother encapsulate these varied possibilities. By creating in-law relationships, women as sisters effectively created structure in the local group. As mothers women ensured the continuity and reproduction of the bilateral family. But even in this context the statuses of mother and sister cannot be completely separated. In Hawaii sisters too were reproducers, for sisters' children might also remain in the *ma* and participate in its continuity.

Chapter 6

The Economic Events

In former times, before Kamehameha, the chiefs took great care of their
people. That was their appropriate business. . . . But from Liholiho's time
to the present, the chiefs seem to have left caring for the people. . . . The
people have been burdened in seeking sandal wood to pay the debts of the
chiefs. . . . On account of this want of care of the chiefs for the people,
some of the people are losing their attachment to the land of their birth.
—David Malo (1839:125–27)

Anthropologists frequently relate gender roles to micro- and macro-
economic conditions. The literature on women, colonialism, and stratification has drawn connections between changes in women's social valuation and processes such as class formation and proletarianization (e.g.,
Beneria 1982; Etienne and Leacock 1980; Gailey 1987; Ong 1987; Stoler
1977). In this chapter I review the economic history of Hawaii between
1778 and approximately 1860 with an eye to factors affecting male and
female roles and the structure of the commoner local group. The major
themes are exchange relations between Hawaiians and foreigners and
the beginnings of Hawaiian proletarianization. During this period the
Hawaiian economy was transformed from production for subsistence
and tribute to production for external markets. In the early years of
exchange with foreigners Hawaiians met the demand for provisions without significant social disruption; production was still organized by customary authorities although, as Sahlins (1981) points out, the trade
created competition between chiefs and commoners as the latter attempted to circumvent chiefly controls over the market. It was during
the sandalwood era, particularly in the early 1820s, that Hawaiians became fully enmeshed in production and extraction for mercantile capitalism. A proletarian class of Hawaiians began to develop in the early
1800s when merchants established fixed businesses in the ports, but most

Hawaiians remained on the land as subsistence agriculturalists until after the Māhele. My review of events ends in the midst of this great land alienation, on the eve of the plantation era (foreign workers were not imported in significant numbers until the 1870s). Chapter 7 will detail the causes of Hawaiian dispossession and explore the role that women played on the land as the Hawaiian diaspora commenced.

I suggested above that the oppression of the commoners by the chiefs, particularly evident from the 1820s on, was a distortion of the chief/commoner relationship, which was formerly characterized by a degree of normative reciprocity and mutual aloha. Before the monarchy there was still a "moral limit" (Sahlins 1972: 147) to chiefly demands. The people did, after all, have the option of leaving the *ahupua'a* and aligning themselves with a different chief. But certainly by the middle of the nineteenth century the notions of common kinship, aloha, and reciprocity between chiefs and commoners appear as a mystifying ideology that cloaked significant political and economic inequities. By removing the ritual buttress for the ruling chief's authority, the *kapu* abolition may have abetted the final breaking of the kinship bond between chiefs and people. Malcolm Webb has pointed out (1965:35) that this event was intimately tied to the transition from chiefdom to state: by secularizing chiefly office the *kapu* abolition eliminated the ethical limits to expropriation and made possible the "new freedom of action" required by a state government.

In the first half of the nineteenth century both the material flow and the spirit of the old relationships were altered. Tax demands escalated dramatically at a time of ever-declining population. Commoner Hawaiians were called upon to provide more labor aand provisions at a time when there were fewer and fewer of them alive on the land to do so. To many Hawaiians, these developments represented the betrayal of their traditional relationship with the chiefs, a loss of aloha. The selective economic history that follows yields insight into the effects of state formation on commoner men and women. Tracing the emergence of social classes is a more difficult matter, since for most of the period under study rank and wealth were coterminous. Through the nineteenth century the chiefs remained materially privileged and the commoners were for the most part poor, a precedented inequality further sedimented by the distribution of lands in the Māhele (the disparity continues to this day, incidentally, as some *ali'i* descendants are supported by the proceeds of large landed estates while most Hawaiians are landless and disadvantaged). A Hawaiian "middle class" of intellectuals, pastors, and professionals without chiefly connections had arisen by midcentury, but the mass of the native population worked the land or labored in the ports.

Assuredly these transformations altered Hawaiian men's and women's economic and domestic roles. Etienne (1980) and Gailey (1987) have argued in analogous cases that colonization and capitalist expansion tend to increase women's dependence on men. The logic here is that men are typically more engaged in the market economy through cash cropping and/or wage labor and thus have differential access to money and foreign goods. While such conclusions are appealingly logical, empirical cases are not always so neatly explained. Hawaiian women were not themselves undifferentiated. It is difficult to believe that differential male/female engagement in the market economy would cause a loss of social status for female chiefs. Even among the commoners, the importance of age hierarchy in the Hawaiian family suggests that the roles and personal authority of older women might contrast significantly with those of younger women. As will be discussed below, Hawaiian women did participate in the external economy and brought money and goods into the family. But the extent to which external economic activity overrides the high valuation of particular roles in the kin group is also problematic. The authority wielded by older women, given their position in the local group (see chap. 5), would not necessarily diminish because they were not themselves bringing in money. An analogy can be drawn here to present-day remittance economies in Polynesia in which young adults working abroad support the national and domestic economies of Samoa and Tonga; the recognized social superiors tend to stay behind while sending the young to engage in the Western economy. As in the political and social economies of Hawaii, the operant ethic extends the notion of service owed from young to old, from inferior to superior.

The New Landlords

Hawaii's transition from a Polynesian redistributive system to a market economy is intimately tied to changes in the basis of Hawaiian political authority. Burgeoning bureaucracy is commonly said to characterize the transition from chiefdom to state: proliferating levels of government officials replace the personal ties between chiefs and people and widen the gap between elite and governed. The chiefs presided over the transformation of Hawaiian society, though they by no means had full control over the process. European meddling played a major role in the creation of the monarchy, and Euro-American merchants opportunistically encouraged the Hawaiian elite to become freewheeling consumers. Chiefly tribute became an oppressive taxation, which ultimately encouraged emigration from rural districts and undermined the commoners' ability to subsist without finding something to sell to the market, whether produce, labor, services, or sex.

Initially the Hawaiian state drew on prior cultural models for the exercise of authority. In Kamehameha's time the monarchy reached out to the local level primarily through the imposition of new landlords. Extending the precedent of conquest land redistribution, Kamehameha solidified his unification of the windward isles by rewarding his loyal supporters with land. These included lesser chiefs and warriors from Hawai'i, personal retainers (including foreigners such as Isaac Davis, John Young, and the harbor pilot Alexander Adams), and the Maui chiefs, Kamehameha's affines, often called the key to his success (see the discussion of Ka'ahumanu *ma* in Sahlins 1981:55–66).

But Kamehameha, always politically astute, added a variation to the old practice. To consolidate his rule, Kamehameha gave his closest relatives and most crucial supporters lands on different islands, thereby placing his own people as rulers over the local level. The effect was most dramatic on the island of O'ahu, which Kamehameha occupied from approximately 1804 to 1812 as a prelude to the invasion of Kaua'i, a plan foiled by the '*ōku'u* epidemic of 1804 and other fortuitous events (see Kamakau 1961:189ff.) Land records from the Māhele document how Kamehameha's chieftains and warriors were settled in over the underlying O'ahu population. Many of those who called themselves *kama'āina* at the time of the Māhele came from Hawai'i during this period, as districts on O'ahu underwent agricultural intensification to feed the occupying army (see Kirch 1979; Kirch and Sahlins ms.).

As the ranks of intermediate *konohiki* swelled, *ahupua'a* were divided into ever-smaller realms of authority to reward state bureaucrats and the king's personal retainers. This process is particularly evident in the districts around Honolulu, where state political authority and foreign trade came to be concentrated. Formerly the *ahupua'a* was the province of a single chiefly owner, but from Kamehameha's time individual '*ili* were allocated to supporting chiefs and royal relatives, who then placed their own *konohiki* on the land under them. The missionary J. S. Emerson, stationed on Oʻahu's north shore, described the superstratification of *konohiki* in his district at midcentury:

> many lands have six or eight owners at the same time. For instance, Waialua, containing perhaps one or two thousand acres in all, has seven lords, one above the other, and all of them are over the people, and claim services from them occasionally. (Wyllie 1846:44–45)

It is nearly axiomatic that state governments place increasing material demands on the underlying populace. The Hawaiian chiefs at first drew on established modes of exaction—the exercise of *kapu* and their right to commandeer the commoners' goods and labor—while the proliferation of landlords in politically choice districts drew on the cultural precedent of conquest land redistribution. But "precedented" does not mean that the prior exchange relationship continued unchanged, ethically or materially. By the time of the Māhele many commoners had come to perceive the chiefs' behavior as despotic abuse.

Early Exchanges

Off the coast of Kauaʻi early in 1778, Captain Cook traded some nails and iron chisels for pigs and sweet potatoes, an exchange that proved to be the prototype of early trade between Hawaiians and Europeans. Cook set the precedent of having his own armorers fashion iron into the native dagger (*pāhoa*) and adz (*koʻi*), the latter referred to as toi, toe, towe, or towee in the early journals. Typically, the foreign ships traded for provisions and consumables: pork, yams, poultry, fresh water, firewood, and salt. Several also mention picking up good line and cordage, probably of *olonā* fiber (Boit ms.; Beresford 1789:112, 250–51, 273; Cook 1967:489 n. 2; Ingraham 1971:66; Portlock 1789:59). The Europeans usually cruised offshore, tacking between different parts of the islands so as not to deplete the produce of any one area. Niʻihau was a popular stopping place for outgoing vessels because there they could procure yams, which would keep on shipboard longer than any other article of Hawaiian produce (see, e.g., Beresford 1789:54; Clerke 1967:573). The Hawaiians in their turn wanted the Europeans' superior iron tools; the chiefs avidly sought guns and ammunition when they could persuade or pressure shippers to trade them. In general the explorers, such as Cook and Vancouver, were opposed to trading arms, but few commercial shippers of the time shared their scruples. In 1788, James Colnett (ms.) ransomed a stolen anchor for iron bars, two muskets, two pistols, ball and powder, saws, and a ship's speaking trumpet; in fairness, he considered it a victory to retrieve the anchor at all. Colnett also had the Kaua'i men instructed in the use of the musket.

Some of the initial transactions between Cook and the Hawaiian chiefs took the form of offerings (ho'okupu) as befitting visiting chiefs and gods (Sahlins 1981:37–38). Cook credited the Kona ruler, Kalani'ōpu'u, for the "vast daily supplies of Vegetables & barbecued hogs" delivered to the ships while at Kealakekua—significantly, brought by a priest (King 1967:564). While the chiefs made formal prestations to Cook and later commanders, on the model of reciprocal exchanges between high-ranking personages, "the common people . . . were content to enter into a peaceful commercial exchange" (Sahlins 1981:38). Even in that first year of commerce with Hawaiians, prices for local produce inflated as the islanders quickly developed trading acumen (cf. Ellis 1782:68). In January, 1778, "several small pigs were got for a sixpenny nail or two apiece" (Cook 1967:264). For some nails and bits of iron, they were able to obtain sixty to eighty pigs, a few chickens, potatoes, plantains, and taro (Cook 1967:272). A year later, Hawaiians were more particular in their demands, and the chiefs were initiating their own barter transactions. As Samwell (1967:1190) tells us, Kamehameha would take nothing but iron daggers, "which they have of later preferred to Tois & every thing else," for his feathered cloak: "& all the large Hogs they bring us now they want Daggers for and tell us that they must be made as long [as] their arms. . . . Kamehameha got nine of them for his Cloak." One such iron pāhoa was the instrument of Cook's death (see Sahlins 1985, chap. 4). Cook's ships stopped at Kaua'i for the final time in March, 1779. As they filled their casks with water, one Hawaiian demanded an adz for every barrelful; others attempted to steal the marines' arms (King 1967:586–87).

The Kona chiefs may initially have presented ho'okupu to Cook with no expectation of direct return, but notions that the Europeans were gods appear to have been short-lived. Transactions with subsequent visitors had a decidedly commercial ethos. The chiefs quickly recognized the material advantages of the trade and closely monitored relations between commoners and the shippers. When Dixon touched at O'ahu late in 1786, hogs and vegetables were under a *kapu* until the chief, Kahekili, had opportunity to board. The commoners actively bartered with the Europeans, even uprooting fences for firewood to sell to the ships (Beresford 1789:113). In their turn Dixon's men supplied primarily iron *ko'i* and nails, but buttons were popular among the Hawaiian women, who wore them in bracelets around their wrists or ankles (Beresford 1789:97).

By 1791, about thirty foreign ships had visited the islands, for the most part English and American fur traders (Morgan 1948:58–59). In 1795, the year of Kamehameha's conquest of O'ahu, a single musket bought nine large hogs from a Hawai'i chief (Boit ms.) John Young told Boit that Kamehameha's forces had five thousand muskets, "& many swivels and cannon one of which was a four-pounder." At the time of Boit's visit Kamehameha placed a taboo on pigs, "only to be purchased for guns and ammunition." Vancouver's men had refused similar demands in 1793 (Vancouver 1798, 2:110); eventually the Hawaiians accepted red cloth for their provisions. Besides acting as a political consultant to Kamehameha (see Kelly 1967:402–8), Vancouver (1798, 3:53) left cattle on Hawai'i island. To protect their numbers, he advised Kamehameha to place a ten-year tabu on them and suggested that women not be allowed to eat them. Left in peace, the cattle multiplied and prospered in the Waimea uplands. Vancouver's gift, however, was to have disastrous consequences for small-scale Hawaiian agriculture (see chap. 7).

As Sahlins (1981) has described, trade with Europeans created unprecedented relations of competition between Hawaiian chiefs and commoners. The chiefs initially used their traditional prerogatives in attempting to monopolize European commerce: the right to confiscate the commoners' possessions and the right to declare *kapu*. Trade goods received from foreigners might be seized immediately by the chiefs' enforcers, or a tabu placed on commerce so as to reserve the trade for the chiefs (see Sahlins 1981:43–44). The chiefs' tabus could be quite selective and were employed both to deter the commoners and to pressure the shippers. Colnett (ms.:158) found trade halted after an altercation over a stolen chain, but "women, wood, & water were not in the prohibition," only provisions. Dixon's men attempted to take on water at Kealakekua in 1787, but the watering place was tabued: "the reason they gave . . . was, that all their Chiefs being absent, engaged in war with a neighbouring island, they durst not . . . suffer strangers to come on shore" (Beresford 1789:50). When they visited a village on Kaua'i a chief threw stones to drive the commoners away, then solicited a gift of several nails (Beresford 1789:126). Portlock (1789:310–11) saw a chief demand from a commoner the bits of iron he had bartered from the foreigners, whereupon they were instantly surrendered. Some commoners began paddling farther out to sea to intercept the ships, thus evading chiefly preemption. On O'ahu in 1786 Kehekili tabued Dixon's ships. He had built a storehouse on top of a hill

> for such articles as the natives might obtain in the course of their traffic with our vessels: when this was compleated, he caused the bay to be tabooed . . . [and directed the inhabitants] to bring whatever trade they had got, that it might be deposited in his new-erected edifice. This being effected, he found means . . . to appropriate one-half of these stores to his own use. (Beresford 1789:106)

As a result of such exercises of privilege, the chiefs "had more Iron than they knew what to do with" by 1793 (Bell 1929–30, 1:63; cf. Sahlins 1981:44). According to Edward Bell (1929–30, 1:62), "some of them wou'd not even look at an Axe, that about three or four years ago would have purchased half their property." But they unceasingly importuned the foreigners for guns and munitions. The commoners, in contrast, still eagerly sought iron nails and knives. Scissors were especially in demand, as well as mirrors, colored beads, and woolen cloth. In this and later periods, Western cloth particularly stimulated consumer interest among the Hawaiians. Trading with Vancouver's men in 1793, Hawaiians gave at first "five large hogs" and later eight to ten pigs for a yard and a half of red fabric (Menzies 1920:54, 62; see chap. 8 below).

Kamehameha's Trade

Kamehameha adeptly maintained a monopoly over foreign commerce, exercising the *kapu* to exclude both commoners and lesser chiefs from direct barter with shippers. As early as 1793 he had Vancouver's ships guarded at night by his own canoes. Menzies (1920:88–89) reports that Kamehameha "had taken in a great measure upon himself the supplying of both vessels." Kamehameha was evidently attuned to the status differences between Vancouver and commercial fur traders. The following year he was again solicitous, stationing a chief to remain on board, "and he particularly requested that we should not barter for provisions like other vessels, but that he would himself undertake to be our purveyor" (Menzies 1920:146; cf. Vancouver 1798, 3:4). After the conquest of Oʻahu Kamehameha developed an admirable system of trade control, sending ships from Hawaiʻi to Oʻahu under escort with orders for supplies (see Townsend 1821:12). He personally oversaw transactions with the Russian expedition of 1816 and assigned a "companion" to accompany Kotzebue's ship to Oʻahu (Kotzebue 1821, 1:314). Corney (1896: 96) reported that in 1818 ships were required to stop at Hawaiʻi island to get Kamehameha's permission before proceeding to Honolulu. Moreover, he sent an *aikane* on board Corney's ship "to look after the vessel, and keep the natives from stealing." The Americans supplied "powder and stores" to the Hawaiians in exchange for sandalwood, rope, pork, and produce (Corney 1896:98). Before entering Honolulu, ships had to pay a harbor fee of eight dollars and a pilotage fee of twelve dollars. These fees were instituted in 1816, after Kamehameha's unprofitable attempt to send a trading expedition of his own to Canton (Ellis 1969:418; Stewart 1970:131–32).

Kamehameha thus accumulated immense stores of trade goods and money, from luxury items to schooners to the arms and munitions that sedimented his conquest of the islands. In 1819 Honolulu was protected by an armed fortress with fifty-four cannon. The Hawaiian navy had twenty European-style vessels, some purchased, some built under the direction of European carpenters (Freycinet 1978:90–91; see Kelly 1978:114–15). When Kamehameha discovered the value Westerners set on pearls, he reserved fishing in Pearl Harbor for himself "and employs divers for the purpose" (Campbell 1967:115). Near his residential complex in Honolulu stood two large stone storehouses for his European goods (Campbell 1967:91). Freycinet (1978:8) saw sheds for war canoes and European boats, a blacksmith's shop, a cooper's shed, and warehouses containing "building timber and sandalwood, copper ingots, and an enormous quantity of fish nets." In others were stored liquor, gunpowder, iron, and cloth. Among Kamehameha's domestic furnishings were a mahogany dining table, chest of drawers, and Chinese carrying chair (Freycinet 1978:64; see also Kotzebue 1821, 1:301). And by 1819, Freycinet notes, chiefs' houses were distinguished from the commoners' by the use of padlocks.

Sandalwood

The sandalwood era irrevocably tied the Hawaiian economy to the Western capitalist system. The particularities of this connection can be summarized as follows: the raw material was extracted by commoner labor commandeered by the chiefs and was traded to foreign merchants in exchange for consumer goods which were likewise retained by the chiefs. The Hawaiian sandalwood trade exemplifies the more general historical phenomenon of "merchant capital," as nicely outlined by Gerald Sider (1986). As Sider (1986:34) points out, merchant capital allows for "less uniform directionalities" in the conjunction of the world system and indigenous societies. For Hawaii, the concept can illuminate changes in the chief/commoner relationship as a result of foreign trade. Merchant capital is a type of commodity extraction in which the producing communities "generate these products through forms of work organization that they themselves control and supervise." There is "domination at the point of exchange, not in production." While local production in Hawaii was skewed by the external demand for provisions and then disrupted by sandalwood harvesting, the effect was uneven. Certain ports and coastal areas were differentially involved in foreign trade while districts less convenient to shippers had minimal access to the commerce.

In retrospect sandalwood appears to have had much more disruptive and far-reaching consequences for Hawaiians than the provisions trade. Demand for provisions drew on local subsistence production, but the sandalwood trade was fundamentally a system of extraction; it was not commoner-produced foodstuffs but commoner labor that was demanded, to the extent of even causing the neglect of subsistence production. There was no plan for replenishing sandalwood; when the supply gave out, the trade died. As I argued in earlier chapters, the Hawaiian economy was historically capable of gearing up to meet increased production demands. But removing commoner labor from production was unprecedented. Moreover, this separation of labor from the production of necessities can be seen as the precursor to wage labor and later proletarianization.

The extent and quality of chiefly control differed markedly in the provisions and sandalwood trades. Despite the chiefly use of *kapu* commoners found ways to trade with foreigners on their own account, procuring iron tools and cloth for themselves whenever they could evade the chiefs' watchers. An ordinary Hawaiian could hope to canoe out to a passing ship with a pig or a chicken, but sandalwood was a different matter. The merchants demanded sandalwood in large set quantities that required concerted group labor to procure. Supplying shippers allowed some competition between chiefs and commoners; extracting sandalwood was experienced by the commoners as oppression, to which they responded with passive resistance.

Sandalwood was discovered in the islands in 1791 but did not become an important trade item until after 1800. The commerce was dominated by Americans, with the peak of the trade lasting from 1810 to 1818 (Morgan 1948:61–62). At its height in 1816, the value of sandalwood exports during the year totalled nearly $400,000: "While it lasted, it was a mine of wealth to the chiefs" (Jarves 1843:181). By 1826 sandalwood was already scarce (see, e.g., Hammatt ms.) and the bottom dropped out of the market in the 1830s (Paulding 1970:232; Barrot 1978:107). In Wallerstein's (1974) terms, the sandalwood trade exemplifies the unequal exchange relationship between core and periphery, wherein finished goods produced in the colonial core states are exchanged at considerable profit for raw materials extracted in the periphery. Indisputably, the sandalwood era was disastrous for Hawaiians; the trade stimulated a voracious demand among the chiefs for imported luxury goods and left a legacy of debt from which the kingdom's economy would never recover. In his excellent economic history of Hawaii, Theodore Morgan (1948:73) summarized the effects of the sandalwood trade:

> Now a long list of foreign goods, useful only for war or ostentatious display, was desired by the chiefs to an extent which jeopardized food and shelter to their retainers. Silks, crepes, broadcloths, tobacco, alcohol, dollars, guns and ammunition accumulated among the chiefs' possessions so long as the sandalwood held out, while the welfare of the commoners declined.

In the early years of the trade Kamehameha incorporated sandalwood into his tributary demands, leaving the details of collection to lesser chiefs who pressed their commoners into service. According to Mathison (1825:458) men, women, and children were employed in carrying the logs to the beach: "The expenses of cutting and shipping it are absolutely nothing; the services of the labourers employed being gratuitous, according to the practice of the country." Even during the years of the royal monopoly, the sandalwood trade siphoned off the commoners' labor from subsistence activities. Kamakau (1961:204) describes a famine that resulted from the expropriation of native labor and consequent neglect of cultivation. Around 1810, the chiefs of Hawai'i ordered all the people into the mountains to cut sandalwood for Kamehameha: "This rush of labor to the mountains brought about a scarcity of cultivated food throughout the whole group." To end the famine, Kamehameha put a *kapu* on all sandalwood as the property of the government "and ordered the people to devote only part of their time to its cutting and to return to the cultivation of the land." Whatever its relationship to actual occurrence, this account illustrates how external trade distorted the relationship between chiefs and their people, the chiefly right to the commoners' labor now being exercised to fuel a new and seemingly inexhaustible supply-and-demand cycle in luxury goods.

The lesser chiefs complied with Kamehameha's monopoly but not without some resentment. Significantly, Freycinet notes that the chiefs particularly objected to the king's hoarding of European goods: "Rather than make use of these stores as a source of largess to his vassals, he preferred to let these supplies rot and become pure loss" (Freycinet 1978:20–21). This statement offers insight into the normative behavior of good chiefs toward their subordinates before the monarchy. The fact that lesser chiefs were objecting precisely to the very un-Polynesian character of Kamehameha's hoarding indicates minimally that high chiefs were expected to give back to their retainers and junior relatives. Redistribution of goods to lesser-ranking folk was integral to a chief's role in Hawaii as elsewhere in Polynesia. Freycinet's explanation for the king's churlishness suggests how political strategies change in the context of a monarchy: "It was not at all a matter of avarice but rather fear on his part that in increasing the resources of these men, whom he held under control only by force, he might be furnishing them the means of emancipating themselves" (Freycinet 1978:21).

After Kamehameha's death Liholiho continued to demand sandalwood as tribute (Ellis 1969:415; Stewart 1970:130) and to trade it in his own right for foreign goods. But Liholiho was a weaker ruler and his authority more fragile than his father's, and he had to surrender the trade monopoly to win the support of fractious chiefs (Morgan 1948:65). Freycinet (1978:32), who visited Hawaii in the interval between Kamehameha's death and the *kapu* abolition, relates a telling incident. On Maui, out of the reach of the king and the Kona chiefs, Ke'eaumoku set his own terms for supplies. He tabued all provisions trade, raised the price of pigs over what Liholiho had quoted, and insisted that Freycinet first buy all the small and medium pigs before he would sell the larger ones:

"Finally, he required as a condition *sine qua non* that we should pay him in coined money and not in any objects of trade." Keʻeaumoku relented somewhat when Freycinet threatened to inform the king.

The most egregious aspects of the sandalwood trade date from the early 1820s, when the chiefs associated with Liholiho's court (particularly Kaʻahumanu *ma*) began their own rush to purchase European goods and collect the wood to pay for them, usually in that order (see, e.g., account books of William French, originals in AH; Hammatt ms.). Mathison (1825:467) observed, "the King and his Chiefs compose a united corps of peaceable merchants, whose principle object is to become rich by the pursuits of trade." Although the Hawaiian chiefs at times demanded cash for sandalwood (see, e.g., Freycinet 1978:32) and some were said to have amassed stores of money (Dampier 1971:47; Stewart 1970:136), most of their receipts were in merchandise. Liholiho periodically demanded taxes in dollars (Ellis 1969:415) and is said to have made a goodly cash profit by reselling some of the goods he received, "as a regular merchant, wholesale and retail to the inhabitants" (Mathison 1825:466). In the sandalwood period it was the chiefs' appetite for imported luxury goods that constituted the immediate stimulus to the trade.

The excesses of this time have been well documented by Morgan (1948:61–73) and eloquently interpreted by Sahlins (1981:43–46). The American merchants competed aggressively for their shares of the chiefly market (see, e.g., Hammatt ms.) and were quite aware that the commerce hinged on stimulating consumer demand among the Hawaiians. In 1809, Isaac Davis and other foreigners in Honolulu chided Archibald Campbell (1967:99–100) for building a loom and instructing Hawaiians in its use, saying that "if the natives could weave cloth, and supply themselves, ships would have no encouragement to call at the Islands." Even though the Hawaiians became progressively shrewder in their dealings, the foreign middlemen were experienced entrepreneurs out to maximize their profits, and caveat emptor was the order of the day. John Colcord (ms.), who came to Hawaii on a sandalwood ship in 1821, wrote that on some of the articles traded to the Hawaiians there was a "300 or 400 per cent profit." In 1828 Laura Judd (1928:7) was told that "some of the chiefs had paid eight hundred and a thousand dollars for mirrors not worth fifty." The merchant Charles Hammatt (ms.), bemoaning the apparent saturation of the market, sought to unload worm-eaten cloth at Hawaiʻi for one-half picul (a Chinese unit of weight, equal to 133.33

pounds) of sandalwood per yard. Hammatt's "chief" tribulation, however, was his assignment to find a buyer for a schooner in return for a (promised) quantity of sandalwood.

At Kailua, Hawai'i, Hammatt did succeed in selling forty-two piculs worth of wines, cordials, beads, rice, and cloth to John Adams Kuakini, governor of the island. Hammatt also reports having for sale "knives, flints, twine, blankets, ginghams & calicos, shirting, scarfs, thread, broadcloth." He preferred to find buyers among the chiefs, but would sell to commoners when he could. Arago (1823:149) wrote that the chiefs preferred to receive guns and powder, "hatchets, ermine, and knives, for the other classes . . . and handkerchiefs, glasses, and beads, for the women." The ledgers of the merchant William French (originals in AH), with their day-by-day accounts of purchases and transactions, provide a vivid record of chiefly dealings and conspicuous consumption during the 1820s. Debits for Boki, governor of O'ahu, in the latter half of 1828 include shirts, gin, two sailing brigs, cider, black paint, pepper, cloth, soup plates and other dishes, wine, teaspoons, soap, a tea kettle, rum, tablecloths, white satin, axes, knives, forks, fabric, clothes, and more clothes; credits include cash, sandalwood, and sealskins. John Adams Kuakini purchased brandy, calico, sugar, cotton, shoes, a coffee pot, and cigars, in exchange for firewood, goats, sheep, and the promise of sandalwood.

In 1824, Hammatt complained in his journal that the price of sandalwood was dropping in China and the quality of the Hawaiian wood deteriorating. Kuakini was said to be hoarding "old fashioned good wood," as chiefs increasingly tried to satisfy their creditors with inferior product. By the time of Barrot's (1978:107) visit in 1836, it was "almost impossible to procure a full cargo" of the wood. The value of sandalwood exported from January, 1836, to August, 1841, totalled only $65,000 (Jarves 1843:332), compared with Mathison's (1825:458) estimate of $350,000–$400,000 over eighteen months at the height of the trade. The result was a calamitous shortfall between the chiefs' debts and their ability to pay.

While the merchants apparently did not foresee this result—presumably no good businessman would knowingly invite default on receivables—the outcome is comprehensible if one views foreign trade during this period as creating dependency between Hawaii and Western nations. Dependency as consumerism is largely a matter of new cultural perceptions and created wants, rather than objective needs. To maintain the asymmetrical relationship between the core states and the periphery, nations on the periphery must be turned into consumers as well as producers of raw materials. Laborers on the periphery must be suitably motivated to buy the products exported by the core states. One undergraduate text on tropical development states the problem quite explicitly as one of stimulating new material wants in the indigenous population: "changes in the attitudes of tropical peasants to work can only be effected by making the peasant want to work harder. . . . In primitive societies, extra income . . . may not be enjoyed as much as in more advanced societies because of the limited ranges of possible uses" (Hodder 1968:50–51). But this was not at all how consumerism affected Hawaii's rank society. Western merchants succeeded all too well in generating new material wants among Hawaiians, but the brunt of the work was performed by commoners while most imported products went to the chiefs.

Peter Worsley (1984:32) has criticized the world-system theorists' view of capitalism as a form of exchange rather than production. For Hawaii, at least, the emphasis on exchange is appropriate for the early period of engagement with the external economy. The merchant capital analysis has one further implication for changes in Hawaiian rank and gender relations. Noting that control over production remains in the local community, Sider (1986:36) points out that indigenous forms of authority may be both overdeveloped and undermined:

> The conjoining of these two diverse processes—the collective self-direction of the work to produce commodities, and the imposed constraints to produce— has a double impact. . . . First, it can hyperdevelop . . . "traditional" forms of leadership . . . giving the traditional leaders a power and an authority . . . they never had before, and it can simultaneously undermine and mock these leaders, reducing them to servants of the external (and hostile) demands.

The dilemma of the Hawaiian chiefs at midcentury echoes Sider's analysis. Through state formation they acquired a new power and authority over their own people. This was realized and extended through growing involvement in foreign trade, as the chiefs demanded more and more from the commoners. During the same period the chiefs were coming to be defined as ineffectual or comic by foreigners in the international arena. As I suggested earlier, the *kapu* abolition overthrew a religion in which male chiefs had a primary interest and thus may have subtly undermined their charter and efficacy, creating a crisis of *mana* and authority. In the context of public, secular authority men may have had more to lose than the women.

Rivals in Trade

Sahlins (1981:33–37) has pointed out that Europeans constituted a third term in the relationship between chiefs and commoners and created situations where the two were for the first time brought into direct competition. Even in the early years of trade with passing ships, ordinary Hawaiians took every opportunity to barter for their own account when they could escape detection by the chiefs. To the latter end, they would swim or canoe out to ships several miles distant from shore (Portlock 1789:160, 298). Although the king and the chiefs controlled major dealings with foreigners, direct exchange with the commoners could not wholly be prevented (see, e.g., Campbell 1967:34–35). At least in theory, the *kapu* abolition represented the loss of the ultimate ritual sanction against commoners' relations with foreigners. The chiefs' right of *kapu* was not immediately swept away, however, but was redirected to a secular end, that of securing the advantage in external trade.

There are several reported examples of the use of *kapu* even in the 1820s (Bloxam 1925:27; Chamberlain ms., August 29, 1823; Stewart 1970:132). When Mathison's (1825:452) ship was docked in Honolulu in 1822, Liholiho tabued potatoes to meet the sudden demand for provisions: "All the farmers who had a stock on hand, were then obliged to give them up without remuneration; and by thus monopolizing the trade, he supplied the market on his own terms." In August of 1823 the missionary Levi Chamberlain (ms.) complained that the Hawaiians had stopped selling food door to door: "there is reason to think the trade is tabu'd & that the natives are forbidden to sell anything upon the penalty of forfeiting the article which they offer for sale." Chamberlain saw this as an "an oppressive measure" to the common people. When he applied to Kalaimoku for food as a gift two days later, however, it was provided. Stewart (1970:163) similarly wrote that his family was living on "sea biscuit, salt beef, and pork, brought from America . . . and scarce ever taste a banana or melon" because they could not afford the chiefs' prices.

Despite these examples, from Liholiho's reign on visitors' and shippers' accounts attest to expanding participation in trade by commoner Hawaiians. The chiefs' tactics shifted from sudden and short-term declarations of *kapu* to standing regulations and taxes. But Ellis (1969:410) suggests that only on Oʻahu and in the ports could the king and chiefs exercise strict controls. One has the impression of an ongoing struggle: the commoners now resisting chiefly expropriation by attempting to conceal their transactions, and the chiefs trying to enforce their customary right of precedence. In the mid-1820s street peddlers waited about chiefly houses in hopes of selling their wares to visiting foreigners. They hawked "Idols, Shells, Stone axes, and other Curiosities, for which they invariably demanded a dollar" (Dampier 1971:47). Such door-to-door trafficking was presumably harder to oversee than sales in the public market, where commoners could not evade the chiefs' agents:

> Two-thirds of the proceeds of any thing a native brings to the market, unless by stealth, must be given to his chief; and, not infrequently, the whole is unhesitatingly taken from him. . . . I have seen money just put into the hands of a native . . . for a bunch of fruit . . . taken directly . . . away, by some one appointed to detect traffic of any kind. (Stewart 1970:151; cf. Ellis 1969:410)

This shift in chiefly forms of economic control—from placing a taboo on commerce to regulating and taxing the people's proceeds—is one aspect of Hawaii's transition from a theocratic chiefdom to a state government holding a monopoly of force. No longer able to bar the commoners from trading, the chiefs attempted to contain their transactions within a stationary market, set the prices, and raised taxes. Figure 16 summarizes economic relations among Hawaiians and foreigners in the early 1820s, including exchanges among the king, the chiefs, and the people. Ellis (1969:18–19) reports that Liholiho controlled Salt Lake in Oʻahu's Ewa District. Hawaiian salt was sent to Kamchatka and sold to the Russians to cure sealskins in North America (cf. Stewart 1970:288).

It is indicative of the productivity of the indigenous Hawaiian economy that even in this time of declining population and increasing demands for labor and produce, most commoners were able to maintain a viable life on the land. But producing for an external market invariably introduces distortions in local production. There is often a loss of range and variety in the economy as cultivators turn their efforts to crops that can be sold. Subsistence staples may suddenly become scarce, and trade goods begin to replace native manufactures. A comparison of ethnohis-

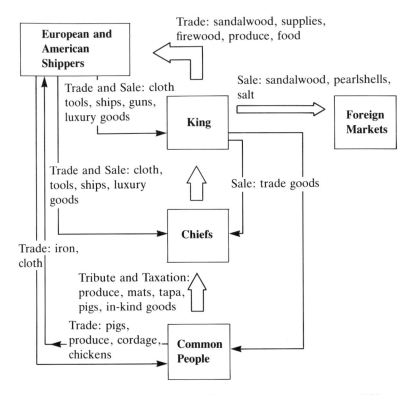

Fig. 16. Trade relations between Hawaiians and foreigners, ca. 1822

torical reports with Māhele testimony indicates wide disparities between the ports and rural areas. In districts remote from markets, Hawaiians still grew and gathered the full range of indigenous cultigens in 1850. But in Honolulu in the mid-1820s, Bloxam (1925:33) observed that "the coconut, breadfruit, and banana are all scarce . . . but they are brought for sale from other parts of the island. The common inhabitants seem principally to feed upon poe and water melons." From the discovery of Honolulu harbor in 1794 (Morgan 1948:60 n. 13) we see the birth and growth of Hawaii's first city, fostered by foreign trade. By the 1820s urban/rural differentiation is clearly evident in the contrast between Honolulu and outlying areas.

What of consumerism among ordinary Hawaiians during this period? What did the commoners do with the goods or money they received from marketing their produce? Except in the ports, most commoners did not participate directly in the market economy. The precedent and the ongoing possibility of chiefly expropriation must have deterred the people from acquiring more than a few imported items, even had they goods to sell and access to a market. According to Dampier (1971:38), in 1825 the natives of Honolulu met their subsistence needs "almost entirely" with the taro and fish that they produced themselves. In 1836 Barrot (1978:75) described production as still geared primarily to domestic needs, with the addition of "some fowls and hogs, which he sells to the ships . . . with the proceeds of these sales he pays his tax to the king, and procures for himself cloth and ardent spirits." Stone adzes were "becoming rare" in Honolulu in 1825 (Byron 1826:137) but in Waimea, Hawai'i, Hawaiians were still using stone *ko'i* as late as 1847 (Lyons, in Doyle 1953:145). In many if not most rural districts, Hawaiians remained isolated from the market economy until the middle of the nineteenth century.

Cloth

The question of cloth—native bark cloth versus foreign substitutes—carries special import for the status of Hawaiian women, for in Polynesia cloth is the quintessential female good. In colonial encounters cloth is also one of the items most readily adopted and avidly sought by indigenous peoples. Visitors from Cook's time on attest to the avidity with which Hawaiians desired foreign cloth. Shippers and merchants hastened to turn this demand to their own advantage. In the 1820s the chiefs ran up their sandalwood debts with, among other things, linen shirting, satin, ginghams, broadcloth, and calicos. If imported fabric rapidly supplanted the native bark cloth (*kapa*), what are the implications for the activities and the general social valuation of Hawaiian women? Before addressing this question (see chap. 8), we must first examine the premise that tapa cloth was quickly displaced. The impact of Western cloth on Hawaiian women's roles in the early postcontact period is a matter of access and distribution: how far and how soon did imported fabrics circulate among the general populace in the early postcontact period? When and where did Hawaiian women give up making tapa?

Although Cook's men traded some "scarlet cloth" at Maui in 1778 (Ellis 1782:171), the most sought-after articles in Hawaiians' earliest exchanges with foreigners were iron nails, tools, and guns. Mentions of payment in cloth become more frequent in accounts of Vancouver's voyage of 1792–94, by which time the chiefs had amassed a surfeit of iron. Bell (1929–30, 1:63) remarked at that time that "all kinds of woolen Cloths, Blankets &c. are in high estimation among them." At Kona in 1793, Hawaiians demanded red and blue wool and printed linen: "Beads and other trinkets were accepted as presents, but were considered as unworthy of any return" (Vancouver 1798, 2:121). Lisiansky (1814:126) reports Hawaiians asking for cloth in exchange for their pigs in 1804. A piece of printed linen would buy a suckling pig (a midsized hog went for two iron axes).

The chiefs at first attempted to monopolize imported fabric and clothing as they had other European introductions. Military uniforms in the mode of Cook and Vancouver became new insignia of authority; Sahlins (1981:30–31) links this to the would-be appropriation of European *mana*. In 1798 Kamehameha greeted a visiting ship's party in an English outfit of pants, coat, and a red waistcoat trimmed with fur (Townsend 1921:8). Further, it is said that Kamehameha "strictly forbade" commoners to wear foreign cloth (Thurston 1921:30). In areas frequented by ships, however, ordinary Hawaiians could not be prevented from bartering for items of Western clothing, and evidence suggests that they sought to emulate their chiefs as far as they might dare, if only by acquiring a single piece of foreign apparel: "some article of European dress has become a matter of necessity, even to the meanest individual; some wear only a shirt, another has trousers, and a third parades in a waistcoat" (this observation dated 1816; Kotzebue 1821, 1:329–30).

But commoners, drawing on familial labor and the produce of their domestic plots, simply did not have the leverage to become rich in European articles even if the chiefs had permitted it. By the early 1820s in Honolulu, according to Ellis (1969:17–18), there were "twelve or fourteen merchants, principally Americans, who have established warehouses on shore for foreign goods, principally piece-goods, hardware, crockery, hats and shoes, naval stores, &c. which they retail to the natives for Spanish dollars or sandal wood." The merchants would deal with commoners but the chiefs were their principal target, both for sales volume and for unloading high-profit goods. Charles Hammatt (ms.), charged with finding a chief who would buy a schooner in exchange for sandalwood, took to plying the islands when trade in Honolulu was slow; in 1823 he bartered with Hawaiians for produce at Kawaihae,

Hawai'i, but gave them relatively common goods: knives, files, chisels, scissors, *pā'ū* and *malo* of blue cloth, "& some other trifles." The traders practiced selective merchandising: fancy goods were reserved for the chiefly market. At a foot race in 1811, Cox (1957:34–35) described Kamehameha's queens "richly dressed" in dresses made for them in England. The "erees of the first and second grades" were distinguished from the commoners by "scarlet and blue cloths, silks, Chinese shawls, calicoes, ribbons, &c." The Western merchants' familiarity with class differences in mass consumption played into a Hawaiian cultural precedent: material finery indexed rank.

During the sandalwood period the chiefs' passion for European fabrics and clothing approached a mania, particularly after Liholiho surrendered the royal monopoly over the trade. By the mid-1820s chiefly fashion in public appearances ran entirely to European garments (Dampier 1971:47; Stewart 1970:136). The English fashion had been the norm for the rulers since early in Kamehameha's reign, but Stewart (1970:136) writes that lesser chiefs were still wearing tapa garments when the missionaries arrived in 1820. When Liholiho greeted Freycinet in 1819, he wore a British naval officer's uniform (Freycinet 1978:14). Although some of his subordinate chiefs had feather cloaks on this occasion, others wore red woolen capes such as given by Cook and Vancouver. But the chiefs' acquisition of cloth went far beyond even the needs of sumptuary display. Hammatt (ms.: Aug. 18, 1823) describes them hoarding "an immense amount of property . . . which the chiefs will not take out of their repositories even to use themselves." Liholiho bought some fabric at a very high price even though he had two or three hundred bolts of the same type "stored away rotting."

The first few decades of the nineteenth century saw a marked and progressive differentiation in the material circumstances of chiefs and commoners—an incipient class distinction, at least in appearance. While Ka'ahumanu dressed in elegant satin, most of the commoners in Honolulu were clothed in tapa in 1828, some adding a single article of European dress (Judd 1928:4–5; see also Freycinet 1978:61; Paulding 1970:197–99). Contrasts also emerged between rural- and urban-dwelling Hawaiians. In Honolulu, most of the people had acquired something European by the 1820s; mirrors were especially popular among women (Byron 1826:136; Dampier 1971:46; Whitman 1979:20). But the sources generally speak of commoners owning a single item of European clothing, even in the ports, through the 1830s. Hawaiians attending church or walking about in town would tend to sport that single article of fancy dress, though it be the only one they possessed. Daily dress for commoners still consisted of the *malo* and *pāʻū* (Barrot 1978:6–7). Given their status and available resources, it is difficult to conceive of ordinary Hawaiians acquiring many European garments, excepting perhaps women living with foreign men (Freycinet 1978:61).

Imported cloth penetrated even more slowly into areas remote from foreign trade. In Waimea District, Hawaiʻi, the predominant dress in 1832 was the tapa *malo* for men and the *pāʻū* for women (Doyle 1953:58–59): "Some of the women are beginning to get bonnets, and the men hats," Lyons wrote in his journal. Some of his students had acquired single items of European dress, as had Honolulu residents ten or fifteen years before. There were no stores in Waimea into the 1850s (letter of Albert B. Lyons, in Doyle 1953:176). Contributions to mission stations in such rural areas were predominantly in kind (including tapa cloth and mats) through the 1840s, revealing the limited circulation of money among commoners during this period. Even on Oʻahu, Hawaiians on the north and windward shores were still claiming *wauke* at the time of the Māhele.

Up until the Māhele, the local Hawaiian subsistence economy was alive and functioning in most rural districts. Despite oppressive chiefly taxation and the ravages of cattle in some areas, Hawaiians living on the land still remained largely self-sufficient until midcentury. After 1850 a series of institutional and legal changes—the Māhele among them—mortally affected the ability of Hawaiians to remain on the land without significant involvement in the market economy. Tapa making, for example, is impossible without a source of the *wauke* shrub. Once Hawaiians left the *ahupuaʻa* or lost access to the uplands and forests where *wauke* grew, they would necessarily become dependent on foreign cloth.

The evidence suggests that by the 1830s tapa making was on the decline in the vicinity of Honolulu. As early as 1819, Arago (1823:145) commented that on Oʻahu he only saw women making mats, while on Kauaʻi and at Kealakekua "most of the women" were "employed in manufacturing cloths." As described with righteous indignation by the missionary Lucy Thurston (1921:46), Hawaiian women who spent the night on foreign ships left garbed in tapa but returned with a "base reward of foreign cloth." In 1849 the *Polynesian* (May 26) complained: "The Hawaiian women who once labored in beating kapa, now lounge and sleep, or ride on horse back, displaying their gay apparel." However, the situation in Honolulu during this period cannot be taken as representative of all Hawaii. Early sources indicate that older women in any case did most of the tapa making. While numbers of young women were consorting with foreigners in the ports, older Hawaiian women in the backs of the valleys and in rural districts were still beating tapa through the period of the Māhele.

Money

Like the distribution of foreign cloth, the circulation of money indexes the intrusion of the market economy into the lives of ordinary Hawaiians. By both measures, most commoners (and certainly those living in districts remote from the ports) had little direct contact with the market up to the time of the Māhele. According to the missionary censuses (Schmitt 1968:42), only about a quarter of the Hawaiian population resided on O'ahu in the 1830s. Judging from ethnohistorical estimates, Hawai'i was the population center of the archipelago well into the 1800s, but foreign trade was largely restricted to the Kona-Kohala coast. In the 1840s Hawai'i lost people while O'ahu's population remained more or less stable (Schmitt 1968:42), a trend that augurs the incipient decline of native agriculture and Hawaiians' increasing participation in the money economy.

Morgan (1948:104) concluded that through the sandalwood period "and into the forties the amount of cash that got into the hands of the commoners were negligible." In the provisions trade of the early 1800s the chiefs increasingly demanded money from foreigners (Freycinet 1978:32, 88; Hammatt ms.), much to the chagrin of the traders. Some of the chiefs' luxury-item purchases were paid for with cash, but both chiefs and commoners seemed to prefer hoarding money to spending it (Campbell 1967:144; Dampier 1971:47). Prices for supplies in the Honolulu market were set in dollars, but most transactions were conducted in kind (Freycinet 1978:88; Hunnewell 1909:16; cf. Morgan 1948:106–7). The Constitution of 1840 recommended tax payment in money, but set equivalencies in kukui nuts, arrowroot, turmeric, pigs, and fish (Hawaii 1894:68–69).

Missionary reports and journals graphically detail the scarcity of money outside the ports. Contributions to the mission stations were predominantly in kind through the 1840s, and the missionaries, having meager cash resources of their own, paid for the Hawaiians' labor in goods. Samuel Whitney's 1823 station report for Waimea, Kaua'i, listed his expenditures for labor and provisions as knives, *pā'ū, malo,* and fishhooks. Lorenzo Lyons's reports for Waimea, Hawai'i, are particularly revealing (Doyle 1953; typescripts in HMCS). Lyons consistently praised the generosity of his flock, but noted: "These people have no money to contribute. . . . Money is very seldom seen, and the contributions they make consist principally in labor . . . cane, potatoes, *kapas, malos, kiheis, paus,* etc. . . . The people give of such things as they have" (letter of 1837, in Doyle 1953:100). Even in 1850, most of the contributions were donations of food and tapa for the missionary's support, although Lyons received one purse containing fifteen dollars (Doyle 1953:157). In Waialua, on O'ahu's north shore, the missionary Emerson paid for labor and supplies with Western cloth in the 1830s and 1840s (letters, HMCS), but by 1846 the Hawaiians were demanding money (letter of August 4, 1846, HMCS).

In 1844 the Hawaiian foreign minister Wyllie estimated the currency in circulation in the port of Hilo, Hawai'i, at only a few hundred dollars, compared to a trade volume valued around $12,000, the exchange conducted "chiefly, of course, by barter" (Wyllie 1844, December). For Kealakekua, he estimated less than $1,000 in circulation, with an annual consumption of foreign goods worth $4,000. The comparable figures for Kaua'i were $5,000 and $20,000. Citing market prices, Wyllie explained: "The above prices are mostly those given in trade or barter; for cash they are much lower." Wyllie's comment points to the divergence of interests between Hawaiians and foreign traders, and suggests that the two parties were continually jockeying for advantage in commerce.

The limited circulation of cash, particularly among the commoners, was not simply an accidental side effect of restricted access to markets. Clearly, keeping transactions with Hawaiians on an in-kind basis was to the advantage of the foreign traders. The Hawaiians initially had no experience by which to judge the monetary value of the things they received. Traders, merchants, and employers, adhering to the Western mercantile ethic of caveat emptor, paid in goods of highly inflated value whenever possible. Wyllie noted: "Except in this and other villages, where foreigners create a demand for domestic service and other particular classes of labor . . . , the daily wage of the natives does not average more than 12 and a half cents *per diem;* and this . . . is paid not in cash, but in goods, given to the natives at a profit to the employer of perhaps

100 per cent" (Wyllie 1844, July). Because of their unfamiliarity with market mechanisms and ethics, the Hawaiians were consistently at a disadvantage in transactions with foreigners, but they were not hapless dupes. That the Hawaiians came to prefer monetary payment and would even lower their prices to obtain it suggests a growing trading acumen, a recognition that cash had a more predictable exchange value than Western goods.

The Late Provisions Market

Producing for an external market invariably distorted and constrained the local economy. Unpredictable shortfalls of subsistence staples arose as cultivators channeled their efforts into cash cropping. Some left the land to become wage laborers or peddlers in the city, where they had to buy the essentials they once produced themselves. At the time of the *Blonde's* visit in the mid-1820s, for example, coconut, breadfruit, and bananas were scarce in Honolulu and had to be brought in from other parts of the island for sale (Bloxam 1925:33). Western contact fostered dependency, a narrowing of alternatives, and a loss of local self-sufficiency. Production became less diverse as imported goods supplanted indigenous equivalents. Fluctuations in external demand seemed arbitrary from the local perspective. And when markets crashed, small-scale producers found themselves caught between two economies, unable to support themselves in either. This was largely the story of Hawaiian agriculture in the middle of the nineteenth century.

After the waning of the fur and sandalwood trades, whaling postponed economic disaster by maintaining a brisk demand for Hawaiian produce. During the 1820s and 1830s Honolulu became the principal stopping place for whalers in the north Pacific, and the necessity of supplying them was "the chief stimulus to mercantile activity" (Morgan 1948:81). The whaling boom in the Pacific began around 1820 with the discovery of the Japanese grounds. By 1823 forty to sixty whalers would lie together in Honolulu harbor at one time, thirty to fifty would visit Lāhaina annually, and between twelve and twenty would stop at other Hawaiian ports (Jarves 1843:331–32). Vendors operated a stationary public market in Honolulu in the early 1820s (Ellis 1969:410) and also sold their wares from house to house. A visitor in 1842 observed: "Early in the morning, a crowd of natives may be seen flocking into

Honolulu, all carrying something to sell . . . *kalo* and *poi,* and fruits and vegetables and milk and eggs," as well as fresh water, pigs, chickens, turkeys, mats, shells, and flower *lei* (Simpson 1847, 2:55). The 1847 New Year's edition of the *Friend* described five "thatched sheds" in Honolulu where one might find "in considerable abundance" a great variety of produce:

> Irish potatoes ($2 to $3 per bbl), sweet potatoes, kalo, Indian corn, cabbages, melons of various kinds, pumpkins, onions, bananas, plantains, beans . . . , capsicums, Chile peppers, tomatos, sallad [*sic*], oranges . . . limes, grapes, citrons, figs, guavas, ohia apples, eggs . . . and fish, both fresh and dried. Pigs, turkeys . . . ducks . . . fowls . . . are usually hawked about the streets. . . . Beef, mutton and goat are common. (cf. Wyllie 1844, September; and *Polynesian,* January 9, 1847.)

This list suggests that supplying shippers encouraged agricultural diversity (cf. Morgan 1948:152), but the dependence on foreign markets engendered a fatal vulnerability to variations in external demand.

Through the late 1830s and 1840s the Hawaiian economy was so intimately tied to the whaling trade that in monetary terms whaling "was as important as all other exports put together" (Morgan 1948:81). Between January, 1836, and August, 1841, the value of "sundries" provided (i.e., shippers' supplies) was three times that of the second-highest export, hides. Four-fifths of the vessels that stopped at Honolulu during this period were whalers, spending between $700 and $800 each (Jarves 1843:331–32; see also Barrot 1978:106–7; Paulding 1970:224–25, 232). Merchant ships also had to be supplied, but the timing and frequency of commercial visits were in turn linked to the whaling cycle (Morgan 1948:150). The whalers stopped at the islands on their way out in the spring, then cruised the Pacific for several months before returning in the fall (Morgan 1948:77). The summer interval saw an "almost absolute doldrum" in the Hawaiian economy (Varigny 1981:7). And despite the whaling trade, the Hawaiian balance of payments remained a disaster, with the value of imports exceeding exports by 400 to 500 percent (Jarves 1843:332).

During the heyday of north Pacific whaling Hawaiian agriculture intensified and diversified in areas with access to markets; the situation was of course different in more remote districts. The *Sandwich Island News* (March 10, 1847) aptly described the contrast:

The whole amount of agricultural production therefore, is by necessity confined to the suppliers of vegetables required by the foreigners who reside or touch at the principal ports, and is limited to the lands in the vicinity of those ports. The great mass of the population . . . cannot by possibility [*sic*] be benefitted by the results of such production.

According to Morgan (1948:140), the Hawaiian whaling trade was at its peak from 1843 to 1860. The provisions market began to collapse in 1858 and was dead by the early 1860s. But there had been earlier warnings of impending crisis in Hawaiian agriculture and in the economy as a whole. The California gold rush of 1848 gave a temporary boost to the Hawaiian market but even then the demand was fitful and there were doldrums in the midst of the boom. In July and August, 1848, the *Polynesian* enthusiastically predicted "a vast population will be suddenly thrown into California; the demand for Hawaiian produce will be greatly increased" (July 22; see also July 15 and August 12). Many of Honolulu's more footloose foreign residents shipped off to make their fortunes. The *Polynesian* reported on October 7, 1848, that "every store in the place, wholesale and retail, is entirely stripped of goods adapted to the California market." But the boom was short-lived, lasting only a few years. California quickly became a net exporter, and Hawaiian imports could not compete in cost with supplies produced in the American mainland (Varigny 1981:6–7, 105).

In July of 1849 the *Polynesian* gloomily reported "such a depression we do not recollect for years": "Business appears to be at a dead stand . . . No ships in, to circulate money; no lumber, for carpenters to work up . . . We look for whale-ships every day, now; and expect a fair fall business for Honolulu" (July 28). According to Varigny, the Hawaiian economy in the 1850s was in a state of "stagnation" but for the visits of whalers. Letters from prominent residents to American consul Joel Turrill (1957) attest that business in Honolulu in the early 1850s was, as W. L. Lee wrote, "utterly prostrate." Late in 1851 C. R. Bishop wrote that because of an unusually small whaling fleet, the market was depressed and "overflowing with goods" (Turrill 1957:48). Lee commented that "there is no cash in town to buy with" and, "when California revives, we shall revive" (Turrill 1957:54). Indeed, 1849 saw a great potato boom in rural Waimea District, Hawai'i. The missionary Lyons excitedly reported in his journal: "Large quantities of sweet potatoes brought to light . . . growing wild for years unknown. . . . Some never had so much cash before—never had any before! Many natives growing rich" (Doyle 1953:153).

The market for provisions encouraged at least some commoners to remain on the land as cultivators and postponed the decline of subsistence agriculture for a time. But when the shipping market evaporated a few years after the Great Māhele, Hawaiians saw their income from the land dwindling precisely at a time of increasing mobility. Morgan (1948:153) has aptly summarized the effect of the collapsing provisions market on small cultivators: "with cattle and staple products comparatively worthless, a large part of agriculture was in an uncertain state of transision . . . with the passing of whaling went the last effective impulse toward general farming." The demise of the shipping trade, coupled with the granting of private land titles, set the stage for the rise of foreign-owned plantations in the latter half of the century.

Wage Labor

Hawaiians first engaged with the market economy as purveyors of supplies, and only later, when the ports presented alternatives to working the land under the chiefs, did they become workers. The chronology of wage labor in Hawaii is intrinsically linked to emigration and land alienation (see chapter 7, where I relate these processes to women's jural and kin roles in the local group). Proletarianization necessarily proceeded slowly as long as most commoners remained on the land.

Like the provisions market, wage labor developed to meet a foreign demand and was centered in Honolulu and Lāhaina. The first Hawaiian "mechanics" were trained by foreigners in the chiefs' employ (Morgan 1948:80). Kamehameha's retinue included "a considerable number" of such skilled tradesmen (Campbell 1967:166–67). From the 1820s on, the lure of wages—although usually paid in kind (Wyllie 1844:63)—drew commoners weary of onerous taxation to leave the land. The missionary Elias Bond described emigration from Kohala during the 1840s: "We were steadily losing our people. Every schooner went crowded to Honolulu and very few ever returned therefrom. . . . the crowning attraction was . . . the fact that there labor was in demand at remunerative wages as it could not be in these outlying districts" (in Damon 1927:172). By the mid-1840s a class of landless Hawaiian laborers had arisen in Honolulu. Although Hawaiians were paid less than half of what haoles earned for the same work—about a dollar a day in 1847 (*Polynesian* January 9)—they could earn from fifty to two hundred dollars a year in the ports and, significantly, "since they held no lands they were excused from the land and labor taxes" (Morgan 1948:114).

In 1847 the *Polynesian* (January 9) reported about 60 Hawaiian "mechanics" in Honolulu and 150 foreign tradesmen ("mechanics" refers here to skilled workers and craftsmen; unskilled laborers are not counted in this total and were undoubtedly far more numerous; see Schmitt 1968:77). Among the occupations listed most frequently for Hawaiians are "tailor," at 19, and "carpenter," at 12. The other trades practiced by Hawaiians, in order of frequency, are bookbinder, shoemaker, printer, mason, engraver, and blacksmith. Hawaiian women in the cities worked as "nurses, houseservants, washerwomen, serving-women" and earned from one to ten dollars a week, about half of men's usual wages (Bates 1854:79), although domestic servants also received clothing and room and board. Hawaiian men and women also worked on the sugar plantations from their inception in the 1830s. The numerical domination of Asian workers after 1880 has often served to obscure the fact that, despite their alleged recalcitrance as laborers, Hawaiians were the bulwark of the early plantation work force. In 1873 more than half the Hawaiian male population was engaged in sugar cultivation (Kuykendall 1953:178). Asian contract laborers were imported primarily because introduced diseases had decimated the Hawaiian population and the native labor supply simply could not keep up with the industry's growth.

Ladd and Co.'s Kōloa plantation, founded in 1835, was the prototype of the self-contained sugar community, and established the paternalistic model that came to dominate relations between planters and workers (see Takaki 1983:6–10). The experience of the Hawaiians who came to Kōloa poignantly encapsulates the historical process of proletarianization in Hawaii and in many other colonized societies as well. To many Hawaiian commoners in the 1830s and 1840s, working for the foreigners' wages seemed a better lot than toiling to meet the chiefs' ever-increasing demands: Kōloa's workers had their taxes paid for them, and though at first the workers received their wages through the chiefs, a sudden strike (the first sugar strike in Hawaii) forced the manager to pay them directly. Kōloa employed a hundred Hawaiians in 1838, among them Hawaiian women who worked at stripping the cane, grinding, and boiling (Takaki 1983:8). William Hooper, the plantation manager, esteemed them as workers but paid them half of what the men earned. Workers at Kōloa were paid in script, redeemable only for goods at the plantation store. Western clothing was one of the most popular purchases. Like American car and clothing manufacturers, Hooper learned to generate wants among the natives by continually bringing in new goods. Takaki (1983:7) insightfully summarizes this new relationship of dependency: "Hooper had created both a wage-earning labor force and a consumer class dependent on a plantation-owned market which had to expand consumer needs constantly."

Ironically, Kōloa was a financial failure. The ascendancy of sugar plantations did not come about until the 1860s and 1870s, particularly after the Reciprocity Treaty of 1875 dramatically boosted the industry's profitability. Earlier in the century the predominant form of Hawaiian wage labor was not work in the cities, but seafaring. In 1789 John Meares (1790, app. 2) recommended to Captain Colnett that "some of the natives of those isles, both men and women, may be embarked and transplanted to America, and made useful in our employ." Though there is little data on the number of Hawaiian women transported to the Northwest Coast (all the other sources I have encountered attest only that the fur and whaling trades took away large numbers of young Hawaiian men), one indicator of the number of seafaring women is given by the 1847 population of San Francisco, which included forty Hawaiians— thirty-nine men and one woman (Schmitt 1968:40). According to Campbell (1967:154), Kamehameha encouraged his subjects to ship on foreign vessels where their skills as seamen were in high demand. Mathison (1825:461) noted that Hawaiians often manned commercial square-riggers under English or American captains. Wyllie (1844, September) described native seamen as "eminently subordinate, docile, good natured and trustworthy," and whalers came to rely more and more on Honolulu for supplying crews.

The net demographic impact of Hawaiian seafaring is difficult to estimate. Honolulu and Lāhaina were the only ports at which native seamen could legally be recruited, but some embarked from other places "in violation of the laws" (*Polynesian* May 29, 1847). Numerical reports vary widely and it is impossible to determine accurately the percentage of Hawaiian men involved, much less ascertain how many of them returned or emigrated permanently (Schmitt 1968:39–40). Wyllie (1844, September) felt that the number was so significant "as to be considered . . . one of the causes of the depopulation of the islands" (cf.

Varigny 1981:133). Morgan (1948:148) estimated that in 1845 Hawaiians made up more than 5 percent of the men engaged in North Pacific whaling, or about 700 seamen. For the year 1843, Wyllie reported that 550 Hawaiian men were serving aboard ships; added to the 300–400 Hawaiians working on the Columbia River as "boatmen, laborers, millmen, cooks, miners" (Blue 1925:20), this would mean that 900 Hawaiians were absent during the year. The *Friend,* however, suggested a vastly greater number than reported in the official sources: 4,000 native seamen "annually afloat" in 1849 (November 15, 1849). If correct, this would equal 5 percent of the total native population in 1850 and 17 percent of males aged between 18 and 53 (Schmitt 1968:39, 43). Whatever the most accurate figure may be, foreign shipping must be considered a significant stimulus to the mobility of Hawaiian men, particularly after the collapse of the agricultural market in 1859. Mark Twain's (1939:63) observations in a letter of 1866 indicate that, in the aftermath of the Māhele, Hawaiian mobility continued to be seen as an impediment to capitalist development:

> In Honolulu it is not a holiday job to ship a crew; natives comprise it chiefly, and the Government frowns upon their employment as sailors, because it causes the agricultural interests to suffer for want of labor, and you see the plantations build up the whole kingdom, while the whaling trade only builds up Honolulu. . . . The bond system, which was intended to keep the kanakas all at home, don't work; the whalers still are obliged to take natives or go without crews.

Given Western normative premises about women's proper roles, it seems logical that proletarianization would create more opportunities for Hawaiian men than for women. Yet putting this supposition to a test is difficult, for we lack occupational data by gender for the first half of the nineteenth century (see Schmitt 1968:77). As noted above, several kinds of service jobs were open to Hawaiian women in the cities, although men dominated the skilled trades and seafaring. And there were other inducements drawing women to the ports: as labor became a marketable commodity in Hawaii, so did the sexual services of Hawaiian women. This later emergence of prostitution must be distinguished from Hawaiian women's sexual advances toward the first Western visitors, many of whom interpreted such behavior as prostitution. Hawaiian women sought and received material rewards for their favors in those early encounters, but they did not necessarily view such exchanges as the commodification of their bodies. Sexuality for Hawaiians was always potentially an instrumental pleasure (Sahlins 1985, chap. 1). If Hawaiian women's seduction of haole voyagers is culturally sensible as marrying up or *'imi haku,* then the giving of gifts may well have been expected, just as chiefs lying with commoner women in the bush might give material tokens of the union (as in the story of 'Umi related in chapter 2). But by the 1840s Hawaiian women seem to have arrived at a different interpretation of short-term sexual exchanges with foreigners, one that more closely approaches the Western definition of prostitution:

> All the women come to Lahaina for it. Some put to them the question, What brings you here? They reply, we came to sell. —What have you to sell? They reply, We sell ourselves. . . . Not a native vessel comes into this harbor . . . that is not crowded with native women from the other islands, so that hundreds and thousands are semi-annually gathered into these places by government helps. . . . After a few weeks . . . they are carried back . . . their persons all filled with diseases. (*Sandwich Island News,* March 10, 1847)

Once again, there is little evidence by which to gauge the social and demographic effects of these short-term movements on the local level. The Hawaiian economy, when it was geared to commoner subsistence and chiefly tribute, had a built-in tolerance for the Hawaiians' wandering tendencies. Periodic short-term absences, particularly of young people, were expected and caused no social disruption, and such cultural attitudes toward mobility are not easily eradicated. Since cultivation was primarily men's work, however, the long-term absences of young men at sea may have been felt more sharply in the *ahupua'a* as those who remained behind were called upon to do more work. Women, no longer engaged in producing cloth, would have increasingly gone into the taro patches. During this period, if not earlier, the movements of people mandated flexibility in the agricultural division of labor.

Conclusion

Having traced Hawaii's early linkage to the capitalist world system and weighed the particular implications of that linkage for Hawaiians—chiefly and common, male and female—two salient points emerge. First, the market's penetration into the local level was quite variable until midcentury. Most Hawaiians were able to participate selectively in the market economy, while residents of *ahupua'a* outside the ports remained largely autonomous. Production for use and in-kind exchanges predominated. Analyzing the 1866 census, Andrew Lind (1980) estimates that "well over half of the natives were still living under a predominately subsistence economy" even a decade after the Māhele. Even if external market conditions suddenly altered, Hawaiians on the land would not starve or be dispossessed, for as long as they performed their work for the chiefs and could pay taxes in kind, Hawaiians could remain largely insulated from market economy. In other words, no irrevocable dependency had as yet developed. Ironically, the extent of Hawaiian land alienation after the Māhele reveals that the commoners were actually more secure in their tenure as tenants under the chiefs than they were as private owners of small holdings.

The second point concerns the impact of Western goods and markets on Hawaiian women. Clearly, there is no simple or single "impact" on the status of Hawaiian women. We have instead a complex encounter where Hawaiian women entered into certain roles in accordance with their own interests and cultural premises, and where the Hawaiian valuation of women's activities appears to have differed significantly from the Western judgment. We cannot say simply that the market economy debased Hawaiian women differentially vis-à-vis men. There may have been more wage laboring jobs for men, but women also had a set of proletarian alternatives whereby they could selectively engage in the market economy for their own ends. Westerners viewed some of these alternatives as legitimate wage-earning jobs and others as prostitution (Ralston 1988; n.d.1).

We cannot say definitively, of course, how the Hawaiians viewed the women who flocked to the ports. Assuredly there were devoted Christians, like David Malo, who condemned them on moral grounds. There must also have been those who could foresee the terrible consequences of the diseases they spread. But those women—young women, for the most part—also returned to their families with money and Western goods in a time when many Hawaiians had come to need and want those things (cf. Ralston n.d.1). Reports of early voyagers (see Colcord ms.) suggest that Hawaiians welcomed liaisons with foreigners for this, among other reasons. When tax payments had to be made in currency (see chap. 7), the monetary contributions of women would have been essential to the viability of the household. Analysis of Hawaiian women's general social valuation in the early postcontact period is further complicated, of course, by their role in land and familial relations, to which I turn in the next chapter as I draw together the themes of earlier chapters— symbolism, productivity, authority, kinship, household structure, and economic transformation—under the theme of women and land.

Chapter 7

Women and Land

Between 1778 and 1850, as the internal dynamic of chiefly conquest politics interacted with foreign plans, motivations, and models, the Hawaiian polity was transformed. The commoners, I would argue, experienced the difference between chiefdom and monarchy as one of degree rather than of kind—more was exacted, even intolerably more, but taxation by the king and government officials was understood on the model of chiefly tribute. Until the middle of the nineteenth century a two-tiered economy persisted, and for most ordinary Hawaiians living in rural and out-island districts, the market remained a remote and little understood institution until certain governmental measures conjoined with economic events to irrevocably alter the commoners' destiny. As we will see, many factors were at work in the disruption of local Hawaiian communities, but with its legacy of dispossession, the most sweeping institutional change of this period was the Māhele.

Women in the Māhele

In chapter 1 I documented a statistical phenomenon: a shift in Hawaiian land transmission patterns in which women came to inherit land (see tables 1 and 2). The trend is noticeable in the first half of the nineteenth century but becomes particularly dramatic during the period of the Māhele. The land division did not in itself cause an increase in female inheritance, but it did create an imperative for someone in the family to come forward as the *haku 'āina*. In the changed social and economic context of midcentury Hawaii, women increasingly came forward to fill this role. If, as is conventional in anthropology, control over land may be taken as an index of jural authority, the statistics point to expanding jural authority on the part of women. Paradoxically, this development occurred during the very period when Western-authored civil restrictions were attempting to disempower women at the national level.

As shown in table 7, the vast majority of the claims in my sample (93.4 percent) were filed by commoner Hawaiians, most of whom were male (table 8). Table 9 shows how many of these claims resulted in Land Commission awards. If we accept W. D. Alexander's (1890:110) figure of 11,309 claims "confirmed" or awarded, the ratio for all Māhele claims would be approximately 84 percent, a figure consistent with my sample analysis of 4,445 Māhele claims. These claims, however, were not randomly selected. In Marshall Sahlins's original research particular land sections were chosen for the quality and quantity of archival materials likely to be available for them. The island of O'ahu and wetland taro-growing areas are therefore overrepresented, but to some extent this bias is inherent in the Māhele corpus, for O'ahu saw a substantial immigration from the outer islands with Kamehameha's military occupation

TABLE 7. Social Standing of Claimants

Claimant's Status	N	%
Maka'āinana (commoner)	4,153	93.4
Konohiki	113	2.5
Ali'i (chief)	79	1.8
Haole (foreigner)	79	1.8
Luna	21	0.5
Total	4,445	

TABLE 8. Gender of Claimants

Claimant's Gender	N	% of Known Gender
Female	206	7.6
Male	2,524	92.4
Unknown	1,715	
Total	4,445	

TABLE 9. Disposition of Claims

Disposition of Claim	N	%
Awarded	3,762	84.6
Not awarded	683	15.4
Total	4,445	

of 1804–12. By the late 1820s Honolulu had become the political and commercial center of the islands, a hub where many chiefs sought land and where many chiefly followers were settled.

Table 10 reveals a significant gender contrast between familial inheritance and land giving by political superiors during the first half of the nineteenth century. The trend for women to be given authority over land is markedly absent in land giving from unrelated donors. In other words, at least from the 1830s on women were much less likely to receive land from chiefs and *konohiki* than from family members, even though many of the prominent land-giving chiefs on Oʻahu during the 1820s and 1830s were women. I suggest that this divergence reflects largely, but not entirely, the postcontact influence of white European and American men on Hawaiian politics and jural attitudes (see Gething 1977; Silverman 1982). In a review of postcontact changes in the legal status of Hawaiian women, Gething (1977:203) has shown "how rapidly the New England view had come to dominate family law" in the kingdom. An 1845 law established coverture, the civil merging of a married woman with her husband whereby she became "civilly dead," without the right to "alienate or dispose of property" (Hawaii 1846:59). A single woman retained the right to buy and sell property and to make contracts. Gailey (1987:186–91) details similar attempts to institutionalize Western gender norms in Tonga.

But the question remains whether these legal disabilities were enforced on the local level, especially since they conflict so markedly with the political influence and active ethos of Hawaiian women as described in chapters 2 and 3. Irene Silverblatt (1987:119–24) notes analogous contradictions between indigenous gender relations and Western imposed law in colonial Peru. In the Andean case, indigenous women were able to manipulate the law to some degree to maintain their land rights

TABLE 10.   Time of Land Receipt by Gender of Recipient, Unrelated Donors Only

| Time of Receipt | Female | | Male | | Total |
	N	%	N	%	N
Before 1820	18	6.6	256	93.4	274
1820–29	22	5.5	380	94.5	402
1830–39	26	3.7	684	96.3	710
1840–47	17	2.9	580	97.1	597
1848–55	3	5.6	51	94.4	54
Total	86		1,951		2,037

at the local level. A striking disjunction is evident between the formal legal status of Hawaiian women and their frequent capacity as household authorities and landholders at the time of the Māhele. Were women discouraged from filing claims before the Land Commission as a result of the coverture law? The preponderance of male claimants suggests so, but in reading nearly five thousand land claims and hundreds of associated archival documents I have found no direct evidence to that effect.

The 1850 Privy Council discussions (minutes in AH) on the subject of sales of government lands may be revealing on this score. Inquiries revolved around whether the land was already allocated to someone else and whether the applicant was offering enough money. There were several female applicants, but their marital status was not questioned. Of the 206 claims in my sample that were filed by women (table 8), 28 are claims of female chiefs, most of whom had husbands at the time of the Māhele. By custom civil restrictions would in any case have weighed lightly on *ali'i* women (see chap. 2). But of the commoner women claimants, it can be established that at least several were married at the time the claim was filed. A more precise statement is difficult because a woman's marital status is not normally mentioned in the testimony and must be determined for each individual case by research in other sources.

At any rate, there was an overall tendency to disenfranchise female claimants during the Māhele (table 11). There is a statistical association between gender and disposition of award such that women were more likely than men to have their claims disallowed. Women filed 7.5 percent of the claims in the sample but composed 12.4 percent of the nonawards. Closer examination of cases where a woman's tenure was disputed reveals that widowhood was frequently the issue. *Konohiki* often objected if a widow did not remarry and no adult male was present to do the chiefs' labor and help meet tax obligations. (Incidentally, such disputes

TABLE 11. Disposition of Claim by Gender of Claimant

Disposition of Claim	Female		Male		Total
	N	%	N	%	N
Awarded	165	6.9	2,234	93.1	2,399
Not awarded	41	12.4	290	87.6	331
Total	206		2,524		2,730

Note: Chi-square = 12.653, degrees of freedom = 1, probability = 0.0004, phi = −0.068

tend to corroborate the conclusion that men did most of the agricultural labor in Hawaiian society.)

The preponderance of male claimants in the Māhele is certainly not wholly the effect of introduced concepts and constraints. As the gender statistics in tables 1 and 12 indicate, there is a male bias in Hawaiian succession just as there is in cognate Polynesian societies. If the statistics indicated a shift from patrilineal to matrilineal inheritance, the Hawaiian case would present a neat anthropological example, but tables 12 and 13 reveal that the situation is not so simple. As indicated by the low frequency of bequests from mother and sister before 1848, the older inheritance pattern is not bilateral (table 12). Before 1848 there is a clear preference for males to inherit, and men usually receive land from their

TABLE 12.   **Donor Relationship by Time of Receipt, Combined Male and Female Heirs**

Donor Relationship	Before 1848		1848–55	
	N	%	N	%
Parents, ancestors, grandparents	234	55.3	8	3.3
Father, *makuakane*	97	22.9	85	35.0
Wife's relatives	25	5.9	10	4.1
Wife	19	4.5	5	2.1
Husband	19	4.5	97	39.9
Brother	15	3.5	16	6.6
Mother, *makuahine*	3	0.7	6	2.5
Sister	3	0.7	2	0.8
Child	2	0.5	4	1.6
Other relative	6	1.4	10	4.1
Total	423		243	

Note: N = 666. *Makuakane* can refer to any related male in the parental generation. Similarly, *makuahine* can mean Mo, MoSi, FaSi, or any related women in that generation.

TABLE 13.   **Donor Relationship by Time of Receipt, Female Heirs Only**

Donor Relationship	Before 1848		1848–55	
	N	%	N	%
Husband	19	48.7	97	69.3
Parents, ancestors	9	23.0	1	0.7
Father	8	20.5	32	22.9
Brother	1	2.6	6	4.3
Mother	1	2.6	2	1.4
Other relative	1	2.6	2	1.4
Total	39		140	

Note: N = 179.

father, parents, or ancestors, with about a 10 percent incidence of a man receiving land from his wife or wife's family. Characterizing Hawaiian land inheritance as patrilineal, however, would be inaccurate (cf. Gailey 1987:66 on Tonga), for by far the largest category of donors is that of parents (*mau mākua*) or ancestors (*nā kūpuna*)—and these are inherently bilateral concepts.

The breakdown of donors in table 13 shows that most of the increase in female inheritance at midcentury reflects widows receiving land from their husbands during a period of terrible depopulation. Transmission from husband to wife increases from 4.5 percent of all bequests before 1848 to 39.9 percent in 1848–55 (table 12), and fathers, brothers, and matrilateral relatives also increasingly leave their property to women during this period (table 13). These sorts of bequests occur in earlier years, but as distinctively minor patterns. During the mid-nineteenth century these secondary forms of inheritance became dominant. Another significant characteristic is the increase in donations from mother, brother, child, and "other relatives" (table 12). The latter category includes donors such as adoptive, distant collateral, and stipulated kin. In part because of recurrent, severe epidemics in the Māhele period—notably measles in 1848–49 and smallpox in 1853—approximately 10 percent of the people claiming land in 1848 had died by 1854, and in many cases their lands fell to individuals who would not normally have stood to inherit. The statistics indicate that many of the next-of-kin remaining on the land were women. In this chapter I will discuss why this was so.

In Pursuit of Taxes

Increased emigration from the land, both short- and long-term, was one immediate cause of an alteration in Hawaiian land transmission patterns, although emigration did not dictate the form of that change. From the earliest years of Western contact the money economy attracted Hawaiians to nonagricultural work (see chap. 6). Some left the land permanently for Honolulu, Lāhaina, or the sea. Yet Dampier (1971:38) noted in 1825 that Hawaiians in Honolulu still subsisted "almost entirely" on the taro and fish that they produced at home. Visiting in 1836, Barrot (1978:108) described the commoners' life-style as little changed from precontact times except for a "much higher rent to pay the chiefs." The ordinary Hawaiian's production efforts were still geared primarily to domestic needs, with the addition of "some fowls and hogs, which he sells to the ships . . . with the proceeds of these sales he pays his tax to the king, and procures for himself cloth and ardent spirits."

Four statutes enacted in 1850 forever ended the economic isolation of rural subsistence communities and further stimulated emigration, which had been recognized as a worsening problem since the 1830s. The Kuleana Act resolved the question of "the rights of native tenants" in the Māhele and made it possible for commoners to be awarded their lands in fee simple (Hawaii 1850:202–4). Another 1850 law gave foreigners the right to own land in the kingdom (Hawaii 1850:146–47). Thus commoners were enabled to sell their lands at precisely the time that foreigners were given the right to buy them. Two other statutes had the effect of driving commoners into the cash economy. One opened the ports of Hilo, Kawaihae, and Kealakekua on Hawai'i to foreign commerce, previously restricted to Honolulu and Lāhaina (Hawaii 1850:159–60). Fee collectors and port regulations were established for these towns the same as in Honolulu. The second statute, even more fateful for Hawaiians in remote areas, was the law abolishing the payment of taxes in kind and requiring Hawaiians to remit all taxes in "current coin of this kingdom" (Hawaii 1850:168–69). Land taxes had been payable only in currency since 1846 (Hawaii 1846:165). The combined effect of these laws was to make it impossible for commoners to subsist on the land without participating in the market economy, either through produce sales, cash cropping, or wage labor.

The escalating tax demands of the 1830s and 1840s had already induced some Hawaiians to leave rural *ahupua'a* for the ports. Elias Bond (in Damon 1927:172) described emigration from Kohala in the early 1840s: "we were steadily losing our people. Every schooner went crowded to Honolulu and very few ever returned therefrom. . . . the crowning attraction was found in the fact that there labor was in demand at remunerative wages as it could not be in these outlying districts." The missionary Lorenzo Lyons recounted how the chiefs and *konohiki* found ever more creative ways to tax the people while the local population dwindled. In 1832 commoners in Waimea worked four half-days a week for their various political overlords (cf. Barrot 1978:104–5): "Tuesday is for the king, Wednesday for the Governor, Thursday for the head people, and Saturday for the konohiki. . . . The women are excluded. They make tax mats, kapa" (Doyle 1953:65). In their turn the commoners devised means of passive resistance, as reported by the missionary Seth Andrews of Kailua ("Answers to Questions," July 8, 1846, F.O. & Ex.):

> I have thought that this kind of labor might have a tendency to encourage a habit of unfaithfulness in the laboring class. For six days each month they make a pretence of laboring. . . . On such days I believe they spend much time in idleness, and make the work as light as possible. For instance, I have seen a company engaged in carrying sand on the labor day of their landlord. A strong able bodied man would go with a small calabash or a fragment of one carrying a pint, or a quart at once. After such an exertion he would of course expect to take an ample resting season. Such I believe to be the character of the exertions put forth on labor days.

Lyons also describes the bizarre "Lualimalima system," whereby commoners received redistributions of foods they themselves had produced on their workdays for the chiefs, and then had to pay taxes on the "gift": "for everyone that receives, a tax of perhaps a kapa or something as valuable is levied. The one who refuses is fined. For instance, a hog is divided into several small pieces and sent to different individuals in the district as a gift. Then in return the receiver has a heavy tax to pay" (Doyle 1953:65). In 1849 the king, as "owner" of Waimea district, added a levy on every head of livestock pastured on his lands. Lyons commented: "At this new regulation the people grown [*sic*]—but it will wake them to buy land for themselves" (Doyle 1953:153).

Besides the labor tax, Hawaiians were subject to land and poll taxes. In 1841 an adult man was assessed seventy-five cents, a woman half of that, a boy over the age of fourteen half of a woman's tax, and a girl over fourteen half of the boy's amount (Richards 1973:26). Exempt were the old and sick, school teachers, and students unless they held land. Fathers were progressively relieved of tax obligations if they had three or more children; six children meant an exemption from all taxes (Richards 1973:27). Any of the taxes could be commuted for money—twenty-five cents for a day's labor in 1839 (*Hawaiian Spectator,* July). Richards estimated the annual tax burden on a family as about $11.30: $9 paid in labor, $1 in produce, and $1.30 in cash.

As stated earlier, most taxes could be paid in kind through the 1840s. Little currency was in circulation outside the ports. The laws of 1840 and 1841 recommended payment in money but set cash equivalents for locally available produce such as arrowroot, cotton, turmeric, fishnets, hogs, and fish (see Richards 1973:24–26). In spite of the various taxes on the people, most government revenues came from shipping dues and, until 1840, a 50 percent levy on produce brought to the Honolulu market (Morgan 1948:108–9; Richards 1973:25). Writing in 1841, Richards (1973:27) noted that not more than a sixth of the anticipated revenues were actually collected—about $50,000, of which the king received $14,000 annually. Richards reported that most of the land tax was remitted in hogs, "which can be turned to very little amount as there is no significant market for the pork." Richards's comments reveal the rationale for abolishing payment in kind: "The defect in the system therefore is very manifest, and is discovered by the chiefs, and they design to change it as rapidly as possible. The want of a circulating medium, and of those productions which can be at once made available in the market, are the obstacles in the way."

The laws of 1846 required monetary payment of the land tax, and some local chiefs were already independently demanding other payments in cash. As early as 1839 David Malo (1839:127) related the growing rootlessness of the Hawaiian people to oppressive taxation: "some are driven from their lands for the want of money. . . . the property of the people is sold at a sacrifice that they gain their tax-money and save their lands." Resident missionaries such as Elias Bond, Lorenzo Lyons, and John Paris have left moving testaments to the profoundly disruptive effects of taxation. Bond's district of Kohala, Hawai'i, exemplifies the plight of the *kua'āina,* the 'back land' regions where cash was scarce:

> There was none of the latter in the district. Barter was the only form of trade. There were no employers wanting work done and of course nothing to be earned by bodily labor. All our supplies we purchased with cloth, cotton handkerchiefs and other articles in trade. (Damon 1927:75)

In 1846 Bond recorded cash contributions to the church from sales of livestock and produce, but noted that transporting the goods to market entailed considerable loss "owing to the remoteness of our station" (Damon 1927:134). In a letter of April, 1844, he lamented:

> The people are, in the largest meaning of the word, *poor.* No *money* is in circulation, and our remoteness from any market, of any kind, is painful assurance that we can get none. Our people can get timber, prepare the

ground, and thatch the building. But *money* they cannot get. (Damon 1927:125)

John Paris's station reports from Ka'ū, perhaps the most remote district of Hawai'i, are equally plaintive on the subject of taxation. In Ka'ū tax payments in kind were ended in 1846, and Paris cited the change as an immediate impetus to local depopulation:

> They require that all taxes be paid in Silver & gold & nothing else. But there is no silver in Kau. . . . The soil is good but it is not adapted for the cultivation of silver and gold. Consequently all our able-bodied men have gone money hunting—Some with their whole families & not a few of them have taken up their abode in the Cities of dollars and cents. If the people are compelled to pay their taxes in money only, I am satisfied it will be the cause of draining Kau of its inhabitants. (Station Report of 1846, HMCS)

Though their tax burden progressively worsened in the 1830s and 1840s, most rural Hawaiians engaged little with the market economy as long as they could pay their taxes in locally available products. Those who stayed on the land appear to have lived much as they had always done. The 1850 tax law was unavoidably a spur to emigration and land abandonment. Describing the isolation of "the great mass of the population" from markets, the *Sandwich Island News* (March 10, 1847) specifically attributed the growth of prostitution in the ports to the necessity of procuring tax money: "remote districts . . . are, consequently . . . obliged to send off the largest part of the female population, to the towns where foreign ships resort, in order to obtain the means of paying their taxes, which are exacted of them equally as of those who raise potatoes and squash." As emigration came to be perceived as a problem in the 1840s, foreign residents and missionaries pressed for the establishment of individual land titles, arguing that private property would result in pride of ownership and would motivate commoners to remain on the land: "The people must become proprietors of the soil. . . . Men and women, in these circumstances, would stay at home, instead of gadding about, as they now do, from place to place, and from one island to another" (letter to the *Polynesian*, June 2, 1849). In retrospect it is ironic that emigration was thus used as a justification for the individualization of title, for the land division was perhaps the single event most responsible for Hawaiian land abandonment.

Leaving the Land

The latter half of the nineteenth century probably witnessed the most extensive land alienation in Hawaiian history. Land abandonment and dispossession were fostered both by circumstances external to the Māhele and by the way the land division was implemented. In the face of oppressive taxation the ports lured many with the promise of cash wages and relative freedom from the chiefs. Epidemics, market instability, uncertainty over land tenure, and threats to small-scale agriculture were not new at midcentury, but these conditions intensified during the Māhele. Working in conjunction with the effects of establishing individual land titles, these exigencies ultimately created a landless people. It is during this period of accelerated land alienation that women increasingly came to hold family property. In order to understand landholding by women as an attempt to preserve a family's legacy, we must examine this historical context in greater detail.

By the time of the Māhele subsistence agriculture was at risk in many localities, due in large part to the ravages of roaming livestock. Cattle were introduced to Hawai'i by Vancouver in 1794 and made *kapu* by Kamehameha (Vancouver 1798, 3:53; Kuykendall 1938:40–44). Left unmolested, the cattle multiplied and were taken to the other islands, where they became a destructive menace to small holders, though the chiefs derived "no inconsiderable revenue" from sales of their products (*Sandwich Islands Gazette,* September 17, 1836). Both Campbell (1967:118) and Kotzebue (1821, 1:333) remarked on the rapid increase of wild cattle on O'ahu, "the fences not being sufficient to confine them" as Campbell noted. The worsening problem was recognized in the 1840 Constitution (Hawaii 1894:74–78), which imposed fines for unfenced livestock in a "Law Respecting Mischievous Beasts." In Waimea in the 1820s cattle were hunted or caught in pits ("bullock traps") for their meat, which was packed in salt and shipped to Honolulu from Kawaihae (Doyle 1953:45, 53; see also Kuykendall 1938:317–18). The king commandeered the commoners' labor to transport the beef, hides, and horns to the shore for loading onto his ships (Doyle 1953:63). Despite this harvest, the swelling herds made small-scale agriculture in Waimea nearly impossible. As a letter to the *Polynesian* (August 26, 1848) complained:

> the native population of Waimea has decreased to almost nothing. Agriculture, with the exception of Macey's sugar plantation, has entirely vanished from the district, which is supplied with vegetable food from Waipio and Kohala, and in itself, is what Mr. Lyons aptly calls one great cattle pen.

As described earlier, the Hawaiian subsistence economy depended not only on extensive irrigation agriculture but also on foraging and scattered cultivation in the uplands and forests. Before the Māhele the uplands and open, unirrigated *kula* lands of the *ahupuaʻa* were effectively common lands, although they were perceived as belonging to the chief or *konohiki*. Commoners could not, for example, erect fences or buildings on such lands, though they could go there freely to gather such things as firewood, house thatch and *olonā* for fishnets or to plant scattered cultigens. In the first half of the nineteenth century the utilization of *kula* lands was transformed as both foreigners and Hawaiians came to use open tracts for pasturing livestock. By the 1840s a commoner landholder typically owned a horse or a mule and a cow or two, as well as pigs and goats. The larger animals were branded with the owner's mark; each brand had to be registered with the government for a fee, and registering the brands was an important enough activity to occupy the Governor of Oʻahu (P. J. Gulick to R. Anderson, December 25, 1846, HMCS).

The threat to local agriculture came not only from wild cattle but also from livestock owned by foreigners, many of whom had acquired large upland tracts from the chiefs or the government. Lyons (Doyle 1953: 124) noted that Hawaiians did not normally enclose their cultivated plots. Waimea residents were thus "driven to the mountains to cultivate secure from cattle" (Doyle 1953:139). Even before the Māhele there were attempts by chiefs and foreigners to reserve the uplands and *kula* for their own use. Lyons's journal for 1847 records that two-thirds of Waimea was precipitously converted into government pasture land, dispossessing people from their cultivated fields and further exposing them to depredations by cattle. Commoners on the leeward side of Oʻahu were told, before the passage of the Kuleana Act, that they were to lose their customary gathering rights:

The word has gone forth from the chiefs to all their konohikis to forbid all such makaainanas who get their land titles, the privileges they formerly enjoyed from the kula of the landlord. . . . They are not to pull grass for their feasts or ilima for fuel, nor go into the mountain for any ki leaf or ki root or timber of any kind. Their horned cattle are prohibited from ranging in the kula. . . . It has nearly raised a rebellion among the people of Waianae . . . they say the chiefs have no [aloha] for them. (A. Bishop to R. Armstrong, April 30, 1850, Interior Department Lands File, AH)

Most chiefly and foreign landlords appear to have cared little for the people's *kuleana* and made no effort to fence in their animals. Māhele testimony from the north and windward shores of Oʻahu yields numerous accounts of marauding cattle and horses. In 1835 sixty Hawaiians in Waialua created a large "collective enclosure" where potatoes and melons could be grown securely (FT 11:448; J. S. Emerson, Report on Waialua Station, 1835, HMCS). In Hauʻula, on the windward side, several claimants describe coffee trees flattened and *kula* lands abandoned by their holders because of repeated crop destruction (LCA 8271, 8341, 8414, 8418). By traditional precedent, carried over into the Māhele guidelines, the commoners could not claim such abandoned or fallow lands, which reverted to the *konohiki* of the *ahupuaʻa*. Incidentally, this provision for reversion remained in *Hawaii Revised Statutes* until 1987. For one hundred thirty years abandoned *kuleana* were allowed to revert by default either to the government or to the owner of the surrounding land—yet another method, and undoubtedly the most effortless, by which large landowners have been able to swallow up Hawaiian *kuleana* since the Māhele.

The files of the minister of the Public Instruction (AH) are filled with petitions and letters protesting the foreigners' use of the *kula*. Large landowners frequently barred Hawaiians from the uplands while their own livestock grazed further and further down the valleys. If the commoners' cattle or pigs trespassed on the foreigners' lands, however, they were liable to be shot or confiscated, with apparent government sanction (letters of April 11 and May 9, 1853, Public Instruction, AH). Documents of the early 1850s poignantly express the despair of Hawaiian small holders who lost their livelihood and their self-sufficiency:

Here in Makaha, plants do not grow. . . . The patches are . . . trampled upon, the furrows hopelessly ruined, the crops crushed irreparable, by hoofs. . . . some of the people who live on the land . . . go somewhere else to live permanently, because the crops have been destroyed by animals. (Letter of October 26, 1853)

While such contingencies were making small-scale subsistence agriculture difficult to sustain, the Māhele directly contributed to land alienation through its guiding premises and procedures. Numbers of Hawaiians were disenfranchised during the process of filing claims and receiving awards, although it is difficult to estimate how many thus lost their rightful *kuleana.* It is often said that many Hawaiians failed to file claims because they did not understand the implications of private property or could not manage to meet the deadline for registration. For commoners, the registration date of February 14, 1848, was final (generous legislative extensions were later granted to chiefs and *konohiki*). Those who did not apply by that date lost any claim as an original interest holder in the lands of Hawaii. Their only recourse was to purchase government lands after the Māhele if they could raise the cash, an alternative specifically provided for in the Kuleana Act (see Hawaii 1850:203).

As the land records demonstrate, some Hawaiians did not understand that the Māhele would irrevocably alter the basis of their tenancy and thought they could continue to live under the *konohiki* as before. Some withdrew their claims in favor of local *konohiki,* some of whom appear to have encouraged or pressured their people to do so. No fewer than ten of the thirty-four claims made in Ka'a'awa, on the windward side of O'ahu, were renounced by commoners who said that they wanted to live under their *konohiki,* Ka'eo. The alacrity with which Hawaiians sold their lands after the Māhele also suggests that many commoners did not fully comprehend the long-term implications of alienating their property.

Although most Hawaiians probably did not comprehend the Western notion of private property, I do not believe that land alienation during the Māhele was caused primarily by the commoners' ignorance, naivete, or gullibility. There is evidence that, at least initially, even Hawaiian political leaders did not view the Māhele as categorically extinguishing all tenancy relations. A curious joint resolution passed in 1846 (Hawaii 1925, 2:2193–95), after the establishment of the Land Commission but before the 1850 Kuleana Act, seems to allow for the optional continuation of tenancy coexisting with fee-simple ownership. The resolution, which was repealed in 1859, preserves the tenants' gathering rights in the uplands and constrains the landlord from disposing of open lands if the sale would leave tenants "destitute." The phraseology providing for applications for land titles is voluntaristic rather than imperative, suggesting that tenancy was perceived as a continuing option.

There was no immediate mass disruption of local populations in the wake of the Māhele. I suggested earlier that most Hawaiians lived out their lives as tenants of someone else, even under other commoners. In the immediate aftermath of the Māhele many commoners who were not awarded land continued to live under others or on chiefly lands as they had always done. The rate and the timing of evictions varied according to local circumstances and the disposition of the landowner. Some chiefs and haoles "took immediate steps to get rid of those natives," in the words of American consul Joel Turrill (1957:77), but consensual tenancy relationships among the commoners often persisted for many years after the Māhele.

The Polynesian notion of a land-giving hierarchy is crucial for analyzing the commoners' alleged failure to apply for *kuleana.* The question is, how many adult members of a commoner Hawaiian household believed that they had the *right* to file a claim under the operant cultural understanding of land tenure? Hawaiians recognized a *haku 'āina* 'landlord' in the family, usually a senior member who had the right to control and allocate the family land. Junior siblings, added-on affines and dependents, and tenants (*hoa'āina* or *lōpā*) were subordinate to that individual. Given historical estimates of household size and the Hawaiian population at the time of the Māhele, it may be that most commoners were in fact represented by claims to the Land Commission. For the purposes of calculation, I will assume that commoners comprised perhaps 95 percent of the population. Admittedly, this is a guess. No one has devised a reliable estimate of the proportion of chiefs to commoners. Ethnohistorical sources claim that the ratio was very small, and I have taken a cue from the low proportion of chiefs and *konohiki* in my sample (see table 7). Schmitt (1968:43) gives approximately 80,000 as the native population in January, 1850, so we can estimate the number of commoners at 76,000. If approximately 12,000 claims were filed by commoners, then there would be about one claim for every five or six *maka'āinana,* and the ratio of claims to adult commoners would be approximately one to four. Given the prevalence of tenancy arrangements, one claimant for every four or five adults may not indicate a high incidence of failure to claim, except by those who did not believe that they had the right to do so.

In retrospect we can see that the Hawaiian cultural understanding of rightful authority over land, by which claims were filed on behalf of an entire extended family, worked against the commoners' long-term interests. It is easy to say that every adult member of a commoner household should have filed a claim for land, but such action would have been antithetical to Hawaiian cultural premises. Some families applied under a single claim in order to save the expenses of survey and title transfer. And in any case, disputes in Māhele testimony suggest that such claims would have been challenged by chiefs and *konohiki*. The crux of the matter is that the Māhele was intended to create no new rights in land, but simply to define and sediment the existing interests of all parties. Although the haole architects of the division initially foresaw the commoners receiving a third of the acreage in the kingdom, in the final plan the vast majority of lands went to the king, the chiefs, and the government. The Māhele was never intended to effect a proletarian revolution or equalize the distribution of resources in Hawaiian society. The king and the chiefs had always controlled the most and the best of everything—rightfully so in the indigenous cultural scheme—and the Māhele once again institutionalized their priority.

This hierarchy of privilege is vividly apparent when we compare what commoners received in the Māhele, on the average, to what was received by chiefs and others of high status (table 14). Only 3 percent (133) of those in the "commoner" category (which includes claimants of unknown social rank) received more than 10 acres. The range is from 0.008 to 87.0 acres, and undoubtedly some of those receiving more than 10 acres are local *konohiki* whom I have not yet identified. Since the stratification in size of award is so pronounced, it is unlikely that those receiving

TABLE 14. **Area of Award by Social Status of Awardee**

Status of Awardee	N	Mean Area (in acres)	Median
Chief	59	1,523.2	4.61
Haole	73	141.2	4.13
Konohiki	100	73.5	4.62
Luna	17	5.8	2.77
Commoner	3,500	2.7	1.54
Total Awards	3,749		

Note: In cases where haoles are identified as *konohiki*, they are classified as "haole." Nonawards (where the area awarded is zero) and missing values for area are excluded from this tabulation. Total number of awards equals 3,749.

more than 10 acres are commoners. I estimate that the mean area of awards to commoners is closer to 1.5 acres. The mean area for chiefs shown in table 14, on the other hand, is probably too low. The precise acreage of chiefly lands was not always readily available, and many are carried in the database as missing values. By an 1852 statute (Hawaii 1852:28) lands to chiefs and *konohiki* could be awarded by the land name, without survey; some of these lands exceed 10,000 acres in size.

As suggested above, the viability of the rural Hawaiian economy was intimately tied to the fate of the uplands and *kula*. Local self-sufficiency depended on access to the wild and open regions of the *ahupua'a,* where Hawaiians gathered numerous articles and pastured their animals. The constitution of 1840 (Hawaii 1894:40–41) recognized the people's rights in these areas by restricting the landlord's ability to place *kapu* on wild-growing things. But in the Māhele commoners effectively lost their access to the uplands and *kula*. Under the Kuleana Act commoners were entitled to claim only lands actually occupied and cultivated for subsistence. "Clumps" of scattered and semiwild cultigens in the uplands were not awarded, nor were lands lying fallow. Even household *kula* plots and previously cultivated taro patches were usually not awarded. Privy Council discussions in 1850 (Privy Council Minutes, vol. 3B, AH) reveal that King Kamehameha III fought to preserve the people's gathering and access rights, which the chiefs opposed. At his insistence the Kuleana Act included a section protecting the commoners' access to the uplands and forests. To this day the section (S. 7-1) remains in *Hawaii Revised Statutes,* where it reads:

> where the landlords have obtained . . . allodial title to their lands, the people on each of their lands shall not be deprived of the right to take firewood, house-timber, aho cord, thatch, or ki leaf, from the land on which they live, for their own private use, but they shall not have a right to take such articles to sell for profit. The people shall also have a right to drinking water, and running water, and the right of way. The springs of water, running water, and roads shall be free to all, on all lands granted in fee simple. (cf. Hawaii 1850:203–4)

To Westerners it is evident that this part of the law conflicts with the notion of fee-simple property as private, exclusive, and inviolable. The chiefs in the Privy Council quite correctly perceived that the retention of residual rights by the commoners would abridge their new ownership rights. Given the examples cited earlier of chiefs and foreigners attempting to restrict commoners from the uplands and open tracts, it is difficult to believe that large landowners respected this clause in the aftermath of the Māhele, or that rural Hawaiians would have been quick to bring challenges to court. A Honolulu lawyer who works extensively with land cases expressed the opinion that section 7 of the Kuleana Act was "virtually ignored" in the latter half of the nineteenth century (see Linnekin 1987a).

Despite the small size of the commoners' *kuleana,* the Land Commission awards might have sufficed to support Hawaiian households after the Māhele if taxation in kind had remained an option and if commoners had retained access to the full range of productive zones. But *kuleana* were frequently located adjacent to, or surrounded by, large tracts of chiefly or government land, which increasingly fell into the hands of foreigners after the Māhele (see Morgan 1948:139). Isolated and beset by marauding livestock, small holders abandoned their *kuleana* or succumbed to the temptation to sell or lease. Rising prices due to land speculation after the Māhele made cash purchase offers hard to resist (Morgan 1948:137). Once the native owner leased the property, sugar cultivation or cattle grazing often obliterated the boundary markers of the *kuleana,* thus making it impossible for Hawaiians to locate the land even if they wanted to return. For these reasons, the sale of the uplands in a district usually heralded the forcing out of small landholders. In Kohala, Elias Bond acted as subcommissioner to the Land Commission when the government lands were put up for sale: "it was reported that applications for large tracts had been made by certain foreigners. . . . there was no chance for a common native living in a remote district like this" (Damon 1927:256).

Emigration from the land had steadily increased during the early postcontact period, but was greatly exacerbated by the land division. In 1839 Lyons (Station Report, HMCS) issued 122 certificates of dismissal, representing a loss of 2.7 percent of his flock. But for that year Lyons also reports that an additional 100 or more "have gone to other places without any letters of recommendation." The statistics worsen in subsequent years. In his 1854 report Lyons notes a net population loss of 5.8 percent by letter. Besides those leaving with official sanction, he cites 283 "wanderers on other Islands and in other places—formerly apostates but not known what they are now or whether they are dead or alive." Bond similarly complained of a "perpetual stream of emigration" from Kohala to Honolulu and Lāhaina (Damon 1927:172). He reported major periods of emigration during the gold rush, from 1848 to 1851, and in 1853 (Damon 1927:178). In 1859, Bond cited a decrease of 100 percent in the population of his field over the preceding seven years, "chiefly caused by removals and with few exceptions to Oahu" (Damon 1927:159).

With the erosion of local self-sufficiency came further involvement in the cash economy and vulnerability to such events as the collapse of the agricultural market in 1859. Though the people's sources of money were evaporating, government taxes were still due. Lyons noted that in January, 1860, the tax collector was able to take in only $10 of a $1,600 assessment for Waimea: "Meanwhile the people are working with all their might, selling their property, going off to other Islands to beg money of friends, or to sell property. . . . Then for unpaid taxes the property must be attached, and sold at auction at great sacrifice" (Doyle 1953:183). In Kohala, too, foreigners had introduced large herds of livestock, with predictable results; as Bond described in 1864: "The entire tract of country is gradually filling with cattle and sheep belonging to foreigners, and the natives, as a matter of necessity, are rapidly leaving the district, chiefly for Oahu" (Damon 1927:207). Under such pressures entire *ahupua'a* were abandoned by Hawaiians in the latter half of the nineteenth century. The 1867 tax assessment for Kalihi-*uka,* the upper third of Kalihi Valley in Honolulu, illustrates the fate of the Hawaiian uplands and *kula*. Of forty-eight landowners assessed in this section, only one is a Hawaiian *kuleana* holder (Honolulu Tax Books, AH). And as early as 1872, Hawaiian land alienation was viewed internationally as a worst-case example (Gilson 1970:281).

Demographics

The missionaries' annual census reports attest that from the 1830s the rural districts of the islands were undergoing a progressive loss of population, with episodes of locally varying intensity. Before 1850 Hawaiians left the land because of oppressive taxation, the lure of the cash economy, or encroachments on their *kuleana* by chiefs and foreigners. The Māhele conjoined with these forces and with the legal changes of 1850 to produce a landless people within a few decades. Hawaiians deserted rural districts in favor of market centers where they might find salaried work or relatives with whom to live. Residence with relatives can be illustrated with a statistic published in the *Polynesian* in 1847 (January 9): 1,337 houses in Honolulu housed a population of approximately 10,000 Hawaiians and 600 foreigners; this yields an average household size of about eight persons, suggesting that Honolulu Hawaiians hosted more than their share of dependents and guests.

If higher mobility had resulted in an excess of adult women at the local level, the rise in female inheritance during the late 1840s and early 1850s could be explained by emigration (cf. Gonzalez 1969:54–56, 140–41). In many ethnographic annals, after all, changes in inheritance are often precipitated by disruptions in population, but while such upheavals mandate some general alteration in customary modes of transmission, the specific form of the change must be explained by reference to cultural precedent and prior social arrangements. Population statistics do not support a simple demographic determination of the inheritance shift in Hawaii, for, paradoxically, the native Hawaiian population of the nineteenth century is characterized by an excess of males over females, in nearly all age categories and in both urban and rural areas (see Schmitt 1968:43). Even though depopulation had removed many potential heirs and wage labor drew others to the ports, in absolute terms there was no dearth of Hawaiian males.

The disparity in the Hawaiian sex ratio has puzzled demographers. At the time of Turnbull's visit, 1803–4, women were reputed to be "more numerous than the men" (1805, 2:68), suggesting that the imbalance is a nineteenth-century development (Schmitt 1968:31). The widening gap between the sexes appears to parallel the process of depopulation (see Schmitt 1968:45) and proceeds even as large numbers of Hawaiian men were going to sea or points abroad. The editor of the *Polynesian* (August 2, 1862) attributed the excess of males to differential mortality: "If we compare the progress of death between the years 1853 and 1860, we shall find that its richest harvest has' been among the young and among the females." Marques (1894) similarly commented: "the ordinary rate of decrease among them follows very closely their ratio of excess of males"; table 15 derives from Marques's figures on the imbalance among native Hawaiians from 1850 to 1890. As Schmitt's (1968:72–74) statistics show, the ratio for the islands' total population becomes skewed by the influx of single male plantation workers from the 1870s on. (With a few exceptions sex ratios are unavailable before 1850, since the missionary censuses did not provide counts by age and sex; see Schmitt 1968:46.)

Differential female mortality is a logical inference from the census data, although, as with many other ethnohistorical questions, there is no conclusive supporting evidence (Schmitt 1968:31–32). The missionary Ellis (1969:326–32) attributed the imbalance of the sexes to female infanticide, and later authors echoed his statements, sometimes nearly verbatim (see Bates 1854:343; Freycinet 1978:65; Kamakau 1961:235; Malo 1839:123–24; Stewart 1970:251). Schmitt (1968:37) wrote that abortion and infanticide increased dramatically during the periods 1819–25 and 1832–36, although he gives no specific source for this statement. Cook and his officers (see Samwell 1967:1182) believed that Hawaiians knew nothing of infanticide, and there are no documented cases (for the only convincing "confession" that I have encountered, see Judd 1928:29). Marion Kelly (in Freycinet 1978:116) has pointed out that nearly every author who discusses infanticide parroted Ellis. Ellis received his information in Tahiti from Hawaiian converts, who might be expected to oblige their haole preceptors with lurid details of their previous heathen life. Paulding (1970:231), who visited the islands in 1826, criticized contemporary observers for needlessly invoking "acts of inhumanity" to account for Hawaiian depopulation. In his view Hawaiians' lack of immunity to introduced diseases was the chief cause of their postcontact decline.

Although I will offer here only a brief summary of Hawaiian depopulation, the terrible loss of life due to European-introduced diseases cannot be overemphasized as a disintegrative force in local communities. From an estimated 250,000 to 300,000 inhabitants in 1778 (see Schmitt 1968:18–24), the population of the islands had declined by at least 75 percent by 1853 (Schmitt 1968:74). The first scourge was venereal disease, which Cook's men left behind in the initial European encounter

TABLE 15. **Sex Ratios by Year, Native Population**

Year	Equivalent Sex Ratio Male to Female
1850	104.39:100
1853	104.42:100
1860	105.48:100
1872	106.50:100
1878	106.56:100
1884	107.48:100
1890	106.66:100

Source: Marques 1894:20.

with Hawaiians at Kaua'i in 1778. Kamakau (1961:236–37) lists decimating epidemics occurring in 1804, 1826, 1839, 1844, 1848, and 1853 (see also Doyle 1953:147–53). The most severe of these were influenza in 1826, measles in 1848, and smallpox in 1853. It is significant for the issue of inheritance by women that the latter two came during the period of the Māhele. Many of those who had filed claims in 1848 were dead by the time the testimony was required or the award granted. In this context many women came to hold family lands originally claimed by their husbands, fathers, or brothers. The occurrence of major epidemics during the land division also contributed directly to Hawaiian land alienation. As stated earlier, widows were particularly vulnerable to dispossession at the hands of local *konohiki*. When entire families were wiped out by measles or smallpox, their lands were absorbed by large landowners or the government.

The *Polynesian*'s comparative figures (August 2, 1862) suggest that the death toll from disease was higher among girls and young women; the ratio of males to females under twenty years old increased from 109:100 in 1853, before the smallpox epidemic, to 117:100 in 1860. Hawaiian birthrates were also very low during this period; the 1860 census showed only one birth for every eleven women (*Polynesian,* August 2, 1862). Infant mortality among Hawaiians was very high, however, as reported by Seth Andrews, missionary in Kailua, Hawai'i: "In this district rather more than one half of the children die before the period of first dentition closes. In the district of Hilo . . . a very little less than one half die during the same period" (Answers to Questions, July 8, 1846, F.O. & Ex.).

Tables 16, 17, and 18 summarize population data from several different sources to illustrate the degree of the sex ratio imbalance and variability from district to district. Hawaiian male/female ratios for several

TABLE 16. Sex Ratios by Age, Total Native Population, January, 1849

Age Bracket	Males	Females	Ratio of Male to Female
0–16 years	10,773	9,593	112:100
17–29	6,327	5,719	110:100
30–49	10,819	9,696	101:100
50 +	8,353	8,121	102:100
Overall	36,272	33,128	106:100

Source: Census figures published in the *Friend,* January, 1849.

cities are given in table 19. Here it is important to note that none of the samples indicates a lack of adult males at the local level. The increase in female heirs may stem in part from greater mobility among men, if not from their numerical minority. Accompanying the growing imbalance in the sex ratio was a rise in the proportion of unmarried men. In the *Polynesian*'s (August 2, 1862) statistics on the declining native population, the ratio of unmarried men to unmarried women is 123:100 (16,523 to 13,384) in 1853 and 129:100 (16,317 to 12,643) in 1860.

In general, the male/female disparity is most acute in the younger age cohorts—again supporting the inference of different mortality rates (see also figures for Kaua'i in 1839; Jarves 1843:373–75)—but this does not entirely explain the unmarried/married contrast. The ratio of men to

TABLE 17.   **Sex Ratios, Waialua, O'ahu, 1841, Male to Female**

Ahupua'a	Adults	Juveniles	Overall
Kawailoa	102:100	100:104	100:100
Pa'ala'a	109:100	177:100	128:100
Kamananui	116:100	135:100	122:100
Mokuleia	111:100	146:100	121:100
Overall	110:100	138:100	118:100

Source: Computed from census and account book of the Rev. J. S. Emerson (Census file, AH).

TABLE 18.   **Sex Ratios, Lāhaina and Waioli, Kaua'i, Male to Female**

Location	Year	Adults	Juveniles	Overall
Lāhaina	1846	100:112	122:100	110:100
	1866	104:100	113:100	106:100
Waioli	1849	115:100	100:101	110:100

Source: Lāhaina computed from census enumeration sheets (AH); Waioli from E. Johnson, Station Report for 1849 with census of field (HMCS).

TABLE 19.   **Sex Ratios for Various Cities, 1872, Native Population**

City	Males	Females	Ratio of Male to Female
Honolulu	5,776	5,434	106:100
Hilo	2,065	1,522	136:100
Lāhaina	1,402	1,145	122:100
Wailuku, Maui	1,820	1,623	112:100
Waimea, Kaua'i	642	578	111:100

Source: Computed from census of December 27, 1872, in Thrum 1877:21.

women under the age of 20 is 109:100 (15,623 to 14,300) in 1853 and 117:100 (11,231 to 9,588) in 1860. In the 1866 Lāhaina census (enumeration sheets in AH), the ratio is 127:100 for unmarried Hawaiians, but 100:106 for married men and women. Interestingly, women outnumber men in the over-40 bracket in Lāhaina by 259 to 251, yielding a ratio of 100:103. In the 1850 census of the total population, the male/female ratio among Hawaiian adults aged 31 to 52 is approximately even (11,018 to 11,047; Schmitt 1968:43). Jarves's (1843:373–75) figures for Kaua'i in 1839 show "old women" outnumbering "old men" in every district. And for the district of Ewa, west of Honolulu, Jarves (1843:376) gives "removals during [1840] to other places" by sex: 73 men, compared to 45 women.

These figures suggest that men were more mobile than women, that men were less likely to marry than women, and that there was less of an imbalance in the sex ratio among older Hawaiians. Older women may even have outnumbered older men in some localities. Taken together, these demographic characteristics would tend to promote landholding by women, particularly given the likelihood that authority was vested in older members of Hawaiian households. Nevertheless, demographics cannot fully account for the increase in female heirs. Census data indicate less of a sex ratio disparity in older age brackets, but not a significant numerical majority of women. If older women did outnumber older men in areas particularly subject to "removals," as Jarves's Kaua'i figures suggest, then this could be a result of greater mobility among men: a result, not a cause, of the tendency for women to stay behind on the land. The question remains, why did women stay behind to inherit? The answer must be cultural as well as historical. The sex ratios do not indicate how Hawaiians on the local level adjusted landholding arrangements as rural populations dwindled or why certain structural alternatives came into play rather than others.

Why Did Women Inherit?

Increased inheritance by women in nineteenth-century Hawaii occurred through the interplay of historical events and cultural precedents. A shift in land inheritance was undeniably precipitated by economic, political, and demographic factors, for by removing potential heirs, depopulation and emigration compelled the emergence of alternate modes of land inheritance in mid-nineteenth-century Hawaii. But the particular form of this inheritance shift can only be explained by invoking cultural premises and precepts: Hawaiian symbolic associations of women with land, the relative egalitarianism in Hawaiian gender relations, the bilaterality of local-level social organization, and concepts of land tenure. With the growing proportion of single, mobile Hawaiian men, women were more likely to remain as stable figures on the land, a role presaged by their mythic and symbolic association with land and permanence. As an adjustment motivated by historical vicissitudes, landholding by women served to keep land within the family in the face of historical challenges to the indigenous social order. Hawaiian social organization and cultural precedent determined that women, and particularly women in certain relationships, should inherit control of familial lands rather than distantly related men.

The increase in female inheritance at first appears as a radical departure from the pattern obtaining before 1848 (see table 1). Yet in the context of Hawaiian land tenure, which envisioned a succession of keepers, of persons "having charge" of the property for the next generation, the change is less than dramatic. For from this point of view, possession is but temporary guardianship. Qualitative evidence in Māhele testimony and later court cases suggests that women inheriting land did in fact see themselves as temporary caretakers on behalf of their own or their siblings' offspring. Thus the apparently unprecedented rise in female inheritance was thoroughly grounded in customary modes of land transmission. Rather than overturning traditional norms, landholding by women had a conservative intent: that of keeping land within the family for the descendents of the adult sibling set, the children and grandchildren of the *ma*. But as women became central figures at the local level, this attempt at social reproduction effected gradual changes in social organization and household authority.

Widow inheritance accounts for most acquisitions by women, with daughter inheriting from father the second most frequent category and sister from brother the third (table 13). There is no increase in Mo/Da inheritance, which would suggest the emergence of matrilineality, but the incidence of Mo/So transmission doubled over the pre-Māhele period (table 12). During the Māhele women were actually more likely than men to inherit land within the family, although men continued to be overwhelmingly favored in receiving land from political superiors (table 10). The suggestion that women who inherited land did not view themselves as the permanent, long-term holders, but as caretakers for a minor child or absent male relative, is also supported by the increase in inheritance from child to parent (table 12). The nature of this place-holding is illustrated by the testament of a Hawaiian woman who died in 1853, leaving a son and a *kuleana* from her husband, the original claimant. After her husband's death she had held the land for her son, and she addressed her will in turn to her husband's younger brother:

> our child is to be with you; you to be the parent. The land is the child's however, the kanaka there, by brother Paakonia, who lives there you are to hooponopono ['regulate, make right']. And so with the horses; you are hooponopono them. All of the things that belonged to me and my husband are to be in your care, just as the staying of our child with you. (P-472, January 1854, AH)

Increased landholding by women occurred as emigration and disease decimated both the parental generation and those who would norma-tively have been the primary heirs. As Hawaiian families were reduced by the epidemics of 1848 and 1853, more distant relatives became poten-tial heirs (see table 12). It is also important to emphasize that the Māhele ended the system of *konohiki* control and forced labor, thus removing an impediment to the commoners' mobility. With the granting of fee-simple title the local *konohiki* lost their special authority and became merely *kuleana* holders, though they received on the average more land than did the commoners under them (table 14). Before the Māhele Hawaiians who neglected cultivation risked losing their land, but once a Land Commission Award was granted an adult male's pres-ence was no longer required. In place of *konohiki* stewardship the Māhele instituted a laissez faire system where landowners might do whatever they chose with their property. Given contemporary pressures on small holders (described above), this new freedom was disastrous for Hawaiians. Landholding by women enabled men to leave the land with-out losing their *kuleana;* they did so with increasing frequency, entrust-ing "care" of the property to others.

In this context women as sisters and as mothers became placeholders on the land. In chapter 5 I described the sibling set as the core of the Hawaiian household group and suggested that at a particular time a Hawaiian woman would be coresident with either her brother or her husband. In the absence of local lineages or descent groups women as

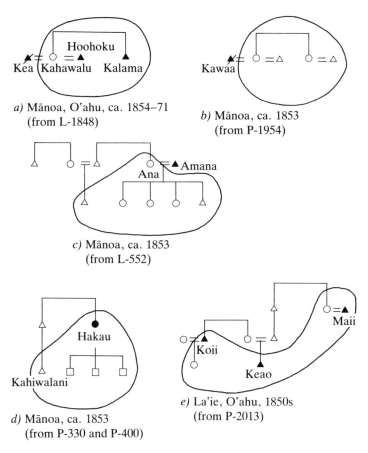

a) Mānoa, Oʻahu, ca. 1854–71
(from L-1848)

b) Mānoa, ca. 1853
(from P-1954)

c) Mānoa, ca. 1853
(from L-552)

d) Mānoa, ca. 1853
(from P-330 and P-400)

e) Laʻie, Oʻahu, 1850s
(from P-2013)

Fig. 17. Variations in household composition after 1850

older sisters were authority figures in their natal *ma* and were rightfully superior to junior male collateral relatives and affines who might be attached to the household. With her brother's death or departure a woman would take charge of the land for his or her own offspring. If the land right was traceable to her husband, a woman would hold the land for her child at her husband's death. In either case she would eventually pass on the *kuleana* to the rightful heirs if they should survive.

Landholding by women thus represents a recurrent stage in Hawaiian family histories—recurrent, because women would continue to take care of the land and household when the rightful *haku ʻāina* was absent. Figure 17 diagrams several empirical examples of fluctuations in land-

holding and household structure dating from the early 1850s, as reconstructed from testimony given in post-Māhele court cases on Oʻahu. The
examples substantiate the inference that women were often temporary
placeholders who would eventually give up control of the land to another family member, usually male.

The priority of cross-sex siblingship is particularly evident in four of
these cases (figs. 17*a,* 17*c,* 17*d,* 17*e*), where a woman landholder defers to
her brother's son (or, in one case, a grandson), who is recognized as the
household authority or rightful heir. But figures 17*a* and 17*b* also illustrate
that a woman as heir and landholder was often a node of relationships in
her own right, someone to whom others attached themselves, either as
husbands or as household dependents. In figure 17, Kea's land fell to his
widow Kahawalu, who lived there with her brother Kalama and second
husband Hoohoku, both also *kuleana* holders in Mānoa. At Kahawalu's
death Kalama returned to his own land. Hoohoku continued to cultivate
Kea's land until his own death, when it fell to Kalama, and thence to
Kalama's son (L-1848). In a second Mānoa case (fig. 17*b*), a widow lived
on her first husband's land with her second husband and brother-in-law
(presumably also with her sister, but this is not specifically stated). Her
second husband called himself "the nominal owner" of the land—
probably because of legal constraints—but acknowledged, "I have no
claim upon any of the property" (P-1954). In figure 17*c* (L-552), Ana
Manoha inherited her husband's Royal Patent Grant. Her brother resided uxorilocally in Kahuku, but his son lived with Ana Manoha and
"took charge" of the property; Ana's children and their spouses lived
under him. Figure 17*d* (P-330, P-400) illustrates a similar case, where a
brother's son lived with his father's sister and "had possession of the
land." After Hakau's death "Kahiwalaṇi was the head of the family, he
was the oldest." He continued to hold the land and remained "as guardian
of the children." The composition of a *ma* in Laʻie (fig. 17*e*) further
underscores the importance of cross-sex siblingship in the local group.
Keao, a minor, lived with his FaFaSi and her husband Maii, who "had
charge of" the boy's property. Also living with them were Keao's MoBr
Koii, also a Laʻie landowner, and Koii's daughter (P-2013).

I have characterized female inheritance in mid-nineteenth-century
Hawaii as initially conservative rather than transformative in nature.
But anthropology has documented many instances where such attempts
at continuity, in the face of radically changing external circumstances,
also result in transformation (cf. Sahlins 1981). The family histories just

cited augur structural changes in the local group, as well as a possible shift in interpersonal authority relations. In the remainder of this chapter I will discuss what happened within the Hawaiian local group after the Māhele and what role women played in the transition.

Women and Land after 1855

The status of Hawaiian women after the Māhele cannot be discussed apart from the fate of all Hawaiians. Although major events such as the ascendancy of sugar, the influx of plantation immigrants, and the overthrow of the monarchy are well known, it is difficult to reconstruct the transformation of local communities. To my knowledge there is no body of data comparable to the Māhele claims that would shed light on the changing composition of particular *ahupua'a* in the late nineteenth century. Documentary sources for the latter half of the century consist primarily of court cases, tax rolls, legal records (such as property conveyances), missionary writings, and occasional accounts in periodicals. I have not analyzed these materials extensively with an eye to reconstructing post-Māhele economic history except for the area in which I did fieldwork (see Linnekin n.d.), but in general this was a transitional period that saw the demise of rural subsistence agriculture. The last tenancy relations were eventually dissolved in the wake of the Māhele. Pressured by expanding plantations and ranches, most Hawaiians abandoned the land to become a largely urban proletariat by the early twentieth century. By 1896 Hawaiians owned only 14 percent of the taxable land although they made up 63 percent of the landowners in the kingdom (Morgan 1948:139 n. 59).

The chronology of emigration and proletarianization after the land division varied with local economic conditions, however. Leaving the land was not the only recourse open to rural Hawaiians. In some areas land abandonment was forestalled for several years, even decades, through cash cropping. In the process, Hawaiians' dependency on the market deepened and localities began to specialize more narrowly in a single product. These trends resulted in the impoverishment of local agriculture and heightened vulnerability to external market conditions, both of which made rural subsistence more difficult to sustain over the long term. But for some time after the Māhele, cash cropping was a local solution to the problem of money. In Ke'anae, Maui, where I did fieldwork, evidence suggests that Hawaiians sold *olonā* for ships' rigging and lines (Linnekin n.d.). In the uplands of Maui, people grew Irish potatoes for the external market, and on Hawai'i, sweet potatoes. Major taro-growing *ahupua'a,* such as Ke'anae and Waipi'o on Hawai'i, supplied food to the towns and to Hawaiian communities that no longer produced enough to feed themselves.

On Hawai'i *pulu* fern enjoyed a brief heyday as an export in the late 1850s and early 1860s (Kelly 1980:13–15). Used as mattress filler and a dressing for wounds, *pulu* was a boom crop, initially an easy source of money but quick to collapse when the world market found a substitute product. In Kohala in 1859, Elias Bond (Damon 1927:157) described a great rush to the uplands to gather *pulu:* "entire families enter into the picking. . . . they leave lands unplanted, houses desolate, schools neglected . . . to go away into the woods and live for months." Lyons (Doyle 1953:164) similarly wrote of "famine at Hamakua, in consequence of the people being all devoted to picking pulu." The *pulu* saga typifies the dangers that cash cropping presents for a previously subsistence-oriented economy; when the market suddenly and irrevocably collapsed Hawaiians were worse off than they were before. Lyons (Doyle 1953:167) related how a company of foreigners contracted to build two churches in return for promised amounts of *pulu,* "but before the buildings were completed, the price depreciated and the firm dissolved." To raise funds, Lyons resorted to giving luau feasts and passing round the collection plate.

A few years after the *pulu* debacle, around 1865, sugar took off in Kohala as it did in many other areas (Doyle 1953:200). Numbers of Hawaiians then turned to wage labor for the plantations, particularly when cash cropping failed. The alleged unsuitability of Hawaiians to plantation labor has been overemphasized. Hawaiians made up the bulk of the sugar work force for the industry's first few decades. It was not so much the Hawaiians' recalcitrance as their lack of numbers that motivated the planters to import Asian laborers. When the industry mushroomed after the 1875 Reciprocity Treaty, the native population could not keep up with the sudden demand for workers (see Schmitt 1968:75–77). It should also be noted that the planters excoriated every immigrant group in turn for sloth and rebelliousness, suggesting that the labor "problem" was not faulty national character but the conditions of employment.

For *kuleana* owners one alternative to plantation work was leasing to foreigners, an alternative that sometimes but not always resulted in the loss of land. In the 1880s and 1890s, for example, Keʻanae Hawaiians leased their lands extensively to Chinese for rice production. The Chinese were the first wave of immigrant laborers brought to Hawaii, but they tended to leave the plantations as soon as they fulfilled their contracts. The Chinese initiated numerous mercantile and entrepreneurial ventures, both in the cities and in rural communities, where they intermarried with Hawaiian women. In Keʻanae, when the Chinese husbands died their Hawaiian affines and offspring converted the pondfields back into taro *loʻi*. But Keʻanae is one of very few areas in the islands where Hawaiians retained ownership of their lands. Geographical remoteness, rugged terrain, and an overabundance of rain played a part in Keʻanae's continuity, as did the purchase of the uplands by cooperatives (*hui*) of Hawaiians after the Māhele (see Linnekin 1983). On the whole, however, leasing was merely the prelude to sale or abandonment.

In this historical context, is it possible to assess the long-term destiny of women landholders after the Māhele? What of the women reflected in the statistics, those who had inherited land from their husbands, brothers, or fathers? In the last section I pointed out that Hawaiians, like many non-Western peoples, viewed land tenure as caretaking and use. Land *holders* were precisely that—custodians in a chain of caretakers from ancestors to grandchildren. When women inherited land during the period in question, they saw themselves as placeholders on behalf of their own or their siblings' children (who are also their "children" in Hawaiian kinship terminology). Landholding by women had particular implications for residence, marriage, and authority relations within the *ahupuaʻa*. As detailed in earlier chapters, residence options in the Hawaiian system were intimately tied to usufruct rights. Members of the *ma* attached themselves to the land giver, who was by definition the superordinate figure in the household group.

As a result of the inheritance shift women were again pivotal figures for access to land, but not as they had been aboriginally. From the male point of view *ʻimi haku*—seeking land, residence rights, and patronage outside one's natal *ma*—would now operate not through attachment to the wife's father but to the woman in her own right as heir to the land of her husband or siblings. As land giver, the woman became both structural focus and authority figure in the *ma*. In absolute numbers women were still a minority of landholders, however; for although women predominated in familial inheritance during the Māhele, land giving from political overlords overwhelmingly favored men. This is clear in the land transmission statistics for earlier periods as well as in the preponderance of male Land Commission awardees. Thus after the Māhele most land owners were male.

But the Hawaiian local group was in a continuous state of flux after the land division (for an indication see the local endogamy graphs in figs. 9 and 10), and many male landowners were periodically absent from the land. Landholding by women must be interpreted against the backdrop of ongoing, often dramatic fluctuations in the population of the *ahupua'a* and in the makeup of constituent household groups. It is in this context that women's landholding was viewed not as a permanent arrangement, but as short-term care. Some corroboration for this interpretation can be found in contemporary tax assessment rolls. After 1858, the annual tax enumeration differentiated landowners from persons having other forms of property, such as horses, mules, dogs, or, infrequently, cash. The procedure was to list taxable persons by name, followed by details of the assessment. The latter were based on the subject's own testimony or, if absent, the word of a spouse, relatives, or neighbors. The tax collectors were Hawaiian, often local residents who could corroborate the assessment with their own firsthand knowledge. In using this material as data, we must keep in mind that idiosyncratic factors, such as a new tax collector, could have significant but unpredictable effects on the enumeration. While all able-bodied men were assessed at least one dollar, women were exempt from the head tax and were assessed only if they owned some form of taxable property. Table 20 shows the proportion of women landholders assessed in five *ahupua'a* on O'ahu, from 1859 through 1869.

The format and content of these records tell us as much about changes in local populations as do the numbers per se. The tax rolls effectively give a year-by-year list of adult householders residing in the *ahupua'a*. The total number of landholders assessed in any one year bears an uncertain relationship to the number of legally distinct parcels in the *ahupua'a*. Even after the granting of individual titles most Hawaiians did not emphasize the distinction between ownership and customary care in their day-to-day affairs. The person paying the tax for a particular *kuleana* often varies from year to year; there are few cases where the legal owner appears on the rolls throughout and few *kuleana* that show no change in landholder during the decade. What is particularly striking about the tax assessments are the dramatic changes in personnel over time. This is especially true for Mānoa and Kalihi, valleys behind Honolulu town, where so many new names appear every year that the list of taxable persons in 1869 bears scant resemblance to the enumeration of 1859.

Despite the limitations of the data, the tax assessments have certain regular characteristics. In all the *ahupua'a* there is wide variability in the total number of landholders from year to year. A steady increase or decrease in the number might suggest a constant process at work, either subdivision or consolidation. Instead, the Hawaiian tax rolls point to a seesaw effect over time. The most dramatic example is the assessment for Waipi'o (Ewa district), which jumps from the lowest figure of the decade to the highest in a single year, 1859–60, an increase of 37 or about 250 percent. Undoubtedly local vagaries of the collection procedure must account for this particular instance, but year-to-year changes of from 5 to 15 percent are common in these figures. After rising to 52 in 1860, the number of landholders in Waipi'o diminishes to 30 five years later and then climbs again to 43 in 1868. Fluctuations such as these reflect high short-term mobility on the part of Hawaiians during this period, as well as the interplay of two simultaneous processes, partitioning and consolidation. The courts, through decrees in probate cases, and Hawaiians themselves, through oral bequests, were subdividing *kuleana* among various heirs and caretakers. At the same time foreigners were buying up Hawaiian lands and amassing large tracts for ranches and plantations.

TABLE 20.　Women Assessed Taxes for Land in Five O'ahu *Ahupua'a*, 1859–69

	Mānoa			Kalihi			Waipi'o			Kawailoa			Pa'ala'a			Total		
Year	N	F	%F	N	F	%F	N	F	%F	N	F	%F	N	F	%F	N	F	%F
1859	34	3	9	40	4	10	15	1	7	67	6	9	49	2	4	205	16	8
1860	40	4	10	40	2	5	52	15	29	72	7	10	50	2	4	254	30	12
1861	40	4	10	38	1	3	50	12	24	68	10	15	49	2	4	245	29	12
1862	40	6	15	44	9	20	43	12	28	64	7	11	43	3	7	234	37	16
1863	50	5	10	45	3	7	37	13	35							132	21	16
1864	46	9	20	55	6	11	31	8	26	56	4	7	38	3	8	221	30	14
1865	50	13	26	42	8	19	30	9	30	56	5	9	43	4	9	221	39	18
1866	50	15	30	40	7	18	31	7	23	56	8	14	42	5	12	219	42	19
1867	42	10	24	40	6	15	32	8	25	48	6	13	42	3	7	204	33	16
1868	38	11	29	39	7	18	43	12	28	57	10	18	40	3	8	217	43	20
1869	39	13	33	43	6	14	42	11	26	54	6	11	38	7	18	216	43	20

Source: Compiled from Real Property Tax Books (AH).

Note: N = total number assessed for land; F = number of women assessed for land; %F = percentage of women landholders; empty cells indicate missing information.

The proportion of women holding land also swings dramatically over time within each *ahupua'a,* varying by as much as 50 percent from one year to the next (e.g., Kawailoa, 1860–62). These temporal variations, I suggest, point to the high short-term mobility of Hawaiian men. Given jural limitations on women's property rights under the coverture law (Hawaii 1846:57; see Gething 1977:202–3), it is likely that a married woman would not have been assessed for land if her husband were present. (I must add, however, that we cannot be certain that the law was observed even to this extent; the enrollment would depend on the tax collector, and the family's particular circumstances.) Although locally extreme, fluctuations in the number of women landholders seem to cancel out when the figures for all the *ahupua'a* are tallied. The total column reveals a general trend for more women to come into possession of land during this decade.

While inheritance statistics derived from Māhele testimony represent primarily oral bequests and cultural adjustments made by Hawaiians, the same is not necessarily true of post-Māhele land transmission. From the 1850s on the estates of deceased *kuleana* owners began to reach the courts more often, enabling the law to intervene actively in inheritance. By law, a woman retained a one-third right of dower in her husband's real and movable property (Hawaii 1852:57–59; cf. Hawaii 1846:57–62). If a man died intestate and without issue, half of his estate would go to his widow, half to his parents. With no living parents, half would go to the widow, half to collateral heirs. If the deceased had no living kin, the widow would inherit the entire estate (Hawaii 1850:181–85). Given high male mobility and declining population—particularly the decline in the number of surviving children—the effect of these inheritance laws operating over time would be to equalize land ownership between the sexes.

Assuredly, for decades after the Māhele the estates of many and perhaps most Hawaiians in rural and remote areas never reached probate court. For these *kua'āina* it is impossible to gauge with any precision what effect inheritance laws had on familial land transmission, if any. But in the land and probate cases that I have encountered the pattern is overwhelmingly bilateral. With the death of the female landholder the heir was likely to be a "child," either her own or that of a sibling. The land histories that I have reconstructed for Ke'anae—one of the few remaining areas with unbroken Hawaiian landholding—support a trend for more land to come into the possession of women since the Māhele. In Ke'anae today the numbers of men and women owning land are about equal and it is common for both spouses in a marriage to own or otherwise control land.

The Lāhaina census of 1866 (originals in AH) offers further insight into women's roles after the Māhele, although as a port city Lāhaina cannot be viewed as representative of rural Hawaii. The census is effectively a snapshot of the Hawaiian population of Lāhaina on the night of December 7, 1866, and gives detailed data on the age, sex, marital status, and occupations of household members. With 161 *kuleana* owners, there were approximately 2 households for every land-owning Hawaiian. To be more precise, if we presume only one *kuleana* owner in a household, then only 57 percent of the Hawaiian households in Lāhaina owned some land. Most of the Land Commission Awards in Lāhaina were houselots with minimal land for cultivation. Of the Hawaiians listed as owning *kuleana,* 74 percent (119) were men and 26 percent (42) women. Of 281 households, 11 percent (30) were headed by women and 89 percent (251) by men. Eighty percent (24 of 30) of the women household heads were single women; 20 percent (6 of 30) of the women householders were listed as married. In approximately the same proportions most of the female household heads were women over 40. Men were much more likely than women to live in single-person households: only 3 households (about 1 percent of the total) were composed of single women living alone, while 18 (6 percent) were occupied by single men living alone.

As might be expected in a port where Hawaiians came to find wage employment or sell whatever they could, the sex ratio in the Lāhaina population is skewed toward men. The imbalance is especially acute in the ratio of single men to single women—127:100 (159 to 125)—and in the 15-to-40 age bracket, where it is 113:100 (227 to 200). Among men and women over 40, however, women predominate by a ratio of 100:103 (251 to 259). The ratio of married men to women is even more skewed toward women, by 100:106 (313 to 331). These figures further substantiate my earlier statements about mobility among Hawaiian men and support the argument that a woman was more likely to remain as the stable figure in the household. The occupational data in the Lāhaina census also tend to confirm these interpretations. Since the detailed breakdown is fascinating and important as a portrait of a people in a time and place, I present the compilation in full in table 21. The most frequent occupation for men is farmer (50 percent); the largest category among women (34 percent) is housekeeper (*mālama hale* or *mālama 'ohana,* literally 'one who cares for the house/family') and the second largest, farmer (14 percent). Men and women who called themselves farmer were most likely cultivating both for their own household subsistence and for the market.

The occupational data provide valuable insight into the sorts of proletarian activities that urban Hawaiian women engaged in. In terms of

TABLE 21. Occupation by Gender, Lāhaina, 1866

Occupation	Female		Male	
	N	%	N	%
Farmer	36	14	266	50
Housekeeper	86	34	2	
Contract laborer	20	8	39	7
Merchant	1		23	4
Seamstress	26	10	0	0
Manual laborer	15	6	15	3
Fisherman	7	3	17	3
Matmaker	17	7	0	0
Washerwoman	14	5	0	0
Worker	6	2	13	1
Hatmaker	7	3	0	0
Carpenter	0	0	7	1
House guard	4	2	0	0
Child care	6	2	0	0
Peddler	1		6	1
Shoemaker	0	0	5	1
Tailor	4	2	1	
Paddler, oarsman	1		4	1
Milk seller	0	0	5	1
Luna	0	0	3	
Stable hand	0	0	3	
Blacksmith	0	0	3	
Janitor	0	0	2	
Cook	0	0	2	
Ship's mate	0	0	2	
Tax collector			2	

Other Female Occupations (1 each): Tapa beater; Pig feeder.

Other Male Occupations (1 each): Governor; Caneworker; Attorney; Clerk; Cooper; Plasterer; Principal; Pig seller; Sedge carrier; Sailor; Investor; Secretary; Kava seller; Beef seller.

Total	255 Female	534 Male

Source: Lāhaina Census of 1866 (AH).

Note: Empty cells indicate occupations representing less than 1%.

women's economic activities, it is noteworthy that 66 percent of the women cited money-earning occupations other than housekeeper. The proportion of women working as contract and manual laborers actually exceeds that of men. The proportion of women engaged in fishing equals that of men. Women in Lāhaina were also making and presumably selling mats, hats, and garments—activities akin to their indigenous economic roles—although men predominated as merchants and peddlers. Even though the most frequent women's occupation was housekeeper, the majority of women in Lāhaina in 1866 were also active in the market economy.

After the Māhele the Hawaiian woman became increasingly central in the household as caretaker and as land giver. In these capacities she became both the point of attachment and the superordinate figure in the *ma*. Given the limitations of ethnohistorical data, we cannot resolve questions of domestic authority and actual decision making in nineteenth-century Hawaiian households. And though it would be wrong to conclude that Hawaiian society became matriarchal in the nineteenth century, or that it is matriarchal today, it would be equally wrong to conclude that nineteenth-century Hawaiian women, even when they deferred to a male heir, were passive or deferential in interpersonal relations and family affairs. In the case of Ana Manoha cited earlier (see fig. 17c), Ana's brother's son was titular owner and heir of Ana's husband's property. He testified that he "took care of Ana Manoha till the time of her death." The phraseology suggests the Polynesian ethic that respect and service are owed to family elders. In such cases the young heir, male or female, had authority over siblings and dependents but still owed deference to the older woman who was the source of the property.

Although initially considered temporary guardianship, the woman's placeholding could lengthen into permanent possession when eligible heirs and consanguines died or failed to return to claim the *kuleana*. If the estate went into probate the legal process contributed to Hawaiian land alienation in yet another way: when the owner died intestate and the law recognized multiple heirs, such as the widow and collateral relatives, the court ordered the land to be sold and the proceeds divided among them. In some cases the female landholder was the last Hawaiian to possess the land before sale or abandonment to foreigners. Further research is needed, but I suspect that even in the late nineteenth century the proportion of *kuleana* held by women in any given locality never exceeded 50 percent. In general we know little about how major events affected the local level in the last quarter of the century. How, for example, did rural Hawaiians adjust to the labor drain of the sugar industry, which in its early years grew on the labor of Hawaiian men *and* women?

Despite the dramatic rise in inheritance by women evident in the Māhele statistics, the census and tax data suggest that landholding by women obtained in a minority of Hawaiian households through the 1860s. Over time, however, more land fell to women. Was this due to the inheritance laws operating in conjunction with demographic imperatives, or does the trend signal changes in Hawaiian cultural norms? The answer must be both. The historical factors that produced a rise in female inheritance through the 1840s and 1850s continued to obtain after the land division. If we can believe modern ethnographers, both Hawaiian and haole, matrilaterality has been increasingly prevalent in Hawaiian social organization. Howard's (1971:21–23) study, for example, demonstrated a high frequency of coresidence for such relationships as Mo/Da, MoMo/DaCh, MoBr/SiCh, and MoSi/SiCh. Modern Hawaiian adoption patterns also reflect a matrilateral bias (Howard et al. 1970:37–38; Linnekin 1985:186–87). The changes in social organization and patterns of jural authority are the result of internal social dynamics and not simply the artifact of introduced laws and external constraints. These changes—one of which is a more bilateral pattern of land inheritance—are founded on certain Hawaiian cultural precedents, notably the structural role, personal authority, and categorical *mana* of women.

Colonization and Gender

Indisputably, the Hawaiian people as a whole suffered a tremendous diminution of status in the aftermath of the Māhele. Along with land alienation and proletarianization, the latter half of the nineteenth century saw the further weakening of the monarchy and the ascendancy of foreign business interests. By the time of annexation in 1898, Hawaiians had lost their land, their traditional livelihood, and their political autonomy. They became a numerical minority in their own land between 1884 and 1890 (Schmitt 1968:74). The haole leaders of the 1893 revolutionary government introduced so many restrictive qualifications that most Hawaiians could not vote in the republic's first election. The landless and economically disadvantaged status of Hawaiians was publicly recognized as a social problem in the debate preceding the Hawaiian Homes Act of 1920.

Were Hawaiian women differentially devalued as a result of Western colonization, vis-à-vis Hawaiian men? The answer depends on context and perspective—devalued in whose eyes? Rather than attempting an overly simple answer to a contentious question, it seems more fruitful to examine specific contexts where women may or may not have had explicit authority or instrumental power. A distinction is appropriate here between the formal legal status of Hawaiian women during this period and their position in local-level social organization. The former largely reflects a Euro-American male ideology, but this did not immediately supplant the indigenous cultural valuation that, minimally, recognized women as powerful beings. From the 1840s through the 1860s, a number of laws inspired and often authored by foreigners successively abridged the legal rights of Hawaiian women. As I suggested earlier, however, the impact of these statutes on the local level is debatable and the extent to which Hawaiians internalized the white male view of women is even more questionable. There appears to have been some dissonance, in other words, between women's legal disabilities and their active role and valuation within the rural, commoner Hawaiian community, as well as between women's legal standing and the actual political power of high-ranking chiefesses through the nineteenth century.

Judging from twentieth-century sources, such as the work of Mary Kawena Pukui and other ethnographers, the pivotal role of Hawaiian women within the household seems to have been if anything strengthened, with women often becoming authority figures as well as nodes of social relationships (see Gallimore and Howard 1968; Handy and Pukui 1972; Howard 1971, 1974; Howard et al. 1970; Linnekin 1985). If this interpretation is correct, Hawaii is not the first colonized society where the local and domestic importance of women has been enhanced even as they have been devalued by the dominant ideology. Other writers have pointed out that colonization introduces a domestic/jural distinction in gender relations that was lacking in the indigenous society. This segregation of men and women in different domains of activity is effected both by the introduction of foreign manufactured goods and by the institutionalization of Western ideology regarding male and female roles (see Boserup 1970; Sanday 1981). For Tonga, Gailey (1987:105) argues that the relegation of women to the kinship sphere "contributed to the degradation of women's authority as classes and state institutions emerged."

But I would maintain that the notion of local response is pertinent here, for indigenous cultural schemes were not eradicated by the world system and did have some impact on what Sahlins (1981) has called "the structure of the conjuncture." From 1778 to annexation, the Hawaiian people as a whole were progressively devalued from the point of view of colonial nations and the expanding world system. From this perspective, which was institutionalized when resident white males overthrew the monarchy in 1893, women were devalued with respect to Hawaiian men. But another perspective was (and, arguably, still is) operational in Hawaii, one that I have characterized as a view from the "inside," from within the Hawaiian community, in contradistinction to the perspective of the "outside," the Western political economy. Though Hawaiians as a people are no longer rurally based, they still constitute a community, not in the sense of a geographical entity, but as a perceived and self-ascribed cultural identity, an indigenous people who have suffered in common the effects of colonization. In the Hawaiian perspective women are still active, authoritative, and instrumental. Given the numbers of Hawaiian women who exercise personal and political leadership today, "inside" as I use it here is emphatically not the same as the "domestic domain." In the Hawaiian case the salient historical issue seems to be whether, in the encounter between different cultural constructions of women, one ideology wins out to the exclusion of the other. Does the powerful intruder's philosophy necessarily supplant the indigenous, or is there a mutually creative encounter between the two, resulting in a unique local version of gender roles that is neither wholly indigenous nor wholly foreign?

I suspect that in such conflicts of values decisive victories are rare. Certainly the historical encounter between gender constructions continues to play itself out in Hawaii today, as the state government, dominated numerically by non-Hawaiian men, confronts many strong and vocal Hawaiian women in political leadership roles. My subjective impression is that women of all ethnicities are more active in politics in Hawaii and are more likely to be taken seriously as leaders in the public domain than are women in most of mainland America. An explanation for such a contrast, if it is plausible, would be complex and would have to take into account other cultures and other, later events than those addressed here. But the cultural-historical encounter narrated in this book—between Hawaiian women's cultural standing and certain nineteenth-century events—would make up at least part of the story.

Chapter 8

Status, Gender, and Colonialism

Where both ideological and behavioral differentiation exist, a balance of power is most likely to occur. . . . Assuming that each sex group in this case controls essential resources, one cannot dominate the other because they are equally interdependent and complementary. Furthermore, because differentiation is stressed on the ideological level, the two groups may not be related hierarchically, because they are perceived as two different things. . . . I would suggest that the first pattern (ideological and behavioral differentiation) is the most common cross-culturally, and the one in which a dominant/subordinate relationship between the sexes is least likely to occur.

—Susan Carol Rogers (1978:155–56)

Imported cultural baggage gives priority to men. However, we must give indigenous peoples some credit. . . . There is a reinterpretation that makes it difficult to predict what the ultimate effects will be on the indigenous system.

—Jill Nash (1984:119)

The gender literature since the 1970s has been dominated by a limited set of major issues, and most of these are variants of the sexual asymmetry question. The mentalist/materialist theoretical divergence surfaces here too, though a sense of sisterhood seems to have muted the debate somewhat. The anthropology of women has not (so far) been characterized by the acrimonious invectives that have been hurled between Marxists and symbolists in other academic debates. This may be because the two perspectives appear, in this context, as different emphases rather than as contradictory and opposed modes of explanation. There are of course many points of view in the anthropology of gender, but a broad contrast is discernible between cultural and symbolic analyses on the one hand (e.g., Ardener 1972; Ortner 1974; Ortner and Whitehead 1981) and studies that derive women's status primarily from production and distribution of material resources (e.g., Beneria 1982; Boserup 1970; Etienne and Leacock 1980; Friedl 1967; Leacock 1981; Sacks 1979). With the exception of Gailey (1980, 1987), most of the literature on Polynesian women falls into the former group, focusing largely on women's symbolic and ritual standing. Weiner (1982, 1985) has focused on women's creation of cloth wealth, but from an implicitly cultural rather than materialist standpoint: she argues that articles such as fine mats and cloth have to do with societal reproduction, "the regeneration of some fundamental aspect of kinship identity" (1985:213).

It should be evident from my earlier discussion of Hawaiian women's activities in production and exchange that I see women's control over resources and material things—including domestic necessities as well as cultural valuables and exchange goods—as a key aspect of their social position. Hawaiian women's production of high-ranking articles has been notably overlooked by contemporary ethnographers, and this omission has led to a somewhat skewed view of their cultural valuation. I do not believe, however, that there is a necessary relationship between control over resources and ideological valuation. The anthropological literature attests that individuals in certain social categories may be esteemed very highly though they neither produce nor allocate important goods. And in certain societies women may contribute substantially to the food supply and yet count for little in male ideology. Extending this premise to the case at hand demands the recognition of cultural-historical particularities within the general processes and impacts associated with Western colonialism. Recent works emphasizing political economy argue precisely this point, and I am merely extending the insight to the study of gender relations.

Compared to other theoretical pursuits in anthropology, the gender literature seems flawed by a tendency to seek simplistic equations explaining women's status. Perhaps this is because male/female appears as an unambiguous binary opposition to Western writers; surely there must be an equally clear relationship between the two terms and a simple order of determinations at work. But the status of Polynesian women in general, and of Hawaiian women in particular, calls into question any such simple accounting. If we examine the division of labor, ritual roles and ideology, political authority, social organization, and the ethos of interpersonal relations, then countervailing and even contradictory indications are evident in Hawaiian gender relations. In Hawaii the overweening social differentiation between chiefs and commoners appears more salient than gender in determining the practical aspects of one's life situation. Women also have different "statuses" depending on social position and on their place in the life cycle (cf. Oboler 1985:304). In Hawaii older sisters are respected and wield greater authority than junior siblings—including male junior siblings—and the same can be said for older women in general relative to young men and women.

Perhaps in reaction to some of these conceptual problems, the anthropology of women has shifted its focus toward more cultural concerns, in the Geertzian sense. The dominant problematic has shifted from the "status of women," narrowly defined, to the more holistic concept of "gender," with its focus on the symbols and meanings of male/female relations (see, e.g., Ortner and Whitehead 1981). "Status of women" always implies the asymmetry question: what is women's status *vis-à-vis men?* Phrasing the study of women in terms of "status" tends to direct us to issues of public, jural authority, where women are at some disadvantage—ideological or statistical—in most known societies. We then become preoccupied with explaining why this is so: is it differential control over production, control over distribution, a colonial phenomenon? As I suggested in the first chapter, since Rosaldo and Lamphere's (1974) pioneering collection this has come to seem less fruitful as a research question.

The notion of gender implicitly broadens the scope of the inquiry beyond the extent of women's public authority and control over resources. Gender, as opposed to sex, is firmly cultural rather than biological and sees female as, a term in a semiotic system rather than as a naturally determined state. A study of gender relations can address fundamental cultural constructs of what it is to be a man or a woman in a particular society, as well as the symbolic attributes of "male" and "female." Gender may also suggest an analysis of symbolic and social relationships as complementary rather than as necessarily hierarchical. Even in cases of extreme male dominance, women are never without power. The pressing empirical question now seems to be the nature of that power: what is its basis, in what contexts is it manifested, and how do female and male power mutually define each other?

The Hawaiian materials point to gender differentiation throughout the details of life—men and women having different tasks and attainments, different deities, different realms of responsibility. Also evident is a degree of gender politics: some vying and competition between men and women for personal control. Overall, my sense of Hawaiian women's valuation vis-à-vis men accords with Susan Carol Rogers's statement quoted above: they are socially equivalent and complementary. In an analysis of Andean gender ideologies Silverblatt (1987) has used the phrase "gender parallelism." This term aptly describes Hawaiian gender relations as well. The structural and ideological similarities between Hawaii and the Inca are striking. Both were politically hierarchical societies with a pronounced degree of "gender segregation" (Silverblatt 1987:64). In both societies high-ranking women controlled material resources of their own and exercised considerable independent authority, albeit in spheres parallel to those of men. Both Hawaii and Inca Peru are ethnographic footnotes for the institution of "royal incest." Among the Inca, too, the "sexual division of the cosmos" (Silverblatt 1987:38) portrayed male/female complementarity and interdependence and women dominated in the transmission of ritual knowledge (Silverblatt 1987:67). Thor Heyerdahl notwithstanding, there are no homologies between Hawaii and the Incas, but there are important structural analogies. Both were highly developed chiefdoms with bilateral (or dual, in the Inca case) kinship systems. The similarities in gender ideology raise intriguing cross-cultural questions. In this sort of society, parallelism in gender relations may be inevitable.

Cloth and Colonization

The literature on women and colonialism has tended to emphasize the sexual asymmetry question over the holistic examination of gender relations. In this as in other problematics, our initial phrasing of the issue defines the tenor of the analysis; an emphasis on gender tends to produce more culturally detailed studies that pay greater attention to women's separate spheres. Silverblatt's work is notable in that she explores the status implications of the conflict between the gender ideologies of rulers and ruled. Other colonial studies have focused on women's production of material goods, control of resources, and changing economic roles. Before arriving at a concluding statement about historicity, colonialism, and changes in gender relations, I will examine a few of the analyses that view women's role in the division of labor as a major component of their status. These studies argue that as this role changes through Western contact and class formation, women's status is diminished.

In several case studies of women in colonized societies (Etienne 1980;

Gailey 1980; Petersen 1982), anthropologists have shown that the introduction of Western goods has a negative impact on women's status. In Polynesia this is largely a question of cloth: the supplanting of handcrafted cloth by imported fabric. The logic of this argument is compelling if we assume that material productivity is a major determinant of women's position in society. Where subsistence agriculture is primarily men's work and women produce cultural valuables and exchange goods, the introduction of manufactured items can be expected to devalue the products of women (Gailey 1987:220–36). First, women's products are likely to count little in the context of the external market, where foodstuffs—not handicrafts or "curiosities"—are demanded in exchange for foreign goods. Second, imported factory-made goods displace women's manufactures both as valuables and as everyday goods. When women no longer produce a society's high-exchange goods and domestic necessities, a distinction develops between jural and domestic domains. Women tend to be left only tasks associated with housekeeping and child care. Petersen (1982: 137) nicely summarizes the effect of this progression in Pohnpei: "Where once Ponapean women had produced the exchange goods that knit together their society, now they relied on men's agriculture or wage labor to produce the capital to purchase exchange goods. From a position of equal partnership in production, women were turned into consumers."

The scenario Petersen describes is recognizable as a classic description of the effects of Western economic expansion along the lines of the world system model (Wallerstein 1974, 1979; see also Wolf 1982), and his statements about Pohnpeian women are applicable to indigenous peoples in general. In the process of colonization societies such as Hawaii were economically and politically subordinated, transformed into the "periphery" of the world system, "that geographical sector of it wherein production is primarily of lower-ranking goods" (Wallerstein 1974:301–2). In Wallerstein's formulation societies on the periphery provide raw materials and agricultural commodities to the core states. But as the Hawaiian case illustrates, even before becoming significant suppliers indigenous societies are drawn into the world economy as consumers of Western imported goods. In Hawaii the creation of economic dependency preceded the loss of political sovereignty by several decades. The first material transactions between Hawaiians and Europeans were the genesis of an asymmetrical exchange relationship whereby "high-profit, high-capital intensive" goods produced in the core states were exchanged for agricultural commodities ("low-wage . . . low-profit, low-capital intensive goods") produced in the indigenous society (Wallerstein 1974:351). Certainly the sandalwood trade exemplifies the developing relationship of core and periphery, but the Hawaiian economy can be analyzed in these terms through the heyday of the sugar industry and up to the present-day dependence on tourism. In providing services to the mass tourist industry, Hawaii still offers "*cheap labor far away*" (Wallerstein 1974:86, emphasis in original).

The strength of dependency theory is that it places local economic transformations in the context of global historical processes, notably the expansion of Western capitalism. But this strength is also the anthropological weakness of this perspective. World system theory has been widely criticized for being "over-deterministic" (Worsley 1980) and for neglecting issues of local adaptation and resistance (see Roseberry 1988:165–67). The emphasis on international capitalist exchange also provides few tools for understanding internal processes of differentiation and specific mechanisms of causality. Etienne (1980) and Gailey (1987) offer more nuanced treatments of economic and political developments affecting women within indigenous societies. Etienne (1980) traces how the introduction of imported thread and cloth, cash crops, and money altered domestic gender politics among the Baule on the Ivory Coast. Baule women, who once controlled cloth production, have been rendered economically "inessential" as their husbands have gained new autonomy through commodity production. Since men participate differentially in the cash economy, the marriage relationship has been transformed from one of interdependence to female dependence on men. Etienne argues that the balance of power in the family depended on equivalent and complementary productive roles. Colonial conquest and development schemes have tipped the scales in favor of men.

Gailey (1987) sees the subordination of Tongan women resulting not only from the replacement of cultural valuables by imported goods, but also from the supplanting of indigenous rank and kinship by invasive class structures. As in Etienne's African example, Tongan women's cloth making was rendered inconsequential by the importation of foreign substitutes. Here, too, Gailey (1987:220) argues, "changes in the division of labor by gender . . . skewed authority relations in the household and helped to create dependency of women upon men." Although women were categorically inferior to men in indigenous ideology, Tongan women as sisters were explicitly superior to men as brothers (Gailey 1987:47, 61–62). The state resolved the native ambiguities of Tongan gender relations in favor of men, introducing civil restrictions on the prerogatives of sisters: "Today . . . rank considerations have been superseded by class prerogatives; and material and labor claims by sisters are illegal" (Gailey 1987:xv). Gailey sees the continuity of women's importance in the kinship sphere in negative terms, as manifesting "the degradation of women's authority." (For other views of Tongan gender relations see Herda 1987; James 1988; Ralston n.d.2.)

Hawaiian-European relations in the early postcontact period exemplify certain global processes that have historically tended to affect women negatively: the "peripheralization" of indigenous societies, state formation, and class stratification. Throughout this study, however, I have emphasized that the culture in place also determines the particularities of any contact situation. When applied to gender relations, this insight means—contra Gailey—that women's subordination and powerlessness do not universally follow from colonization and state formation (Stoler 1977 has made this point in a Javanese context, as has Peletz 1987 for Malaysia). In order to make judgments about women's status in colonial situations one must closely examine women's total realm of activities, the resources they controlled, and the contexts in which they were important, before and after Western contact. In the following discussion I will use the example of cloth to substantiate and underscore this point. In brief, I argue that the supplanting of tapa by imported cloth did not result in a loss of status for Hawaiian women for reasons having to do with their other roles, both economic and structural.

It seems logical to conclude that, beginning with the earliest encounters between Hawaiians and Europeans, the differential market demand for the products of men and women would gradually alter the categorical relationship between the sexes. For the most part the foreigners wanted food, the production of which was largely the province of Hawaiian men. This would tend to concentrate foreign trade goods and money in the hands of men (cf. Gailey 1987:230). On many ships officers and crew were reminded that supplies were their primary goal and were specifically cautioned against procuring "curiosities" (Meares to Captain Colnett, April 17, 1789, in Meares 1790; app. 2; see also "Instructions of the Merchant Proprietors," app. 1). Vancouver's men were forbidden to trade directly with the Hawaiians until the ship had all necessary supplies because, as he explains in his journal,

> Whilst the prohibition was in force . . . all the essential articles were brought to market, and perchased by us as fast as they could conveniently be received. . . . But no sooner were these restrictions discontinued, and our people at liberty to indulge themselves in the purchase of what at the moment

they esteemed to be curiosities, than almost all our essential supplies ceased to be brought from the shore, and the few articles . . . which did appear . . . were increased in price four or five hundred percent. (1798, 2:163)

Vancouver termed the native handicrafts "insignificant articles, which were no sooner possessed than they were neglected, and often in a few days were thrown overboard." Of all the Hawaiian "curiosities," the feather cloaks and helmets were more showy than fine mats and tapas and garnered greater attention from foreigners. The feathered artifacts were more likely to be preserved with care and to end up in museum collections, and I do not think this is solely due to different rates of deterioration.

The other important factor in the differential valuation of men's and women's manufactures after European contact was the chiefs' adoption of imported cloth and luxury items for sumptuary display. Chiefly high status came to be indexed not by fine tapas and mats but by silks, silver service, and tea sets. One reason that we know so little about Hawaiian fine mats and tapas in comparison to the analogous articles in Samoa, for example, is that in postcontact Hawaii the fine-quality traditional manufactures rapidly lost their functions as ceremonial gifts and markers of high status. The making of fine mats and tapas declined as the chiefs turned to Western markers of status; Brigham (1911:2) estimated that fine tapas ceased to be produced soon after the arrival of the missionaries in 1820.

It would be logical to infer from the evidence that the chiefs' enthusiasm for foreign luxury goods relegated Hawaiian women's products to domestic and common use. In the 1820s the ruling chiefs adorned themselves with European garments when they went about town or appeared in formal gatherings, but mats and tapas still served as the primary furnishings of chiefly dwellings. Among commoners in rural areas, mats and tapas retained their domestic uses into the last half of the nineteenth century. Brigham writes that when he arrived in Hawaii in 1864, "kapa was worn only in the outlying districts, and only the plainer forms were made. . . . on Oahu foreign cloth was almost universally worn" (1911:3). According to Brigham, the production and use of tapa had ceased by 1890. Certainly after 1850, when tax payments had to be made in currency, the demand for the weaving and tapa making skills of Hawaiian women must have greatly diminished.

One might be led to conclude that by the 1860s the only economic task left to Hawaiian women was that of producing coarse domestic furnishings in remote areas. Evidence presented in preceding chapters indicates that this was not so. As the Lāhaina census attests, in the cities women engaged in numerous wage-earning activities, as well as in the production of craft items and apparel for sale. At least by the 1850s rural Hawaiian women were working in the fields, and given the effects of emigration and mobility on the local group it is likely that they did so increasingly in the latter half of the century. But even if it were true that women's direct economic contribution diminished in the postcontact period, the question remains: does the devaluation of women's manufactures lead to the devaluation of women themselves? If there was relatively small market demand for Hawaiian women's products, would this necessarily affect the categorical relationship between the sexes? The linkage here seems problematic.

I suggest that the replacement of tapa by foreign cloth had in itself little impact on the native valuation of women. The status of Hawaiian women, both in pre- and post-European times, is much more than a question of cloth. First, in early transactions with shippers the issue of women's manufactures is nearly irrelevant, for Hawaiian women had something else of value: they had sex. In a significant contrast to Etienne's African example, there is no clear evidence of the *dependency* of Hawaiian women on their men. Second, the cultural estimation of women in Hawaii was not simply derived from their material productions, though women produced things of no little value. In earlier chapters I described the structural salience of women in Hawaiian social organization, the political hierarchy, and the sentimental complex celebrating women as mothers and as sisters. As heirs and landholders after the Māhele women became increasingly important as the stable figures in the local group, and in this status their authority was not simply relegated to the domestic domain. I do not dispute the fact that from the 1840s Western-inspired civil restrictions worked to abridge Hawaiian women's public status. I do suggest that Hawaiian women, both chiefly and common, resisted such pressures with some success.

Women in Global and Local History

The case of Hawaiian women aptly demonstrates that "sexual meanings," to use Ortner and Whitehead's (1981) term, are critically bound up with the material and political aspects of women's status, and suggests that the explanation of any facet of women's lives must be multivariate. Hawaiian women were favored in land inheritance during the period of the Māhele *because* women were symbolically associated with land, *because* women were valued as producers of high cultural goods, goods that men needed, *because* an ideology of male interpersonal dominance and superiority was weakly developed in Hawaii, *because* the gender tabus of the native religion founded a separate domain of female ritual and social power, *because* women were seen as powerful, autonomous beings in the indigenous society, *because* from the male perspective women were points of access to rank, land, and political power, *because* women could assume positions of the highest jural authority though men were favored in such roles, and *because* depopulation and economic events disrupted normal chains of inheritance in local communities. With the accelerated dislocation of the commoners, alternate jural figures—women—emerged as landholders and household authorities, though they saw themselves as temporary guardians of the family's destiny.

Since I see the problem of women as multifactorial, I cannot agree that "women's authority and status *necessarily* decline with class and state formation" (Gailey 1987:ix; emphasis added), though I concur that women's subordination has often followed from Western colonization. Gerald Sider's (1986:34) caution against assuming a one-way "directionality" in capitalist expansion is appropriate here. Sider felicitously calls for an awareness of "more complex processes, with less uniform directionalities, in the history of hinterland societies—processes of both loss and creation, adaptation and distancing, collusion and confrontation." In order to assess changes in women's status one must ask questions that are culturally nuanced: authority in what areas? Status in what contexts, and from whose point of view? Did women have particular practical alternatives, and how successful were these as modes of resistance (see, e.g., Ong 1987)?

From the perspective of white foreigners, all Hawaiians were devalued in the colonial encounter, and women particularly so. The early seamen saw them as whores. Missionaries and mid-nineteenth-century government advisors sought to mold them, practically and jurally, into the domestic ideal of the Western middle-class woman. But the Hawaiian cultural response had some force in this confrontation. Westerners learned of necessity to respect Hawaiian chiefesses as political authorities, and Hawaiian women were not transformed into meek, acquiescent quilt makers. In Hawaii as elsewhere, Western "impact" is perhaps better phrased as a contest. Hawaiians, like other indigenous peoples, were destined to lose the contest politically, but they have nonetheless retained a certain cultural and community integrity, even in gender relations.

"The problem of women"—whether synchronic or historical—must encompass gender constructs and symbolism as well as an evaluation of male/female political authority and control over resources. The question is not simply one of ritual status, nor of cloth, nor of household composition, nor even of land, but of all these arenas. The concept of "gender hierarchy" must be unbundled into specifics. Similarly, colonial history is only intelligible as a structural and cultural history. Hawaii lacked the explicit, normative denigration of women found, say, in some African and Mediterranean societies. Moreover, the segregation of men and women under the *kapu* system gave women a degree of autonomy, even a certain ritual leverage over men. The social standing of Hawaiian men *and* women has been radically abridged since 1778. A society with far different notions of women's proper place became dominant in the islands. Nevertheless, cultural ideas such as gender constructions can prove remarkably resilient. The devastating social impact of colonization on all Hawaiians is undeniable. Whether Hawaiians have internalized the Western model of male-and-female is quite another question, and one that is yet to be answered.

In some ways this study has challenged both the cultural interpretivist and orthodox Marxist positions regarding the effects of Western contact on indigenous societies. Neither form of analysis seems adequate in itself for understanding colonial situations, where global and local processes are always in dynamic conjunction. William Roseberry (1988:174) has written that scholars of political economy constantly face a dilemma: "They must avoid making capitalism too determinative, and they must avoid romanticizing the cultural freedom of anthropological subjects." The tension that Roseberry so aptly describes has informed the present work, and probably concerns most historical anthropologists. Acting human subjects respond to multiple determinations, both structural and practical. This book has attempted to weigh the constraints and power disparities that impinged on Hawaiian women against the autonomous capabilities by which they defined themselves historically as people of consequence.

Glossary

ahupua'a: land division running from the mountain to the sea
aikane: intimate friend
'ai kapu: the "tabu eating," referring to the pre-1819 period when men and
 women ate apart
'āina: land
akua: god
ali'i: chief
aloha: affection, love
'aumakua [pl. *'aumākua*]: ancestral guardian spirit
'auwai: irrigation ditch

haku 'āina: landlord; family member having authority over household land
hale pe'a: menstrual seclusion house
hānai: adoptive; literally 'feeding'
haole: white person, foreigner
heiau: temple of the indigenous Hawaiian religion
ho'āo pa'a: "binding" marriage as opposed to cohabitation
ho'okupu: offering, tribute
ho'onoa: 'to free' or lift a tabu
hui: corporation, society, cooperative group

'ili: named subsection of an *ahupua'a*
'imi haku: 'to seek a lord,' the custom of attaching oneself to a social superior
 in order to better one's own destiny
imu: underground oven

kāhili: feather standards of the chiefs
kahu: guardian, steward
kahuna [pl. *kāhuna*]: priest; expert; healer
kaikaina: younger sibling of the same sex
kaikua'ana: older sibling of the same sex
kama'āina: old-time resident; literally "child of the land"
kanaka: man, mankind; often used in the nineteenth century to refer to the
 common people in contradistinction to the chiefs

kapa: bark cloth

kapu: tabu, prohibition; sacred, divine

kapu moe: prostration tabu, requiring those of lesser rank to lie face down in the chief's presence

kaukauali'i: lesser chiefs

kāula: seer, prophet

kīhāpai: cultivated garden, usually dryland plantings

kino lau: myriad forms or 'bodies' of the gods

konohiki: landlord; headman, land agent

kua'āina: 'back land,' rural, remote areas

kula: open, unirrigated land, used for dryland plantings

kuleana: claim, right, responsibility; Land Commission Award

kūpuna: grandparents, ancestors

lei niho palaoa: whalebone pendant, sign of chiefly status

lele: discontiguous land parcel belonging to an *'ili;* lit. 'to jump, fly'

lo'i: taro patch

luakini: war temples, where ruling chiefs made sacrifices to legitimize and sediment their authority

lū'au: a Hawaiian feast; taro leaves

luna: local overseer under the *konohiki*

ma: particle meaning 'attendant upon, associates'; used here to refer to the commoner household group

maka'āinana: the common people

makai: seaward, toward the sea

makua [pl. *mākua*]: parent

malo: loincloth, usual male dress

mana: efficacious power

mauka: upland, toward the mountain

mōhai: offering; to make an offering

mo'o: lizard; a common form of *'aumākua;* also, a 'strip' of land

mo'opuna: grandchild

naha: the second-highest chiefly rank, possessing the sitting tabu (*kapu noho*)

noa: common, 'free' of *kapu*

noho pū: cohabitation

'ohana: family, relatives

ōhua: dependents, retainers, added-on household members

olonā: shrub from which a fiber was made for fishlines and nets

pā'ū: sarong or lavalava, usual dress for women

pi'o, nī'aupi'o: the highest chiefly ranks, resulting from the union of true or classificatory siblings

po'e: people
poi: taro paste, the traditional staple food of Hawaii
punahele: 'favorite' of a chief
punalua: co-spouse

ti: cordyline terminalis, a plant used ritually in the Hawaiian religion and for medicinal purposes

wahine [pl. *wāhine*]: woman
wauke: shrup from which tapa cloth was made
wohi: the third rank of ruling chiefs, related as junior collaterals to the ruler; Kamehameha held this rank

Notes

Chapter 1

1. The gender literature in anthropology has become voluminous since Rosaldo and Lamphere's (1974) landmark volume. Other noteworthy collections include MacCormack and Strathern (1980), Ortner and Whitehead (1981), and Etienne and Leacock (1980). For reviews of the literature see Quinn (1977), Rapp (1979), and Atkinson (1982). O'Brien and Tiffany (1984) and Strathern (1987) are recent collections dealing with women in Pacific societies.

2. For other accounts of the Māhele see Chinen 1958 and Kelly 1956.

3. The Crown and Government Lands are a major focus of modern Hawaiian protest and political activism. After the overthrow of the monarchy in 1893 the Crown and Government Lands were merged into a category of Public Lands. When Hawaii was annexed by the United States these were ceded to the federal government. Most of these lands were returned to the State of Hawaii after statehood, but the federal government still retains large tracts for military reservations. Under the provisions of the 1978 State Constitution Native Hawaiians are defined as one class of beneficiaries of the income the state receives from the "Ceded Lands," and the Office of Hawaiian Affairs (OHA) was established in 1980 to manage the proceeds. However, there is still no definitive inventory of the lands that fall into this category, and some state departments have been recalcitrant in meeting their fiscal obligation to OHA. For an excellent summary of modern Hawaiian land issues see volume 2 of the Native Hawaiians Study Commission (1983) report.

Chapter 3

1. For statements and observations bearing on the sexual division of labor see, in addition to sources cited in the text: Arago 1823:145; Campbell 1967: 139–40; Ellis 1782:169, 176; Ellis 1969:109; Judd 1928:9; King 1967:625; Doyle 1953:163; Malo 1951:75; Menzies 1920:82–83; Paulding 1970:213–14; Stewart 1970:146, 150.

2. *Olonā* fiber, made from the bark of the shrub, was resistant to sea water and highly durable. Used for fishing nets, lines, and cord, *olonā* was traded internally in pre-European times and was a medium of tax payment (Kamakau

1976:44). In the nineteenth century *olonā* was sold to shippers for rigging and lines.

Chapter 5

1. Kaomi was a part-Tahitian companion and boon friend of Kauikeaouli, Kamehameha III. In 1833 and 1834, encouraged and abetted by Kaomi, Kamehameha III rebelled against Christian strictures. He made a show of public drunkenness, suspended the law against adultery, and generally engaged in outrageous behavior for over a year. Eventually he succumbed to pressure from his Christian mothers and other chiefs, and put a new set of laws into effect in 1835.

2. This usage was originally suggested by Marshall Sahlins. For a reconstruction of the local group see also Kirch 1984:243–63.

Works Cited

Alexander, W. D.
  1890   "A Brief History of Land Titles in the Hawaiian Kingdom." *Hawaiian Annual for 1891,* 105–24. Honolulu: Thrum Publishing Co.
Andrews, Lorrin
  1836   "Letters from Lorrin Andrews." *Missionary Herald* 33:390–91.
  1865   *A Dictionary of the Hawaiian Language.* Honolulu: Henry M. Whitney.
Anonymous
  1868   "The Story of Kanewailani." *Ke Au Okoa,* February 2–April 2. Bernice P. Bishop Museum. Typescript.
Anonymous
  1839   "Crime in the Sandwich Islands." *Hawaiian Spectator* 2:234.
Arago, Jacques
  1823   *Narrative of a Voyage Round the World. . . .* London: Treuttel, Jun, and Richter. [1819]
Ardener, Edwin
  1972   "Belief and the Problem of Women." In *The Interpretation of Ritual,* edited by J. S. LaFontaine, 135–58. London: Tavistock.
Ardener, Shirley
  1975   "Introduction." In *Perceiving Women,* edited by Shirley Ardener, vii–xxiii. London: Malaby Press.
Asad, Talal, ed.
  1973   *Anthropology and the Colonial Encounter.* London: Ithaca Press.
Atkinson, Jane Monnig
  1982   "Review Essay: Anthropology." *Signs* 8:236–58.
Barrère, Dorothy B.
  1959   Glossary. In *Fragments of Hawaiian History As Recorded by John Papa Ii,* translated by Mary Kawena Pukui. Honolulu: Bishop Museum Press.
Barrère, Dorothy B., Mary Kawena Pukui, and Marion Kelly
  1980   *Hula: Historical Perspectives.* Pacific Anthropological Records, no. 30. Honolulu: Bernice P. Bishop Museum.
Barrot, Theodore-Adolphe
  1978   *Unless Haste Is Made.* Kailua: Press Pacifica. [1836]

Barth, Fredrik
1956   "Ecologic Relationships of Ethnic Groups in Swat, North Pakistan." *American Anthropologist* 58:1079–89.

Bates, G. W. [A. Haole, pseud.]
1854   *Sandwich Island Notes.* New York: Harper and Bros.

Bateson, Gregory
1967   *Naven.* Stanford: Stanford University Press.

Beaglehole, J. C., ed.
1967   *The Journals of Captain James Cook on His Voyages of Discovery,* vol. 3, pts. 1 and 2. Cambridge: Cambridge University Press for the Hakluyt Society.

Bell, Edward
1929–30 "Log of the *Chatham.*" *Honolulu Mercury* 1:7–26, 55–69, 76–96; 2:80–91, 119–29. [1792–94]

Beneria, Lourdes, ed.
1982   *Women and Development.* New York: Praeger.

Beresford, William [and George Dixon]
1789   *A Voyage around the World . . . Performed in 1785, 1786, 1787 and 1788. . . .* London: George Goulding. [1786–87]

Biersack, Aletta, ed.
N.d.   *Clio in Oceania: Toward a Historical Anthropology.* Washington, D.C.: Smithsonian Institution Press. In press.

Bloxam, Andrew
1925   *Diary of Andrew Bloxam.* Bernice P. Bishop Museum Special Publication no. 10. Honolulu. [1824–25]

Blue, George
1925   "Early Relations between Hawaii and the Northwest Coast." *Reports of the Hawaiian Historical Society* 33:16–22.

Boit, John R.
Ms.   "The Journal of a Voyage Round the Globe." Copy of the second volume, HMCS. [1795–96]

Boserup, Esther
1970   *Women's Role in Economic Development.* New York: St. Martin's Press.

Brigham, William T.
1899   *Hawaiian Feather Work.* Memoirs of the Bernice P. Bishop Museum 1(1): 1–86. Honolulu.

1903   *Additional Notes on Hawaiian Feather Work.* Memoirs of the Bernice P. Bishop Museum 1(5): 437–53. Honolulu.

1906   *Mat and Basket Weaving of the Ancient Hawaiians.* Memoirs of the Bernice P. Bishop Museum 2(1): 1–105. Honolulu.

1911   *Ka Hana Kapa: The Making of Bark Cloth in Hawaii.* Memoirs of the Bernice P. Bishop Museum 3:1–273. Honolulu.

1918   *Additional Notes on Hawaiian Feather Work, Second Supplement.* Memoirs of the Bernice P. Bishop Museum 7(1):1–64. Honolulu.

Buck, Peter H. (Te Rangi Hiroa)
    1957   *Arts and Crafts of Hawaii.* Bernice P. Bishop Museum Special Publi-
            cation no. 45. Honolulu.
Burridge, Kenelm
    1959   "Siblings in Tangu." *Oceania* 30:128–54.
    1969   *Tangu Traditions.* Oxford: Oxford University Press.
Byron, George Anson Lord
    1826   *Voyage of H.M.S. Blonde to the Sandwich Islands, in the Years
            1824–1825.* London: Murray. [1824–25]
Campbell, Archibald
    1967   [1822] *A Voyage round the World from 1806 to 1812.* Facsimile ed.
            Honolulu: University of Hawaii Press. [1809–10]
Chamberlain, Levi
    Ms.   "Journal." 24 vols. HMCS. [1822–42]
Chamisso, Adelbert von
    1981   *Voyage autour du monde 1815–1818,* translated by Henri Baatsch.
            Paris: Le Sycomore. [1816–17]
Chinen, Jon
    1958   *The Great Mahele.* Honolulu: University of Hawaii Press.
Colcord, John
    Ms.   John Colcord's Journal. 1826–44. AH, Private Collections.
Colnett, James
    Ms.   "Journal of Captain James Colnett aboard the Prince of Wales &
            Princess Royal from 16 Oct. 1786 to 7 Nov. 1788." Copy, Hawaiian
            Collection, Hamilton Library, University of Hawaii. [November
            1787–February 1788]
Comaroff, Jean
    1985   *Body of Power, Spirit of Resistance.* Chicago: University of Chicago
            Press.
Comaroff, John L.
    1982   "Dialectical Systems, History and Anthropology: Units of Study
            and Questions of Theory." *Journal of Southern African Studies*
            8:143–72.
Conrad, Agnes, ed.
    1973   "The Letters and Journal of Francisco de Paula Marin." In *Don
            Francisco de Paula Marin,* edited by Ross H. Gast and Agnes C.
            Conrad. Honolulu: University Press of Hawaii for the Hawaiian
            Historical Society.
Cook, James
    1967   "Journal of Captain Cook: The Third Voyage." In *The Journals of
            Captain James Cook on His Voyages of Discovery,* edited by J. C.
            Beaglehole, 3:1–491. [1778–79]
Cook, James, and James King
    1784   *A Voyage to the Pacific Ocean, Undertaken . . . in the Years 1776,
            1777, 1778, 1779 and 1780.* 3 vols. London: W. and A. Strahan et al.
            [1778–79]

Corney, Peter
1896   *Voyages in the Northern Pacific*. Honolulu: Thomas G. Thrum. [1817–18]
Cox, Ross
1957   *The Columbia River*. Edited by Edgar I. Stewart and Jane R. Stewart. Norman: University of Oklahoma Press. [1811]
Damon, Ethel
1927   *Father Bond of Kohala*. Honolulu: The Friend.
Dampier, Robert
1971   *To the Sandwich Islands on H.M.S. Blonde*. Edited by Pauline King Joerger. Honolulu: University Press of Hawaii. [1824–25]
Davenport, William H.
1969   "The 'Hawaiian Cultural Revolution': Some Political and Economic Considerations." *American Anthropologist* 71:1–20.
Dening, Greg
1980   *Islands and Beaches: Discourse of a Silent Land, Marquesas 1774–1870*. Honolulu: University Press of Hawaii.
Dibble, Sheldon
1909   *A History of the Sandwich Islands*. Honolulu: Thomas G. Thrum. [1831–36, 1840]
Dole, Sanford
1892   "Evolution of Hawaiian Land Tenure." Papers of the Hawaiian Historical Society no. 5. Honolulu.
Dorton, Lilikalā
1986   "Land and the Promise of Capitalism: A Dilemma for the Hawaiian Chiefs of the 1848 Māhele," Ph.D. diss., University of Hawaii.
Doyle, Emma Lyons
1953   *Makua Laiana*. Honolulu: Advertiser Publishing Co. [Lorenzo Lyons, 1832–86]
Dubisch, Jill, ed.
1986   *Gender and Power in Rural Greece*. Princeton: Princeton University Press.
Ellis, William [surgeon]
1782   *An Authentic Narrative of a Voyage Performed by Captain Cook and Captain Clerke*. 2 vols. London: Robinson et al. [1778–79]
Ellis, William [missionary]
1969   [1842] *Polynesian Researches: Hawaii*. Facsimile ed. Rutland and Tokyo: Charles E. Tuttle Company. [1823]
Emerson, Nathaniel B.
1894   "The Bird-Hunters of Ancient Hawaii." *Hawaiian Annual for 1895*, 101–11. Honolulu: Thrum Publishing Co.
1909   *Unwritten Literature of Hawaii: The Sacred Songs of the Hula*. Bureau of American Ethnology Bulletin no. 38. Washington, D.C.: Government Printing Office.
Etienne, Mona
1980   "Women and Men, Cloth and Colonization: The Transformation of

Production-Distribution Relations among the Baule (Ivory Coast)." In *Women and Colonization,* edited by Mona Etienne and Eleanor Leacock, 214–38. New York: Praeger.

Etienne, Mona, and Eleanor Leacock eds.
1980   *Women and Colonization: Anthropological Perspectives.* New York: Praeger.

Feil, D. K.
1978   "Women and Men in the Enga *Tee.*" *American Anthropologist* 5:263–79.

Firth, Raymond
1957   *We, the Tikopia.* Boston: Beacon Press.

Fornander, Abraham
1865   *Report of the Inspector General of Schools, Island of Maui.* Original in AH.
1878–85   *An Account of the Polynesian Race.* 3 vols. London: Trubner and Co.
1916–19   *Fornander Collection of Hawaiian Antiquities and Folk-lore.* Translated by John Wise. Edited by Thomas G. Thrum. Memoirs of the Bernice P. Bishop Museum, vols. 4–6. Honolulu.

Freycinet, Louis Claude de Soulses de
1978   *Hawaii in 1819: A Narrative Account by Louis Claude de Soulses de Freycinet.* Translated by Ella Wiswell. Edited by Marion Kelly. Pacific Anthropological Records, no. 26. Honolulu: Bernice P. Bishop Museum.

Friedl, Ernestine
1967   "The Position of Women: Appearance and Reality." *Anthropological Quarterly* 40:97–108.

Gailey, Christine Ward
1980   "Putting Down Sisters and Wives: Tongan Women and Colonization." In *Women and Colonization,* edited by Mona Etienne and Eleanor Leacock, 294–322. New York: Praeger.
1987   *Kinship to Kingship: Gender Hierarchy and State Formation in the Tongan Islands.* Austin: University of Texas Press.

Gallimore, Ronald, and Alan Howard, eds.
1968   *Studies in a Hawaiian Community.* Pacific Anthropological Records, no. 1. Honolulu: Bernice P. Bishop Museum.

Gething, Judith
1977   "Christianity and Coverture: Impact on the Legal Status of Women in Hawaii, 1820–1920." *Hawaiian Journal of History* 11:188–220.

Giddens, Anthony
1979   *Central Problems in Social Theory: Action, Structure, and Contradiction in Social Analysis.* Berkeley: University of California Press.

Gilson, Richard P.
1970   *Samoa 1830–1900: The Politics of a Multi-Cultural Community.* Melbourne: Oxford University Press.

Goldman, Irving
    1970   *Ancient Polynesian Society.* Chicago: University of Chicago Press.
Gonzalez, Nancie L. Solien
    1969   *Black Carib Household Structure.* Seattle: University of Washington Press.
Grimshaw, Patricia
    1985   "New England Missionary Wives, Hawaiian Women, and 'The Cult of True Womanhood.' " *Hawaiian Journal of History* 19:71–100.
Hammatt, Charles H.
    Ms.   "Journal of Charles H. Hammatt Two Years' Stay in the Sandwich Islands, May 6, 1823–June 9, 1825." Copy, HMCS.
Handy, E. S. Craighill
    1927   *Polynesian Religion.* Bernice P. Bishop Museum Bulletin no. 34. Honolulu.
    1940   *The Hawaiian Planter.* Bernice P. Bishop Museum Bulletin no. 161. Honolulu.
Handy, E. S. Craighill, and E. G. Handy
    1972   *The Native Planters in Old Hawaii: Their Life, Lore, and Environments.* Bernice P. Bishop Museum Bulletin no. 233. Honolulu.
Handy, E. S. Craighill, and Mary Kawena Pukui
    1972   *The Polynesian Family System in Ka-'u, Hawai'i.* Rutland and Tokyo: Charles E. Tuttle.
Hanson, F. Allan
    1982   "Female Pollution in Polynesia?" *Journal of the Polynesian Society* 91:335–81.
Hanson, F. Allan, and Louise Hanson
    1983   *Counterpoint in Maori Culture.* London: Routledge and Kegan Paul.
Hawaii, Kingdom of
    1846   *Statute Laws of His Majesty Kamehameha III.* Honolulu: Government Press.
    1850   *Penal Code of the Hawaiian Islands, Including Session Laws.* Honolulu: Henry M. Whitney.
    1852   *Constitution and Laws of His Majesty Kamehameha III.* Honolulu: Henry M. Whitney.
    1894   [1840] *Hawaii's "Blue" Laws: Constitution and Laws of 1840.* Honolulu: Holomua Publishing Co.
Hawaii, Territory of
    1925   *Revised Laws of Hawaii,* vol. 2. Honolulu.
    1929   *Indices of Awards Made by the Board of Commissioners to Quiet Land Titles in the Hawaiian Islands.* Honolulu: Office of the Commissioner of Public Lands.
Hecht, Julia
    1977   "The Culture of Gender in Pukapuka: Male, Female and the *Mayakitanga* 'Sacred Maid.' " *Journal of the Polynesian Society* 86:183–206.

Herda, Phyllis
    1987   "Gender, Rank and Power in 18th Century Tonga: The Case of Tupoumoheofo." *Journal of Pacific History* 22:195–208.

Hodder, B. W.
    1968   *Economic Development in the Tropics.* London: Methuen.

Holman, Lucia Ruggles
    1931   *Journal of Lucia Ruggles Holman.* Bernice P. Bishop Museum Special Publication no. 17. Honolulu. [1820–21]

Howard, Alan
    1971   *Households, Families and Friends in a Hawaiian-American Community.* Working Papers of the East-West Population Institute, no. 19. Honolulu: East-West Center.
    1974   *Ain't No Big Thing.* Honolulu: University Press of Hawaii.

Howard, Alan, R. Heighton, Jr., C. Jordan, and Ronald Gallimore
    1970   "Traditional and Modern Adoption Patterns in Hawaii." In *Adoption in Eastern Oceania,* edited by Vern Carroll, 21–51. Honolulu: University of Hawaii Press.

Hunnewell, James
    1909   "Honolulu in 1817 and 1818." Hawaiian Historical Society Papers, no. 8. Honolulu.

Huntsman, Judith and Anthony Hooper
    1975   "Male and Female in Tokelau Culture." *Journal of the Polynesian Society* 84:415–30.

Ii, John Papa
    1959   *Fragments of Hawaiian History as Recorded by John Papa Ii.* Translated by Mary Kawena Pukui. Edited by Dorothy B. Barrère. Honolulu: Bishop Museum Press.

Ingraham, Joseph
    1971   *Journal of the Brigantine Hope. . . .* Edited by Mark D. Kaplanoff. Barre, Mass.: Imprint Society. [1791]

James, Kerry E.
    1988   "O, Lead Us Not Into 'Commoditisation' . . . Christine Ward Gailey's Changing Gender Values in the Tongan Islands." *Journal of the Polynesian Society* 97:31–48.

Jarves, James J.
    1843   *History of the Hawaiian or Sandwich Islands.* London: Edward Moxon.

Judd, Laura Fish
    1928   *Honolulu.* Honolulu: Honolulu Star-Bulletin. [1828–61]

Kaeppler, Adrienne
    1970   *Feather Cloaks, Ship Captains, and Lords.* Bishop Museum Occasional Papers 24(6):92–114. Honolulu.
    1978   *"Artificial Curiosities": Being an Exposition of Native Manufactures Collected on the Three Pacific Voyages of Captain James Cook, R.N.* Bernice P. Bishop Special Publication no. 66. Honolulu.
    1985   "Hawaiian Art and Society: Traditions and Transformations."

In *Transformations of Polynesian Culture,* edited by Antony Hooper and Judith Huntsman, 105–31. Auckland: The Polynesian Society.

Kamakau, Kēlou
1919–20   "No Na Oihana Kahuna Kahiko." In *Fornander Collection of Hawaiian Antiquities and Folk-lore,* edited by Thomas Thrum. Memoirs of the Bernice P. Bishop Museum 6:2–45. Honolulu.

Kamakau, Samuel Manaiakalani
1961   *Ruling Chiefs of Hawaii.* Honolulu: Kamehameha Schools Press.
1964   *Ka Po'e Kahiko: The People of Old.* Translated by Mary Kawena Pukui. Edited by Dorothy B. Barrère. Bishop Museum Press Special Publication no. 51. Honolulu.
1976   *The Works of the People of Old: Na Hana a Ka Po'e Kahiko.* Translated by Mary Kawena Pukui. Edited by Dorothy B. Barrère. Bishop Museum Press Special Publication no. 61. Honolulu.

Kekoa, E.
1865   "Birth Rites of Hawaiian Children in Ancient Times." Translated from *Ka Nupepa Ku'oko'a* (newspaper) by Thomas G. Thrum. Bishop Museum Library: Thrum Collection no. 23.

Kelly, Marion
1956   "Changes in Land Tenure in Hawaii, 1778–1850." Master's thesis, University of Hawaii.
1967   "Some Problems with Early Descriptions of Hawaiian Culture." In *Polynesian Culture History: Essays in Honor of Kenneth P. Emory,* edited by Genevieve A. Highland, Roland W. Force, Alan Howard, Marion Kelly, and Yoshiko H. Sinoto. Bernice P. Bishop Museum Special Publication no. 56. Honolulu.
1978   Notes to *Hawaii in 1819: A Narrative Account by Louis Claude de Soulses de Freycinet* (q.v.).
1980   *Majestic Ka'u: Mo'olelo of Nine Ahupua'a.* Bernice P. Bishop Museum Department of Anthropology Report no. 80-2. Honolulu.

Kelly, Raymond C.
1977   *Etoro Social Structure: A Study in Structural Contradiction.* Ann Arbor: University of Michigan Press.

Kepelino, Z.
1932   *Kepelino's Traditions of Hawaii.* Edited by Martha W. Beckwith. Honolulu: Bishop Museum Press.
1977   "Kepelino's 'Hawaiian Collection': His 'Hooiliili Hawaii,' Pepa I, 1858." Translated by Bacil F. Kirtley and Esther T. Mookini. *Hawaiian Journal of History* 11:39–68.

Kikuchi, William K.
1976   "Prehistoric Hawaiian Fishponds." *Science* 193:295–99.

King, James
1967   "Supplement to Cook's Journal." In *The Journals of Captain James Cook on His Voyages of Discovery,* edited by J. C. Beaglehole, 3:493–718. [1778–79]

Kirch, Patrick V.
1979   *Late Prehistoric and Early Historic Settlement-Subsistence Systems in the Anahulu Valley, Oahu.* Bernice P. Bishop Museum Report no. 79-2. Honolulu.
1982   "The Impact of the Prehistoric Polynesians on the Hawaiian Ecosystem." *Pacific Science* 36:1–14.
1984   *The Evolution of the Polynesian Chiefdoms.* Cambridge: Cambridge University Press.
1985   *Feathered Gods and Fishhooks.* Honolulu: University of Hawaii Press.

Kirch, Patrick V. and Marshall Sahlins
Ms.   "Anahulu: The Archaeology of History in an Hawaiian Valley."

Kirchhoff, Paul
1959   "The Principles of Clanship in Human Society." In *Readings in Anthropology,* edited by Morton Fried, 2:259–70. New York: Thomas Crowell.

Kotzebue, Otto von
1821   *A Voyage of Discovery into the South Sea and Beering's Straits . . . in the Years 1815–1818.* 3 vols. London: Longman et al. [1816–17]

Kroeber, Alfred L.
1948   *Anthropology.* Rev. ed. New York: Harcourt, Brace and World.

Kuykendall, Ralph S.
1938   *The Hawaiian Kingdom: 1778–1854.* Honolulu: University of Hawaii Press.
1953   *The Hawaiian Kingdom: 1854–1874.* Honolulu: University of Hawaii Press.

Laanui, Gideon
1930   "Reminiscences of Gideon Laanui, Reared in the Train of Kamehameha I, 1800–1819. Translated from 'Kumu Hawaii,' March–April 1838." *Hawaiian Annual for 1930,* 86–93. Honolulu: Thrum Publishing Co.

Lapérouse, Jean Francois de
1799   *A Voyage round the World, Performed in the years 1785, 1786, 1787, and 1788, by the Boussole and Astrolabe.* 2 vols. London: G. G. and J. Robinson. [1786]

Leacock, Eleanor Burke
1981   *Myths of Male Dominance.* New York: Monthly Review Press.

Levin, Stephanie Seto
1968   "Overthrow of the *Kapu* System in Hawaii." *Journal of the Polynesian Society* 77:402–31.

Lévi-Strauss, Claude
1963   *Structural Anthropology.* Translated by Claire Jacobson and Brooke Grundfest Schoepf. Garden City, N.Y.: Basic Books.
1969   *The Elementary Structures of Kinship.* Translated by James Harle Bell, John R. von Sturmer, and Rodney Needham. Boston: Beacon Press.

Lind, Andrew W.
  1980   *Hawaii's People.* 4th ed. Honolulu: University Press of Hawaii.
Linnekin, Jocelyn
  1983   "The *Hui* Lands of Keanae: Hawaiian Land Tenure and the Great
            Mahele." *Journal of the Polynesian Society,* June, 10–24.
  1985   *Children of the Land: Exchange and Status in a Hawaiian Commu-
            nity.* New Brunswick, N.J.: Rutgers University Press.
  1987a   "Statistical Analysis of the Great Māhele: Some Preliminary Find-
            ings." *Journal of Pacific History* 22:15–33.
  1987b   "Categorize, Cannibalize? Humanistic Quantification in Anthropo-
            logical Research." *American Anthropologist* 89:920–26.
  1988   "Who Made the Feather Cloaks? A Problem in Hawaiian Gender
            Relations." *Journal of the Polynesian Society* 97:265–80.
  N.d.   "Inside, Outside: A Hawaiian Community in the World System."
            In *Clio in Oceania: Toward a Historical Anthropology,* edited by
            Aletta Biersack. Washington, D.C.: Smithsonian Institution Press.
            In press.
Lisiansky, Urey
  1814   *Voyage round the World, 1803–1806, in the Ship "Neva."* London:
            Longmans. [1804]
Locke, Edwin
  Ms.   "Journal of Edwin Locke." Copy, HMCS. [1830s]
Loomis, Elisha
  Ms.   "The Journal of Elisha Loomis." Copy, HMCS. [1824–26]
Lyons, Curtis J.
  1875   "Land Matters in Hawaii." *The Islander,* July 16, 30; August 6, 13.
MacCormack, Carol P., and Marilyn Strathern, eds.
  1980   *Nature, Culture and Gender.* Cambridge: Cambridge University
            Press.
Macrae, James
  1922   *With Lord Byron at the Sandwich Islands in 1825.* Honolulu: Wil-
            son New Freedom Press. [1825–26]
Malo, David
  1839   "Decrease of Population." *Hawaiian Spectator* 2:121–30.
  1951   [1838] *Hawaiian Antiquities.* 2d ed. Translated by Nathaniel B.
            Emerson. Honolulu: Bishop Museum Press.
Marcus, George, and Michael M. J. Fischer
  1986   *Anthropology as Cultural Critique.* Chicago: University of Chicago
            Press.
Marques, A.
  1894   "Population of the Hawaiian Islands." Copy, AH.
Marshall, Mac, ed.
  1979   *Siblingship in Oceania.* Ann Arbor: University of Michigan Press.
Mathison, Gilbert F.
  1825   *Narrative of a Visit to Brazil, Chile, Peru, and the Sandwich Islands,
            1821–1822.* London: Charles Knight. [1822]

Meares, John
1790 *Voyages Made in the Years 1788 and 1789, from China to the North-west Coast of America.* London: Logographic Press. [1788–89]
Menzies, Archibald
1920 *Hawaii nei 128 Years Ago.* Honolulu: New Freedom Press. [1792–94]
Mintz, Sidney W.
1975 *Worker in the Cane.* 2d ed. New York: Norton.
1977 "The So-called World System: Local Initiative and Local Response." *Dialectical Anthropology* 2:253–70.
1985 *Sweetness and Power: The Place of Sugar in Modern History.* New York: Viking.
Morgan, Theodore
1948 *Hawaii: A Century of Economic Change.* Cambridge: Harvard University Press.
Nash, Jill
1984 "Women, Work, and Change in Nagovisi." In *Rethinking Women's Roles,* edited by Denise O'Brien and Sharon Tiffany, pp. 94–119. Berkeley: University of California Press.
Native Hawaiians Study Commission
1983 *Report on the Culture, Needs and Concerns of Native Hawaiians pursuant to Public Law 96-565, Title III.* 2 vols. Washington, D.C.: The Commission.
Oboler, Regina Smith
1985 *Women, Power, and Economic Change: the Nandi of Kenya.* Stanford: Stanford University Press.
O'Brien, Denise, and Sharon Tiffany, eds.
1984 *Rethinking Women's Roles.* Berkeley: University of California Press.
Olmstead, Francis Allyn
1969 [1841] *Incidents of a Whaling Voyage.* Facsimile ed. New York: Bell Publishing Co. [1840]
Ong, Aihwa
1987 *Spirits of Resistance and Capitalist Discipline: Factory Women in Malaysia.* Albany: State University of New York Press.
Ortner, Sherry
1974 "Is Female to Male as Nature is to Culture?" In *Women, Culture and Society,* edited by Michelle Zimbalist Rosaldo and Louise Lamphere, 67–88. Stanford: Stanford University Press.
1981 "Gender and Sexuality in Hierarchical Societies: The Case of Polynesia and Some Comparative Implications." In *Sexual Meanings,* edited by Sherry Ortner and Harriet Whitehead, 359–409. Cambridge: Cambridge University Press.
Ortner, Sherry, and Harriet Whitehead, eds.
1981 *Sexual Meanings: The Cultural Construction of Gender and Sexuality.* Cambridge: Cambridge University Press.

Paulding, Hiram
1970   [1831] *Journal of a Cruise of the United States Schooner Dol-
         phin. . . .* Facsimile ed. Honolulu: University of Hawaii Press.
         [1826]
Pehrson, Robert N.
1954   "Bilateral Kin Groupings as a Structural Type." *Journal of East
         Asiatic Studies* 3:199–202.
Peletz, Michael
1987   "Female Heirship and the Autonomy of Women in Negeri Sembilan,
         West Malaysia." In *Research in Economic Anthropology,* edited by
         Barry L. Isaac. London: JAI Press.
Peterson, Glenn
1982   "Ponapean Matriliny: Production, Exchange, and the Ties that
         Bind." *American Ethnologist* 9:129–44.
Portlock, Nathaniel
1789   *A Voyage around the World . . . in 1785, 1786, 1787, and 1788.*
         London: Stockdale and Goulding. [1786–87]
Pukui, Mary Kawena, and Samuel Elbert
1971   *Hawaiian Dictionary: Hawaiian-English, English-Hawaiian.* 3d ed.
         Honolulu: University Press of Hawaii.
Pukui, Mary Kawena, Samuel H. Elbert, and Esther T. Mookini
1974   *Place Names of Hawaii.* Rev. ed. Honolulu: University of Hawaii
         Press.
Quinn, Naomi
1977   "Anthropological Studies of Women's Status." *Annual Review of
         Anthropology* 6:181–225.
Ralston, Caroline
1988   "Polyandry, 'Pollution,' 'Prostitution.' The Problems of Eurocen-
         trism and Androcentrism in Polynesian Studies." In *Crossing Bound-
         aries: Feminisms and the Critique of Knowledges,* edited by Barbara
         Caine, E. A. Grosz, and Marie de Lepervanche, 71–81. Sydney:
         Allen and Unwin.
n.d.1   "Changes in the Lives of Ordinary Women in Early Post-contact
         Hawaii." In *Family and Gender in the Pacific: Domestic Contradic-
         tions and the Colonial Impact,* edited by Margaret Jolly and Martha
         McIntyre. Cambridge: Cambridge University Press. In press.
n.d.2   "Deceptive Dichotomies: Private/Public, and Nature/Culture. Gen-
         der Relations in Tonga in the Early Contact Period." *Australian
         Feminist Studies.* In press.
Rapp, Reina
1979   "Review Essay: Anthropology." *Signs* 4:497–513.
Remy, Jules
1979   [1874] *Contributions of a Venerable Native to the Ancient History of
         the Hawaiian Islands.* Facsimile ed. Reno, Nev.: Outbooks. [1853]
Richards, William
1973   "William Richards on Hawaiian Culture and Political Conditions of

the Islands in 1841." Edited by Marshall Sahlins and Dorothy Barrère. *Hawaiian Journal of History* 7:18–40. [1841]

Rogers, Garth
1977   " 'The Father's Sister is Black': A Consideration of Female Rank and Power in Tonga." *Journal of the Polynesian Society* 86: 157–82.

Rogers, Susan C.
1975   "Female Forms of Power and the Myth of Male Dominance: A Model of Female/Male Interaction in Peasant Society." *American Ethnologist* 2:727–56.
1978   "Women's Place: A Critical Review of Anthropological Theory." *Comparative Studies in Society and History* 20:123–62.

Rosaldo, Michelle Z., and Louise Lamphere, eds.
1974   *Women, Culture, and Society.* Stanford: Stanford University Press.

Rose, Roger G.
1980   *Hawai'i: The Royal Isles.* Bernice P. Bishop Museum Special Publication no. 67. Honolulu.

Roseberry, William
1988   "Political Economy." *Annual Review of Anthropology* 17:161–85.

Sacks, Karen
1979   *Sisters and Wives: The Past and Future of Sexual Equality.* Westport, Conn.: Greenwood Press.

Sahlins, Marshall D.
1958   *Social Stratification in Polynesia.* Seattle: University of Washington Press.
1965   "On the Sociology of Primitive Exchange." In *The Relevance of Models for Social Anthropology,* edited by Michael Banton, 139–236. London: Tavistock.
1972   *Stone Age Economics.* Chicago: Aldine-Atherton.
1981   *Historical Metaphors and Mythical Realities: Structure in the Early History of the Sandwich Islands Kingdom.* ASAO Special Publications, no. 1. Ann Arbor: University of Michigan Press.
1985   *Islands of History.* Chicago: University of Chicago Press.

Samwell, David
1967   "Some Account of a Voyage to South Sea's [*sic*] in 1776–1777–1778." In *The Journals of Captain James Cook on His Voyages of Discovery,* edited by J. C. Beaglehole, 3:987–1300. Cambridge: Cambridge University Press for the Hakluyt Society. [1778–79]

Sanday, Peggy Reeves
1981   *Female Power and Male Dominance: On the Origins of Sexual Inequality.* Cambridge: Cambridge University Press.

Schmitt, Robert C.
1968   *Demographic Statistics of Hawaii: 1778–1965.* Honolulu: University of Hawaii Press.

Schneider, David
1965   "Some Muddles in the Models: Or, How the System Really

Works." In *The Relevance of Models for Social Anthropology,* edited by Michael Banton, 25–85. London: Tavistock.

Schoeffel, Penelope
1978   "Gender, Status and Power in Western Samoa." *Canberra Anthropology* 1(2): 69–81.

Sexton, Lorraine
1986   *Mothers of Money, Daughters of Coffee: the Wok Meri Movement.* Ann Arbor: UMI Research Press.

Shaler, William
1935   *Journal of a Voyage between China and the Northwestern Coast of America, Made in 1804.* Claremont, Calif.: Saunders Studio Press. [1804]

Shore, Bradd
1981   "Sexuality and Gender in Samoa: Conceptions and Missed Conceptions." In *Sexual Meanings,* edited by Sherry Ortner and Harriet Whitehead, 192–215. Cambridge: Cambridge University Press.

Sider, Gerald M.
1986   *Culture and Class in Anthropology and History: A Newfoundland Illustration.* Cambridge: Cambridge University Press.

Silverblatt, Irene
1987   *Moon, Sun, and Witches: Gender Ideologies and Class in Inca and Colonial Peru.* Princeton: Princeton University Press.

Silverman, Jane
1982   "Imposition of a Western Judicial System in the Hawaiian Monarchy." *Hawaiian Journal of History* 16:48–64.

Simpson, George
1847   *Narrative of a Journey Around the World.* 2 vols. London: H. Colburn. [1842]

Smith, Deverne Reed
1983   *Palauan Social Structure.* New Brunswick, N.J.: Rutgers University Press.

Stewart, Charles S.
1970   [1830] *Journal of a Residence in the Sandwich Islands During the Years 1823, 1824, 1825.* Facsimile ed. Honolulu: University of Hawaii Press. [1823–25]

Stokes, John F. G.
1906   *Hawaiian Nets and Netting.* Memoirs of the Bernice P. Bishop Museum 2(1): 105–62. Honolulu.

1932   "The Hawaiian King." Hawaiian Historical Society Papers, no. 19, pp. 1–28. Honolulu.

Stoler, Ann
1977   "Class Structure and Female Autonomy in Rural Java." *Signs* 3: 74–89.

Strathern, Marilyn
1972   *Women in Between. Female Roles in a Male World: Mount Hagen, New Guinea.* London: Seminar Press.

Strathern, Marilyn, ed.
1987 *Dealing with Inequality.* Cambridge: Cambridge University Press.
Takaki, Ronald
1983 *Pau Hana.* Honolulu: University of Hawaii Press.
Taussig, Michael T.
1980 *The Devil and Commodity Fetishism in South America.* Chapel Hill: University of North Carolina Press.
Thrum, Thomas G., ed.
1877 *Hawaiian Annual for 1878.* Honolulu: Thrum Publishing Co.
1896 *Hawaiian Annual for 1897.* Honolulu: Thrum.
Thurston, Lorrin A., ed.
1904 *The Fundamental Law of Hawaii.* Honolulu.
Thurston, Lucy G.
1921 *Life and Times of Mrs. Lucy G. Thurston. . . .* Ann Arbor: S. C. Andrews. [1820–1876]
Tiffany, Sharon
1978 "Models and the Social Anthropology of Women: A Preliminary Assessment." *Man* 13:34–51.
1979 "Introduction: Theoretical Issues in the Anthropological Study of Women." In *Women and Society: An Anthropological Reader,* edited by Sharon Tiffany, 1–35. Montreal: Eden Press.
Townsend, Ebenezer
1921 "Extract from the Diary of Ebenezer Townsend, Jr. Supercargo of the Sealing Ship '*Neptune*' on Her Voyage to the South Pacific and Canton." Hawaiian Historical Society Reprints, no. 4. Honolulu. [1798]
Turnbull, John
1805 *A Voyage round the World in the Years 1800, 1801, 1802, 1803, and 1804. . . .* 3 vols. London: Richard Phillips. [1802–3]
Turrill, Joel
1957 "The Turrill Collection, 1845–1860." *Hawaiian Historical Society Report* 66, pp. 26–92. Honolulu.
Twain, Mark
1939 *Letters from Honolulu.* Honolulu: Thomas Nickerson. [1866]
Tyerman, Daniel, and George Bennett
1832 *Journal of Voyages and Travels . . . in the South Sea Sea Islands . . . between the Years 1821 and 1829.* 2 vols. Boston: Crocker and Brewster. [1822]
Valeri, Valerio
1972 "Le fonctionnement du système des rangs à Hawaii." *L'Homme* 12:29–66.
1982 "The Transformation of a Transformation: A Structural Essay on an Aspect of Hawaiian History (1809–1819)." *Social Analysis* 10:3–41.
1985 *Kingship and Sacrifice: Ritual and Society in Ancient Hawaii.* Translated by Paula Wissing. Chicago: University of Chicago Press.
Vancouver, George
1798 *A Voyage of Discovery to the North Pacific Ocean and round the*

World. . . . 3 vols. London: G. G. and J. Robinson and J. Edwards. [1792–94]

Varigny, Charles de
1981   *Fourteen Years in the Sandwich Islands 1855–1868.* Translated by Alfons L. Korn. Honolulu: University Press of Hawaii and the Hawaiian Historical Society.

Verdery, Katherine
1983   *Transylvanian Villagers.* Berkeley: University of California Press.

Wagner, Roy
1967   *The Curse of Souw.* Chicago: University of Chicago Press.

Wallerstein, Immanuel
1974   *The Modern World-System.* New York: Academic Press.
1979   *The Capitalist World-Economy.* Cambridge: Cambridge University Press.

Webb, Malcolm C.
1965   "The Abolition of the Taboo System in Hawaii." *Journal of the Polynesian Society* 74:21–39.

Weiner, Annette
1976   *Women of Value, Men of Renown: New Perspectives in Trobriand Exchange.* Austin: University of Texas Press.
1982   "Plus précieux que l'or: relations et échanges entre hommes et femmes dans les sociétés d'Océanie." *Annales* 37(2): 222–45.
1985   Inalienable Wealth. *American Ethnologist* 12:210–27.

Whitman, John B.
1979   *The Hawaiian Journal of John B. Whitman 1813–1815: An Account of the Sandwich Islands.* Honolulu and Salem: Topgallant Publishing Co. and the Peabody Museum of Salem. [1813–15]

Whyte, Martin King
1978   *The Status of Women in Preindustrial Societies.* Princeton: Princeton University Press.

Wolf, Eric
1982   *Europe and the People without History.* Berkeley: University of California Press.

Worsley, Peter
1980   "One World or Three? A Critique of the World-System Theory of Immanuel Wallerstein." In *The Socialist Register 1980,* edited by Ralph Miliband and John Saville, 298–338. London: Merlin Press.
1984   *The Three Worlds: Culture and World Development.* Chicago: University of Chicago Press.

Wyllie, Robert C.
1844   Notes on the Shipping Trade. *The Friend* 2, *passim.*

Wyllie, Robert C., ed.
1846   *Answers to Questions Proposed by His Excellency, R. C. Wyllie, His Hawaiian Majesty's Minister of Foreign Relations. . . .* Honolulu: Government Printer.

Index

Action. *See* Practice

Adams, Alexander, 158

Adoption, 127, 138, 147; of chiefly children, 108; in exchange model, 108, 143–44, 149–51; norm of, 61, 108, 125; as service, 97–99; women's role in, 5

Adzes. See *Ko'i*

Affines. *See* Households; Marriage

Agriculture, 87–91, 128; cattle's effects on, 161, 199–202; division of labor in, 37–40; dryland, 38–39, 89–90, 118, 120; intensified, 158; market impact on, 156, 166, 177, 179–82; post-Māhele, 156, 217. *See also* Cash cropping; *individual crops*

Ahupua'a, 84–88; ecology, 118–21; land redistribution unit, 129–30, 158–59; social organization, 114–16, 137–52, 217, 219, 221. *See also* Local group

'Aikanaka, 18–19, 104–7

Aikāne, 99–100, 140, 148, 163

'Ai kapu. See Kapu

Akahiakuleana, 17–19

Ali'i. See Chiefs

Alliance, 142–45, 149–52. *See also* Marriage

Ancestors, 91–92, 146, 194, 219. See also *'Aumākua;* Genealogies

Annexation, 226, 228

Archaeology, 76, 93, 117

Arms, military: mat shields, 42; role

in conquest, 76; traded, 23, 159–60, 162–63, 168, 173

Ascription, 75, 92, 95–96. *See also* Rank

'Aumākua, 32. *See also* Religion

'Auwai. See Irrigation

'Ava. See Kava

Bananas, 90; *kapu* food, 15; offerings, 78, traded, 172

Barter. *See* Exchange; Trade

Barth, Fredrik, 117

Basketry, 51

Bathing, 17

Bingham, Hiram, 72

Bird catchers, 50

Birth, 124

Birthing stones, 61, 110

Blood, 17–19

Board of Commissioners to Quiet Land Titles in the Hawaiian Kingdom. *See* Land Commission

Boki, 168

Bond, Elias, 197, 206–7, 218

Bones, 50, 107

Brother: relationships, 139–42; landholding role, 146, 215–16. See also *Kaikaina; Kaikua'ana;* Siblings

Buck, Peter, 47

Bureaucracy, 157

Burial, 85

Campbell, Archibald, 167

Canoes, 21–22, 42, 78, 163